Stylistic Boundaries among Mobile Hunter-Foragers

Stylistic Boundaries

among Mobile Hunter-Foragers

C. Garth Sampson

Smithsonian Institution Press
Washington and London

Smithsonian Series in Archaeological Inquiry

Robert McC. Adams and Bruce D. Smith,
Series Editors

The Smithsonian Series in Archaeological Inquiry presents original case studies that address important general research problems and demonstrate the values of particular theoretical and/or methodological approaches. Titles include well-focused, edited collections as well as works by individual authors. The series is open to all subject areas, geographical regions, and theoretical modes.

This book was edited by Carol Clark,
proofed by Lisa A. Baylor,
and designed by Lisa Buck.

Library of Congress Cataloging-in-Publication Data

Sampson, C. Garth (Clavil Garth), 1941-
   Stylistic boundaries among mobile hunter-foragers.
Bibliography: p.
1. San (African people)—Pottery.
2. Art, San (African people)
I. Title.
DT764.B8S24   1988   968'.004961   87-31431
ISBN 0-87474-838-0

British Library Cataloging-in-Publication Data is available.

♾ The paper used in this publication
meets the minimum requirements of the
American National Standard for
Permanence of Paper for Printed Library
Materials Z39.48-1984.

For my parents, Clavil and Marjorie Sampson,
who introduced me to field archaeology thirty years ago

Contents

Preface 9

Acknowledgments 11

ONE Introduction 13

TWO The Upper Seacow River Valley 29

THREE Archaeology of the Upper Seacow River Bushmen 37

FOUR Sherd Collection and Classification 45

FIVE Introduction to the Non-Rocker Motifs 54

SIX The Comb-Stamp Decorations 67

SEVEN Small Spatulate Stylus and Related Types 93

EIGHT Double Tip Stylus and Variations 106

NINE The Large Plain Spatulate Decorations 117

TEN Porcupine Quill Decorations 138

ELEVEN Motifs with Peripheral Distributions 145

TWELVE The Rocker-Stamp Motifs 155

THIRTEEN Interpretations 171

Appendix 177

Bibliography 182

Preface

Winter 1956 in the suburbs of Cape Town. We huddle over our school desks in a freezing classroom as the history master booms away cheerfully in Oxonian tones about the Congress of Vienna. I peer earnestly down at my textbook, and read the other volume concealed on my lap, pinned between bluish knees (the draconian dress code dictates long pants for us next year) and my grimy desk base. It is George Stow's *The Native Races of South Africa* published fifty years earlier and still available, incredibly, from the local public library. The pages are filled with accounts of battles between Bushmen and Dutchmen, and I'm aghast at the unfairness of it all. The Bushmen are always without guns or horses; it's simply not cricket. Then comes an account of a massacre on the Zeekoe River—hippos are shot as bait; horsemen ride off into the Karoo night; spies posted; horsemen return; blaze away at Bushmen feeding on the carcasses; refugees run down and killed all next day; hundreds dead; children taken as slaves. I'm both excited and appalled.

During break, my friends shrug. The history master looks blank (it's the cane if I'm caught reading in class, but he's a decent bloke). The history textbook doesn't even mention Bushmen—dozens of Kaffir wars, but not a breath about South Africa's Hundred-Year War. Right then, I determine to find out more about this stuff. These poor little guys deserve their own history. So one thing leads to another, and I become a Paleolithic archaeologist.

Now, thirty years later I'm delivering on a schoolboy pledge to the Zeekoe River Bushmen, by trying to find out how they organized themselves on the landscape. It isn't easy. The official archives are scant and make incredibly depressing reading—mainly headcounts and gory anecdotes. The travelers' diaries are full of secondhand summaries and high-minded opinion. Not a single word of the language was ever recorded, although there are hints that there were a couple of Europeans who could converse with them, albeit haltingly. So, these Bushmen belong to archaeology, if not to prehistory in the full sense. Fortunately, the surface traces of their camps and other activities are both superabundant and highly visible on this beautiful and treeless landscape. They left scatters of flaked stone all over the valley floor, as well as other bits and pieces, including broken pottery.

This book is mostly about their pottery decorations. First, I dream up a model of how one decorative motif will be distributed on the landscape by members of a single Bushman band who all recognize this motif as their "signature." The model predicts that the motif will have a restricted distribution, with the highest density at sites inside the band's territorial boundary. Not a very profound idea, but we have to start somewhere. Next, there is a description of the upper end of the valley, plus a quick tour of some Bushman surface archaeology, with a closer look at what is known about Bushman pot making. I go on to describe how we collected the broken pottery from a thousand Bushman campsites in the upper valley, and how this collection was sorted into an earlier and later group of motifs. After that, there is a string of chapters dealing with the details of individual decorations.

It turns out that the decorative patterns stamped on the outsides of their cooking bowls have quite restricted distributions on the landscape. I try to build a case that certain decorative motifs were used by the potters of four different bands and that each motif was passed on to younger potters of the same band. Then I try to argue that their restricted distributions on the map reflect the territorial organization of different Bushman bands who once lived here. Finally, I am racked by self-doubt and start to dream up other possible interpretations for the restricted distributions. The "territorial" interpretation comes out of this introspection still looking pretty good, but the whole exercise sparks off a new set of ideas for further testing of the proposition.

Embedded in all this is a second motive, nothing to do with childhood nostalgia. This whole project grew out of my increasing disillusionment over stone artifact typology and the ever more rancorous debate about "style" and its meaning in Paleolithic prehistory. Everyone seemed to tacitly agree that we were looking for stylistic traits in stone artifacts because we thought that they might be the clue to the identity of socially coherent groups. It was a long time before anyone came right out and said this, but even then the haggling continued. After releasing a few growls of my own into the literature ("typology is dead"—that sort of thing), I was struck by the silliness of it all. What was missing was a sufficiently large and complete map of stylistic traits that would capture *the edges* of trait distributions. Stylistic boundaries in space would at least give us a handle on whether style represents social groups in ancient hunters. What better source for such a map than the abundant archaeological trace of those "poor little guys" of boyhood memory?

So I took a team to the Zeekoe and we walked for fifteen months—five days a week, eight hours a day. We covered an area as big as the state of Delaware and found 16,000 sites, about half of them left by the Bushmen. This is all described in the *Atlas of Stone Age Settlement in the Central and Upper Seacow Valley* (1985). There are enough stone artifacts lying out there to fill several freight trains, but which artifacts carry the stylistic traits we are looking for? As every Paleolithic archaeologist knows, style is easily confounded with function. Is a stone point shaped that way because it was the "signature" of a group, or be-cause it's more efficient that way? To get around this, I needed to map a guaranteed nonfunctional trait. The pottery decorations looked like my best hope.

So I took another team back to the upper Zeekoe and we collected potsherds for eight months—five days a week, eight hours a day. It worked. Now we have a framework of stylistic boundaries within which to seek stylistic variations among Bushman stone artifacts—but that is all for the future. I hope this book is going to open up a whole vista of possibilities for future research elsewhere in the world. It should interest a far wider readership than the two hundred or so individuals concerned with the regional prehistory of southern Africa, because it suggests new ways to tackle spatial problems by surface archaeology. These can be tried out in any semiarid environment where prehistoric hunter-foragers have left a reasonably dense surface trace. Who knows? It may even interest cultural anthropologists with hunter-forager leanings, as well as cultural ecologists involved in the current debate over habitat and territory. It won't interest statistics buffs at all—my conclusions are being tested now, and a specialist paper on the subject should be ready by the time this goes to print.

After twenty years of shuffling stone artifacts from one tray to another, there I was peering myopically at bits of pottery for the first time in real earnest. I did this for five months, in a wonderful field lab on a koppie overlooking the Zeekoe headwaters. At sundown the wind would drop and the Karoo became deafeningly quiet. By the fifth month, alone all day, I inevitably thought I could hear the laughter. The tone was ambiguous, though. Celebration? Mockery? Time will tell.

Acknowledgments

The Bushman camps mentioned in this volume were discovered during an archaeological survey funded by the National Science Foundation, Washington, D.C. through Grant No. BNS-7914153 entitled "Archaeological enquiries into spatial organization of the Zeekoe valley San," and through Grant No. BNS-7914153-AO1 entitled "Population distribution in ecologically simple contexts." The potsherd collections were made with support from Grant No. BNS-8210085 entitled "Detection of territorial edges and mobility patterns" and from Grant No. BNS-8406137 entitled "Prehistoric herder-hunter interactions along a pastoralist frontier." The latter grant also supported preliminary excavations, analysis, and manuscript production. Substantial support for the fieldwork also came from Southern Methodist University, Dallas, Texas in the form of faculty research fellowships in 1980 and 1985. The Institute for the Study of Earth and Man at S.M.U. has also generously funded photographic production, and the purchase of map storage facilities in Dallas. Additional support during the analysis of excavated materials came from a Bursary for Tim Hart, provided by the University of Cape Town.

Nothing would have come of this enterprise without the ceaseless efforts of my wife Beatrix, who directs the entire logistical backup to our fieldwork. Housing, staff, vehicles, payroll, bookkeeping, cooking, equipment, and public relations all fall within her bailiwick. She also manages the ceramics lab and maintains a wide network of friendships and working relationships stretched across five districts. Out of the field, she participates energetically in drafting and proofreading during manuscript production.

The archaeological team responsible for the original survey included David Arter, Britt Bousman, Tim Dalbey, Emily Lovick, Steven Lovick, Les Peters, and Joe Saunders. The potsherd collection team included Britt Bousman, Tim Dalbey, Tim Hart, Conrad Steenkamp, and Reg Webster.

We function in the field thanks entirely to the hospitality and friendship of several sheep farming families who allow us to use abandoned farmhouses and outbuildings as field bases. During this "ceramic studies" phase of our work, we depended heavily on Mr. and Mrs. Tinus Naudé, Mr. and Mrs. Gerald Naudé, Mr. and Mrs. Fred Rubidge, and Mr. and Mrs. Peter Watermeyer. A special note of thanks is also due to the Rubidge family who have taken our project to heart and provided not only housing, but also magnificent laboratory space and live storage for the sherd collections. Over the years, the Watermeyers have also maintained a lively interest in our work and have allowed us to store field equipment between seasons. Out-of-season vehicle storage has also been made possible by Mr. and Mrs. Glanton Maskell and by Mr. and Mrs. Neil Sheard. The practical help, advice, and friendship of Mr. and Mrs. Quintin Naudé has been a constant support to our efforts.

For permission to survey their properties and to collect sherds, also for their constant interest, hospitality, and friendship, I am deeply indebted to the following farmers: F. Aucamp, J. de Klerk, P. de Klerk, J. de Villiers, R. Geldenhuis, A. Keun, D. Moolman, C. Kingwill, D. Kingwill, M. Kroon, C. Lessing, C. Loock, E. Naudé, F. Naudé (jr.), F. P. Naudé, G. Naudé, Q. Naudé, T. Naudé, vZ. Naudé, S. Neveling, H. Prinsloo, F. Rubidge, C. Schwandervelder, N. Sheard, M. van den Heever, B. van der Merwe, B. van der Merwe (jr.), J. van der Merwe, P. van der Merwe, W. van der Merwe, P. van Schalkwyck, D. Viljoen, E. Viljoen, K. Viljoen, A. Vorster, E. Vorster, and P. Watermeyer. For permission to conduct excavations at rockshelters on their property, I also wish to thank F. Naudé and vZ. Naudé. Many families living outside the valley have also provided invaluable support during our comings and goings. In Johannesburg, we are greatly indebted to Mr. and Mrs. Frans van der Wielen who have undertaken to collect our fragmented remains from various cross-Atlantic flights and to put us back together again in preparation for the field. Mr. and Mrs. M. Taylor have also contributed significantly by boarding and reorienting student assistants in transit to the field. In Graaff Reneit, we have come to rely heavily on the unstinting hospitality of Dr. and Mrs. D. Thornton who have allowed us to use their home as a supply base for all of our foraging trips. In Port Elizabeth, our monthly supply runs are made additionally pleasant by the overwhelming generosity of Mr. and Mrs. N. Vimpany, who have enveloped us in their warm family atmosphere and have housed many a homesick graduate student.

Several colleagues have afforded valuable insights and advice while visiting us in the field. I greatly appreciate the time and effort it takes from busy schedules to visit this relatively remote and off-the-track part of the Karoo. In particular, I want to thank: Dr. A. Brooks, George Washington University; Professor H. Deacon, University of Stellenbosch; Dr. J. Deacon, University of Stellenbosch; Professor T. Huffman, University of Witwatersrand; Mr. A. Mazel, Natal Museum; Professor J. Parkington, University of Cape Town; Professor T. Partridge, University of Witwatersrand; Dr. L. Scott, University of Orange Free State; Mr. M. Taylor, University of Witwatersrand; Dr. J. Vogel, Council for Scientific and Industrial Research; and Dr. J. Yellen, National Science Foundation.

During the production of photographs for this volume, Bill Westbury was the source of much patient counsel and experiment. I would also like to thank Dr. John Yellen for reading and commenting on the manuscript, and Dr. Robert McC. Adams and Dr. Bruce Smith of the Smithsonian Institution for their support.

ONE

Introduction

Among the many new research pathways being opened up in hunter-forager archaeology, there has been little or no discussion (cf. Thomas 1986) of the *band-territory*, and how it might be recognized in the archaeological record. There was a flurry of debate in the seventies, but it soon lost momentum, and no consensus emerged on how to proceed. Some discussants thought the archaeological record was just too sparse and too fickle to yield territorial boundaries (Wobst 1978). More stubborn optimists urged that we keep slogging away at the problem until we find a suitable approach (Stiles 1979). Thereafter, all but a few brave souls (see below) "voted with their feet" and opted for research careers in seasonal subsistence/ mobility systems—a very promising avenue opened up by the single-site study of Clark (1954), then at the regional level by MacNeish et al. (1972), and now further developed into a full-blown research paradigm by Jochim (1976, 1981), Binford (1978), and many others. Of late, though, confidence in the ecological approach has begun to erode (Bettinger 1980). Doubts are creeping in about the validity of many supposed seasonal markers in the record (Monks 1981), and even some of the sacred cows among case studies have come under attack (Andresen *et al.* 1981, Grayson 1984).

All this reevaluation is unquestionably a good thing, but attention is still too sharply focused on the details of site formation processes (cf. Schiffer 1983) —all those bones and seeds, and what times of year they really entered the archaeological record. Meanwhile, a larger and more ominous question hangs over this collective endeavor, which no one seems to have noticed (at least not in the current literature) except for the odd over-the-shoulder glance (Bettinger 1980, Jochim 1981). I am referring to the rather obvious fact that *seasonal mobility systems cannot be properly delineated unless they are first circumscribed by the territorial boundaries within which they functioned.*

It is somewhat amazing, therefore, that a "Received Formula" for seasonality research has been allowed to evolve with the need for territorial boundaries going unnoticed or barely acknowledged. Typically, the formula runs something like this: (1) pick a likely looking basin, valley, coastal strip, and so forth as a study area; (2) find the rockshelters, caves, and middens most likely to yield organic remains; (3) search each site's locale for edible plants and animals; (4) figure out the seasonal spacing of all this stuff in modern and historical times; (5) assume the same spacing during prehistoric times, that is, concoct a "model of seasonal resource availability" by analogy with present distributions and timings; (6) conjure up another "model" of a seasonal round whereby hunter-foragers take full advantage of what is available when and where; then, (7) excavate enough material at each site to show what folks ate at each place. If the field data fit the model—lo, the seasonal round is discovered. More prudent fieldworkers dig first, then figure out the "model" afterwards. Either way, the circularity of reasoning is obvious enough—the foodwaste that piles up at a site is going to reflect the food supply around that site, whether or not folks are on a seasonal round.

Of course, this account is compressed almost to the point of parody, but readers well versed in these arduous routines will recognize that all the essential components are in place. Note also that our list contains not a single test of the built-in assumption that the prehistoric folks had equal access to all parts of the *archaeologist's* (not their own) chosen area. It does not allow for sociopolitical (that is, territorial) boundaries across the area—invisible lines that may have blocked free passage across it (Wobst 1974, Bettinger 1980, Price 1981). Once the latter option is allowed into the "model," this opens up the awkward possibility that the archaeologist has built two or more fragments of seasonal rounds of *neighboring* bands into a spurious model for a single, but nonexistent, group.

13

It would seem prudent, therefore, to make certain that the chosen study area is not really a mosaic of contiguous territorial fragments. This is not a hypothetical danger—the otherwise elegant study of Parkington (1972, 1984) on Later Stone Age seasonal mobility patterns in the southwest Cape, South Africa, is in precisely this sort of trouble. Sealy and van der Merwe (1985) have shown through isotopic analysis of human skeletons that the diets of coastal and montane populations were discrete, not mixed. This result conflicts with the expectations of Parkington's seasonal coast and mountain transhumance model, and suggests that a territorial boundary ran across the middle of his study area, thus keeping the two populations within their separate habitats.

At this point is it reasonable to ask why archaeologists have plowed so far into the seasonal and subsistence paradigm without taking boundaries into account? The answer is complex, but can be sorted out into what I call the "Four Discouragements."

The First Discouragement lurks in that aborted seventies debate I mentioned at the outset—most workers just assumed that it was impossible to etch territorial boundaries into the archaeological record, because of the sheer volume of fieldwork involved. Those embarking on case studies who stopped to think about it must have taken a leap of faith that their respective study areas were okay—that is, free of territorial boundaries, but these were private doubts, and I can find no airing of them in the literature. A prudent few chose areas bounded by convincing physical barriers (mountain ranges, sea, and so forth) that fenced off the area, but even this approach leaves no guarantee that the enclosed basin, coastal strip, or whatever, was not crisscrossed by territorial lines mutually agreed upon by its former inhabitants. These can only be discovered once we have amassed a sufficiently complete data-set (from a large enough area) that stylistic marker boundaries can reasonably be expected to appear.

The Second Discouragement derives from the ethnohistoric record. Archaeologists have long assumed that sociopolitical territories would show up in the record as restricted distributions of stylistic elements on a landscape, and that the outer limits of the distribution would approximate the sociopolitical boundary. However, this intuitively reasonable prediction was badly shaken when ethnographic surveys (Driver and Massey 1957) revealed that all kinds of objects (and presumably styles) were moving across such boundaries in quite recent times. Why, then, should prehistoric styles distribute themselves strictly within territorial limits? We now realize that this was premature defeatism, thanks in large part to the pioneering work of Hodder (especially 1977) on cross-boundary traffic in material culture. This, together with Wiessner's (1983, 1984) fascinating work on hunter-forager stylistic distributions, has done much to dispel doubts about the meaning of stylistic distributions. Admittedly, the least ambiguous stylistic differences obtained so far are between San language-groups (Wiessner 1983) rather than between bands (Wiessner 1984), but this is owing to small sample sizes.

The Third Discouragement is embedded in that awful old war-horse called variously the ethnic-functional debate, or the Bordes-Binford debate, as well as other colorful but unprintable epithets. As all hunter-forager archaeologists know, the essence of this debate is: do styles oscillate back and forth within one stratified sequence because (ethnic-Bordes) tribal boundaries shifted back and forth across the site through time? or (function-Binford) was the site used (by only one group) to accomplish different jobs requiring various toolkits, at different times? Commentary on this debate could already fill a book (cf. Sackett 1982), and I have no wish to add to the rhetorical overburden. The point here is that the functionalist argument introduced doubts about the value of style as an ethnic marker. If style did not signal group identity, then a restricted distribution of one element on the landscape could not possibly reflect the range of one group. This doubt can now be laid to rest by the following cross-check—if a stylistic element displays a restricted distribution for functional reasons alone, then its distribution is unlikely to coincide with that of some exotic rock source in the same landscape. When two such distributions overlap, then the style is an ethnic signal (see below). However, it must also be admitted that efforts to test this assumption in the ethnographic present are still fraught with ambiguities (Binford 1979, Gould and Saggers 1985, Binford and Stone 1985, Bamforth 1986).

The Fourth Discouragement that caused archaeologists to delay the search for prehistoric territories must be sought in living hunter-forager studies. In the sixties, many anthropologists were appalled by the current fad for "innate" (phylogenetically adapted) territorial behavior in humans (Lorenz 1963, Ardrey 1966)—so much so that they even managed to rally to the call for a unified riposte (Ashley-Montagu 1973). Thus, in the United Kingdom and the United States at least it became intellectually improper to interest oneself in hunter-forager territoriality, although Australian (Hiatt 1962) and German scholars (Heinz 1972) seem to have been less squeamish about this. The prevailing mood among San scholars, however, tended to foster the "harmless people" image of hunter-foragers, with great emphasis on sharing, fluid movement, and lack of aggression. Little care was taken to document boundaries, and I have found no published interviews with informants on the topic of boundary markers, boundary recognition, or any of the things that might interest an archaeologist looking for material traces of a boundary. It took almost a decade for this attitude to wear off.

Although I know of no archaeologist whose decisions were directly colored by this moralistic basis for ignoring territory, it cannot be denied that there has been a convenient climate of thought within which to forget about territory—a topic that already looked too tough to handle. The Fourth Discouragement was really an intellectual fashion that died on its feet, although the reasons for its demise are significant. Any further debate on the issue (whether territorial behavior in humans was innate or culturally determined) was stymied for want of any archaeological evidence on the *evolution* of territorial behavior. The intellectual climate was discouraging the very activities with which it might have sustained itself!

No longer, though—there is a rising tide of advice in the literature on how to detect "social territories" in the archaeological record (Clark 1975, 1980; Clarke 1968; Jacobi 1979; Price 1981; Gendel 1984). The recommended approach is to combine the distribution maps of distinctive stone artifact styles with the distribution maps of distinctive flakable rock types from solitary outcrops. When both have limited distributions on the landscape, and when both distributions coincide, then their combined rims on the map may be taken as a sociopolitical boundary, across which prehistoric hunter-foragers seldom strayed.

So far, there are only a few completed case studies (Jacobi 1979, Gendel 1984), and these are based on quite limited data-sets. There are also some partially tested cases of either artifact style alone (Close 1977, 1978) or rock sourcing alone (Hughes and Bettinger 1984). Also, the boundaries of whole cultural systems or "techno-territories" have attracted far more attention (De Atley and Findlow 1984, Green and Perlman 1985), but studies at so large a scale embrace areas several times larger than the case studies discussed above. Likewise, the analytical tradition of so-called "exploitation-territories" (site catchments) started by Higgs and Vita-Finzi (1972) operates at far too small a scale, and has far too many inherent flaws (cf. Findlow and Ericson 1980) to be applicable here.

Clearly, the Four Discouragements are losing their grip on hunter-forager archaeology, and we are gradually coming round to the business of detecting boundaries, although not always at the band-territory level. Furthermore, cursory evaluation of what has been achieved so far reveals two common weaknesses. The first is that the territorial boundaries have been etched out of data-sets that accumulated on a random-discovery basis, not out of systematic surveys. Consequently the point-plot for a given stylistic element is thin and uneven because of varying amounts of fieldwork in different parts of the study area. The second observation is that ethnographic analogs for the appropriate territorial size have to be drawn from very far away from the study area (Gendel 1984). For the recommended approach to succeed, what is really needed is a case study that meets all these requirements: a sufficiently large and complete archaeological map of the distribution of some nonfunctional stylistic element, produced by systematic survey, in a region where hunter-forager bands have recently lived.

The Zeekoe Valley Archaeological Project (ZVAP) was designed to apply the recommended approach in an area where stylistic data are numerous and free of functional ambiguities, and where ethnographic analogs are close at hand. However, ZVAP is *not* an exercise in ethnoarchaeology. Instead, ZVAP draws its analogs from the Kalahari San—always

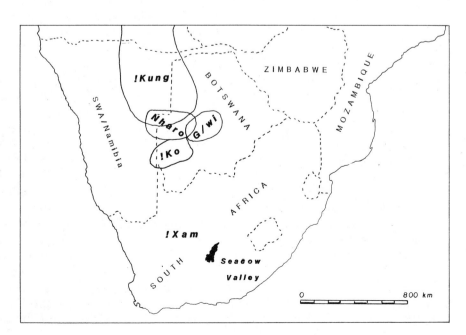

Figure 1-1a. Location of the Seacow Valley in relation to the San language areas.

mindful that they are not "pristine" hunter-foragers (Ember 1978, Schrire 1980, Wilmsen 1983)—who no longer make stone tools or pots, and who thus leave absolutely minimal archaeological residues (Yellen 1976, 1977). ZVAP then cautiously applies these analogs to a group of Northern Cape Bushmen (San) who lived at least 900 kilometers to the south (fig.1-1a) in a quite different semiarid habitat (chapter 2), and whose territorial system was destroyed over a century ago (Willcox 1963:24). Being prolific makers of stone tools and pottery, their archaeological surface trace is staggeringly abundant (see chapter 3).

It follows that ZVAP does not use direct historical analogy (Steward 1942), but is forced to employ a riskier mélange of ethnohistoric scraps and "new" analogy (Ascher 1961). Thus we are passing out of the glittering realm of Living Archaeology (Gould 1980) into an even messier and more confusing matrix of "Dead Ethnology." In this twilight zone there is no convenient body of ethnological or archaeological theory that can be raided for models—these will have to be developed from scratch. As a preliminary step towards this goal, it is useful to briefly review the status of territorial studies in various disciplines.

There are two debates going on simultaneously about territories. Facing off in the first debate are the cultural ecologists and "optimal foragers" versus the structural and cognitive anthropologists. The ecologists, concerned with applying optimal foraging theory to humans (for example, Wilmsen 1973, Dyson-Hudson and Smith 1978, Keene 1979, Winterhalder and Smith 1981, Smith 1983) take it as axiomatic that territorial behavior is an adaptive spacing mechanism for mapping humans onto resources. Structuralists insist that territory is more a cognitive plan or "mental map" of social relations reinforced by the belief system and rules associated with ceremonial activities (Tanner 1973, Peterson 1975, Yengoyan 1976, Blundell 1980). Australian Aborigines display clearer ties between mythology, ritual, rock art, and territory than the Kalahari San (Peterson 1979, Layton 1986), but rock art studies (Lewis-Williams 1984) hint that this needs rethinking for the South African San.

The lineup in the second debate are those archaeologists, invoking demographic theory, who claim that territoriality came about only quite recently as the result of steady population increase (Wobst 1976, Conkey 1978, Hassan 1981) versus primatologists and others who argue that even the earliest hominids must have been territorial (King 1976, Butzer 1982).

Both debates converge with the seemingly moribund issues caricatured above as the Fourth Discouragement. Together, they focus on a single set of problems, namely the timing and mechanisms by which territorial behavior developed away from a phylogenetically adaptive behavior towards a cognitive "mental map" of cultural and social space. The long-term goal of ZVAP is to probe exactly when and

how "the territorial definition of society" changed to "the social definition of territory" (Soja 1971). The present study (prehistoric San territories reflected in pottery design) is but the first incremental step. After San space-time dynamics are better understood, we plan to pursue territorial patterning farther back in time. If geochemical sourcing of San stone tools produces overlapping patterns with the pottery motifs —and prospects are good for this (Pheasant, Sampson, and Waibel n.d.)—then rock-dispersal patterns can be generated for the several earlier industries mapped in the same area (Sampson 1985). Thus the door to Paleolithic territoriality will be finally unlocked.

A theoretical framework within which this can be achieved must now be considered. *Style* theory provides the main vehicle for etching territorial boundaries from the archaeological record. Basically, it allows that hunter-foragers shape and decorate artifacts as identity signals at two levels—individual identity and group membership. Wiessner (1983, 1984, 1985) has coined two terms to designate these levels of stylistic expression: *assertive style*, meaning an individual signature or marker, and *emblemic style* meaning a group signature or marker. Note, however, that Sackett (1985) questions the validity of emblemic style as a concept. At present, I tend to side with Wiessner (1985), who doubts the usefulness of Sackett's "isochrestic style" as an alternative heuristic device. In passing it should also be noted that style theory predicts that group-signals (via decorative motifs) will be expressed more emphatically under conditions of stress and competition for resources. This statement derives from the extensive ethnoarchaeological studies of Hodder (1982) and Wiessner (1984). Although there are no good case studies to back up the reverse of this trend, it is intuitively reasonable to suppose that "emblemic" style (that is, group-signature style) production slackens off when the pressures of contact are reduced or resolved (cf. Wadley 1986). Recent work by Wiessner on Kalahari San bone arrowheads (1983) represents the most promising start towards an ethnographic test of the validity of style theory. However, her published samples are only large enough to determine boundaries between language-groups (for example, !Kung versus G/wi), not between individual bands within linguistic areas. San beadwork shows still more promise (Wiessner 1984) although traffic in beadwork exchange may produce very diffuse boundaries in the end. Nonetheless, the northern Kalahari seems the most likely place where an ethnographic test could be completed, but could a comparable archaeological study be conducted in the same area? This would be ideal, since direct ethnoarchaeological links between living and prehistoric distributions could be established. Alas, this is not to be, since bone points and beads cannot be recovered in sufficient quantities from archaeological surface sites. Furthermore, the living San are not stone toolmakers, and it is stone tools that are the most prolific objects on Kalahari surface sites. Thus a direct past-to-present comparison of territorial boundaries cannot be accomplished here. It must be stressed again that no San band territory has yet been mapped in terms of a density distribution of its emblemic style. Thus, it has yet to be demonstrated that style theory is applicable at the band-territory level. A band-level, marker-object distribution pattern is still a theoretical construct, existing only in the mind's eye. That is nonetheless my next goal—to construct a theoretical model of what the density distribution of a group marker (that is, one artifact type or motif exhibiting emblemic style) might look like on a large enough portion of landscape to have captured an entire San territory. My point of departure is an ethnographic analog—the territorial outline of the !Kung band centered on the Dobe waterhole (fig. 1-1b) as first mapped by Lee (1965). Note two important features in passing: its boundaries overlap with those of two neighboring bands, and at least half of its boundary lines are defined by drainage channels.

Next, we should note that although members of the band could readily list their fellow-members (and describe their territorial boundary) they were seldom seen at home. Yellen and Harpending (1972) plotted the movements of four member-families (fig. 1-2a) that bore no resemblance to the outline of their territory. To show that these wanderings were not merely a symptom of recent band disintegration under modern stresses, the stated birthplaces of the adults were also mapped (fig. 1-2b). Obviously, their movements beyond this boundary were habitual and have persisted for decades.

Band members thus distributed themselves in very "fluid" patterns so that the movements of any two families seldom ran parallel for more than a few weeks. Sets of families acted as independent units moving to different places at different times, meeting only when their schedules overlapped. There was no headman who decided on band movements as a whole, or who owned a waterhole himself. Ownership usually rested with a group of sibs or even cousins (Lee 1972, *pace* Marshall 1960). In this way, an individual acquired residence rights at several waterholes in neighboring territories. In a sparse and unpredictable environment like this, such a loose fluid organization made excellent sense. If a bad year should wipe out the resources of a band's territory and dry up its waterhole, then families were free and entitled by ties of kinship and friendship to move to waterholes some territories away. The adaptational

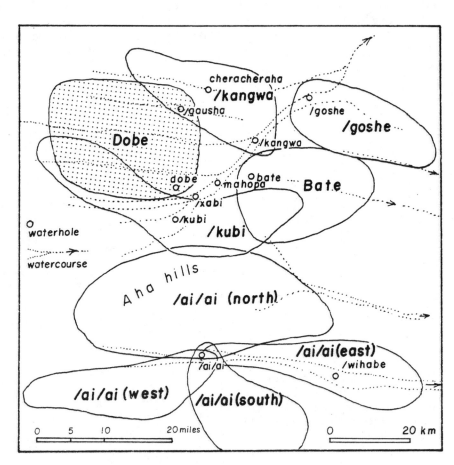

Figure 1-1b. The territorial boundaries of nine bands of the !Kung San as mapped by Lee (1965). The Dobe !Kung territory (stippled) is the focus of figure 1-2.

17

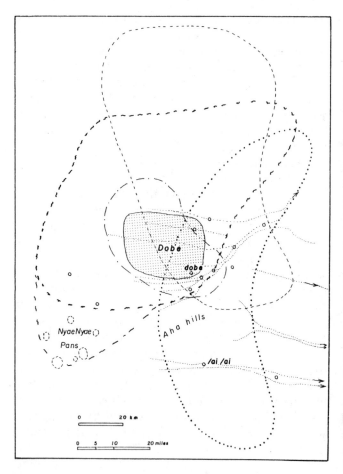

Figure 1-2a. Approximate ranges of five families of the Dobe !Kung band (after Yellen and Harpending 1972) mapped onto the Dobe territory as recorded by Lee (1965).

advantages of this system are obvious.

Equally obvious, however, is the impact of such a system on the distribution of group-markers dropped on the landscape—they will be spread far and wide beyond the margin of the territory itself. Although this was originally seen as a serious theoretical spoiler of the prospects for detecting archaeological territories, it was later realized that the time frame of these observations was too short. In the long term—say, in the lifetime of one generation—it is reasonable to assume that each of the studied families would have spent more time inside the territory than out of it because of periodic return trips to the Dobe waterhole.

This analog will now be modified so that we can consider the hypothetical map of one individual's movements on the landscape throughout his or her lifetime (fig. 1-3 top). It can be plotted as three concentric rings: a core area surrounded by the annual range, surrounded in turn by the lifetime range (Peterson 1975). Most time is spent in the core area (territory or subterritory). The annual range embraces visits to adjacent bands during the seasonal round, and longer visits during bad years for the core area. Least time was spent in the lifetime range. It encompasses rare visits farther afield when drought affected the entire annual range. It is also visited to maintain reciprocity ties, as a hedge against prolonged drought.

Now, this hypothetical map of one person's movements can be converted to a map of "assertive style," reflecting the handiwork of that individual (cf. Hill 1977). Assuming that the style does not change

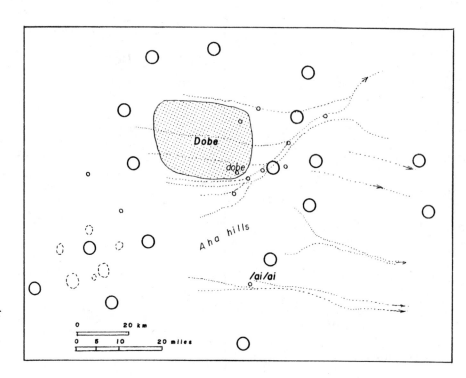

Figure 1-2b. Approximate birthplaces of Dobe band members (after Yellen and Harpending 1972) mapped onto the Dobe territory as recorded by Lee (1965).

Figure 1-3. *Top:* Hypothetical map showing the concentric arrangement of the Core Area (territory or sub-territory), annual range, and lifetime range of an individual hunter-forager; the individual never visited the gift recycling zone. *Middle:* Section showing the relative drop rate of articles decorated with the personal "signature" of that individual. *Bottom:* Note blurring of the frequency "shoulders" when several individual markers are combined.

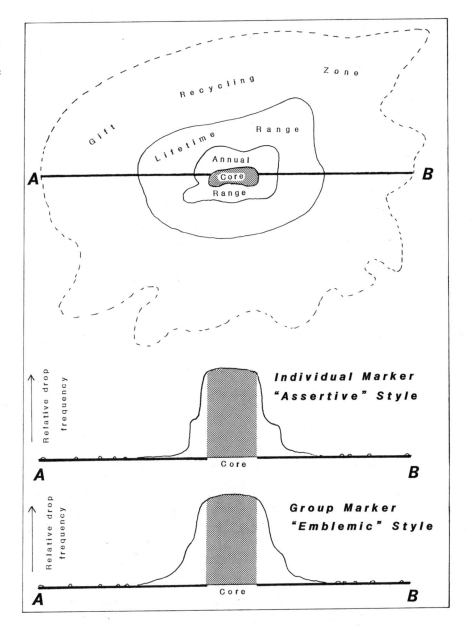

during the person's life-span, different discard rates of the style element will appear in each zone. As Soja (1971:37 and fig. 11b), first predicted about "activity" within a territory, the core area should display a high-density "plateau," and there will be a sharp, well-defined drop-off "shoulder" at the boundaries of the various rings (fig. 1-3 middle). A fourth, outer ring must now be added to account for the individual's gifts being reexchanged (Wiessner 1977) farther out beyond the lifetime range (fig. 1-3 top).

Common sense dictates, however, that low survival rates for individual-markers make this model unworkable in the field, so it is modified again to a map of "emblemic" style (group-marker) elements. Survival rates are very much greater for emblemic style because most band members produce it, thus relative densities across a landscape can now be plotted. However, group-signatures are produced by many individuals for several generations, and their ranges will not perfectly overlap. Thus the drop-off pattern will be far more diffuse, with boundaries between concentric zones becoming smeared. In cross-section, the shoulders will become rounded and less well defined (fig. 1-3 bottom). The modification is now complete. We have a model of a band territory that predicts the distribution of emblemic style. It is still useless to a field archaeologist, however.

Before this model can be field-tested, we need to imagine it within a more complete context, so that its articulation with other neighboring territories is fully grasped. Consider the layout in figure 1-4a, where the core area (shaded) of band number 4 in band cluster E, or "nexus" E (Heinz 1979), has been highlighted. Its collective annual range spreads to

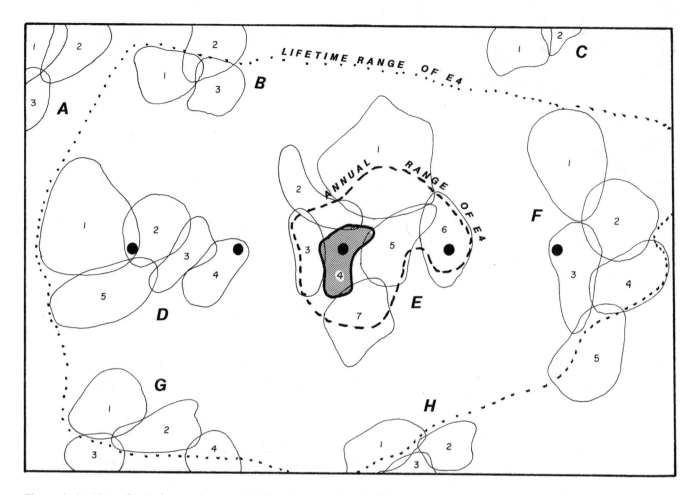

Figure 1-4a. Hypothetical map showing the distribution of several band clusters, with "dead ground" between them. Only one band (E4, stippled) has its collective annual and lifetime ranges plotted. The five black circles represent a sample of waterhole localities, treated in figure 1-4b. Such a map would probably measure more than 500 kilometers across in a semiarid environment.

parts of all the neighboring territories in the band cluster, and its collective lifetime range spreads to five neighboring band clusters. A scale is deliberately omitted from the map, but in a Kalahari setting it would be several hundred kilometers across. In areas with more densely packed resources, it might be less, but more of this later. The most likely reason that nobody visited clusters A and C would be a language barrier, but other reasons might apply in more densely packed habitats (see below). Also omitted are the annual and lifetime ranges of each of the other plotted territories, and the viewer is invited to imagine the chaos of lines resulting, if they were all included.

Let us now consider the frequency distributions of group-markers (emblemic style) collected from the camp surfaces clustered around five different waterholes spaced out across the landscape (fig. 1-4b). Again, common sense dictates that individual sites will yield too few objects to provide reliable percentage calculations, so site clusters are combined to produce adequate samples. It is assumed that the site cluster represents a valid settlement unit, and that all

bands using the waterhole were equally likely to use any campsite around the waterpoint.

Marker object E4 is dominant at the waterhole within territory E4, and there are distinct drop-off shoulders on either slope of the shaded graph where more distant waterholes reflect their positions in the annual and lifetime ranges. Note also that the E4 waterhole yielded dozens of items representing other bands—the relative frequency of each reflecting the position of the E4 waterhole in their own annual or lifetime ranges. Now consider the waterhole in D1 and 2 on the left side of the graph. This was shared by two contiguous bands (fig. 1-1b) so there is an equal proportion of both marker objects. However, their frequencies are suppressed by that of D4, whose members were in the habit of visiting both bands annually and who spent almost as much time at this waterhole as the host pair did together. Next, the reader's attention is drawn to the vertical frequency scale on the far left, which terminates short of 100 percent. This allows for a residue of marker objects (not necessarily all exactly ten percent totals) coming

Figure 1-4b. Hypothetical graph of the relative frequencies of E4 group-markers (stippled) recovered at each of the five waterholes plotted across the map in figure 1-4a. Percentage values are deliberately vague, but they do not reach 100 percent to allow for the peripheral distributions from territories off the map.

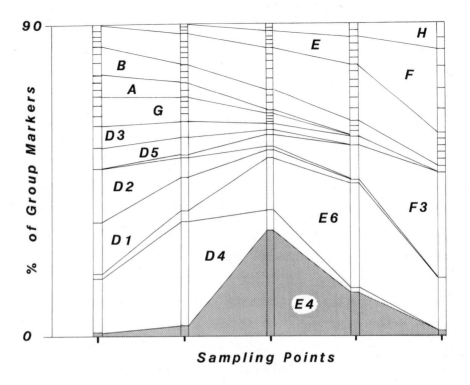

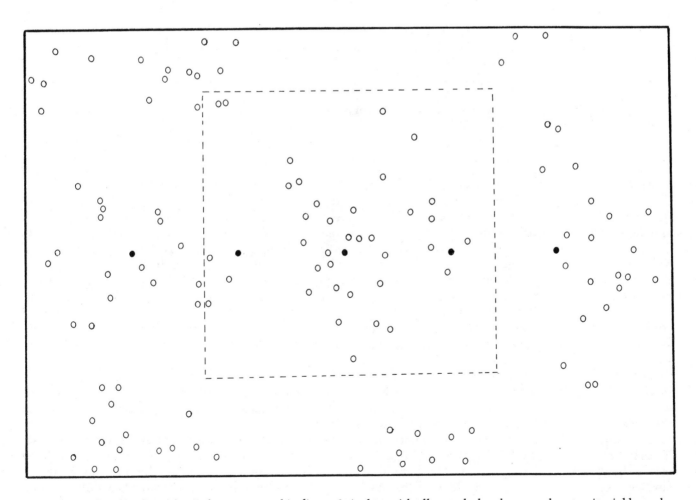

Figure 1-5. The same hypothetical area mapped in figure 1-4a, but with all waterholes shown and no territorial boundaries indicated. The five waterholes shown in figures 1-4ab are in black. The dashed line is the boundary of the area discussed in figures 1-8 through 1-10.

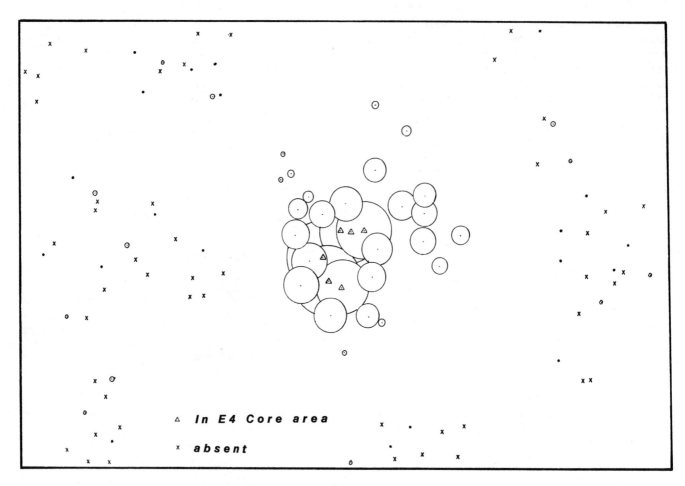

Figure 1-6. Hypothetical map of the relative frequencies of group-marker objects made by members of band E4 that were recovered at the waterholes plotted in figure 1-5.

from more distant bands that are positioned beyond the margins of the map. Fringes of their annual and lifetime ranges will be intersected by these margins, and their lines would further clutter the map in figure 1-4a, if added. In a semiarid landscape like the Kalahari, territorial configurations are dictated by the whereabouts of reliable waterholes. Figure 1-5 plots *all* the waterholes on our imaginary landscape, with the same five locations highlighted. Let us now consider the frequency distribution of marker object E4 at every waterhole on the map (fig. 1-6). Circles of various sizes represent the number of E4 objects expressed as percentage values (unspecified) of total marker objects collected at each waterhole. The highest values occur at band E4 waterholes; about half those values occur at waterholes within the annual range of E4; and decreasing fractions occur at waterholes as we move out across the lifetime range. Towards the rim of the lifetime range the chances of finding even a single specimen decline, so the outer limits of distribution become only a ragged shadow of the actual range limit.

One last manipulation will convert this map into an archaeologically visible record of the territory and its annual range. In this exercise the waterhole loci are used as data-points around which to plot an isopleth map (fig. 1-7), in which the rapid frequency drop-off at each margin is rendered as closely spaced isolines. This diagram emerges as the key to recognizing group-markers in the field—*their frequency isopleth maps will yield clearly defined double shoulders* (cf. Soja 1971: fig. 9). This is the main criterion used throughout the following chapters for determining whether or not a particular motif was indeed an emblemic style.

A few field tests of this "shoulder" concept have already been conducted. Hodder and Orton (1976) plotted the density drop-off profiles for British Late Iron Age Dubonnic and Cunobelin coins, the distributions of which were thought to map out tribal territories (Rivet 1964). The profiles failed to produce shoulders, but suggested to the analysts a simple density-decay relationship instead. Similar results were produced by Hogg (1971) for Durotrigian coinage in an adjacent area. The trouble here is that the data-set is still too limited, and the function of coinage is too ambiguous to be accepted as a true marker object. Hodder and Orton (1976) also raise the very real possibility that boundary changes have blurred the shoulders in the density profile, and point out that finer chronologies will be required to resolve this menacing question (see below). Returning again to our hypothetical case, it would be rash to suppose that a single field test will suffice, and some independent cross-check is advisable. Two related double-checking procedures have been used throughout this study, and examples of each will be applied to a fragment of our imaginary landscape. A portion (delineated in fig. 1-5) containing all the data points in band cluster E, plus a few neighboring ones, is used in this sample exercise. Step 1 demands that a percentage value for every marker object at every waterhole (data point) be computed. In step 2 the column of values for every two contiguous waterholes is compared, and the difference between the values for each pair of marker objects in the two columns is recorded. In step 3 the sum of the differences is computed and plotted midway between the two data points (fig. 1-8). In step 5, lines of varying thicknesses, expressing the accu-

mulative percentage differences between waterholes, are plotted (fig. 1-9). A minimum cutoff value is chosen, to screen out minor differences between closely related waterholes.

Obviously, the intervals and line thicknesses must be chosen with care, and can be manipulated to bring out differences or to suppress background (or statistical) noise. Although hand fitted and somewhat subjective, this is nonetheless an invaluable device for seeing the picture whole, because it involves all the marker objects in the study area, not just one. As such, it provides an independent test of the validity of the "shoulders" first depicted in figure 1-7 for a single market object. Note also that it displays various subdivisions within the individual territories of band cluster E, which tend to confuse the picture.

A third related test will help resolve this within-cluster confusion. Here, the same steps are carried out, except that the accumulative percentage difference between every waterhole and every other waterhole on the map is now computed. Some maximum allowable percentage difference is then chosen—usually close to the minimum allowable value in the

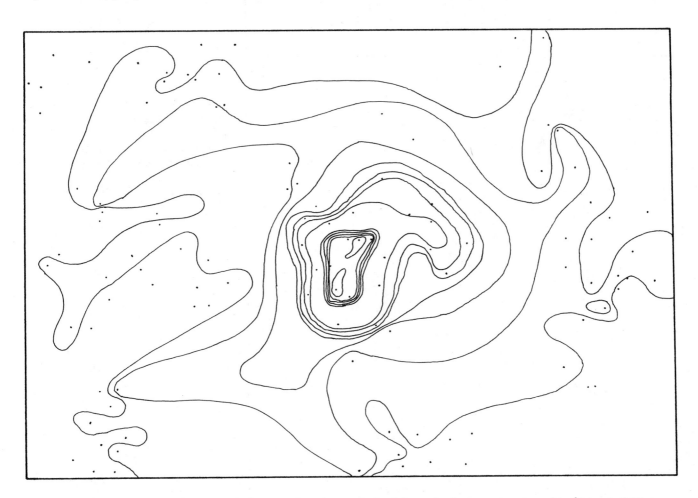

Figure 1-7. Hypothetical isopleth map of E4 marker objects derived from the frequencies plotted in figure 1-6. Note that the clustered isopleth lines, reflecting rapid frequency drop-off "shoulders," coincide with the core area boundary and the annual range boundary shown in figure 1-4a.

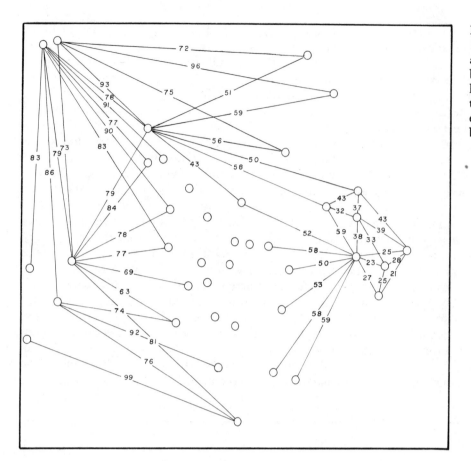

Figure 1-8. Sample area (see figure 1-5) showing waterholes in and around band cluster E. The values between (selected) contiguous waterholes are the hypothetical accumulative group-marker percentage differences between those two assemblages.

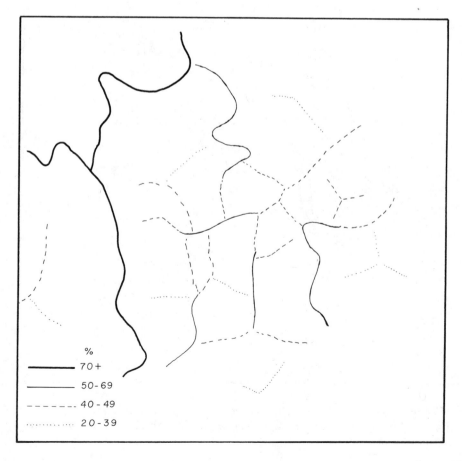

Figure 1-9. The area given in figure 1-8 with accumulative group-marker percentage differences between all contiguous waterholes shown as lines of varying thickness. Only differences greater than 20 percent are plotted.

Figure 1-10. The area given in figure 1-8, with accumulative group-marker percentage differences between all contiguous waterholes shown as clustered hierarchies. Only differences less than 50 percent are plotted.

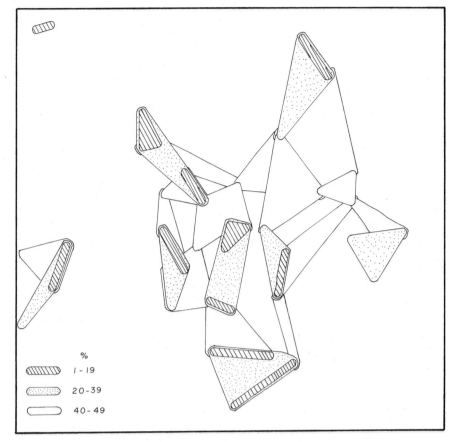

%
1 - 19
20 - 39
40 - 49

previous test. This time, the waterholes most like each other (in percentage frequencies of each marker object) are clustered in a hierarchy of values (fig. 1-10) such that waterholes most closely linked (that is, with the smallest percentage difference) are highlighted. Inevitably, contiguous waterholes inside the core area of a territory are prominent because they share a dominant high value. Two waterholes on the rim of the core area will be less tightly linked because they will each be "contaminated" by marker objects from two different neighboring bands. The only situation where a bogus linkage might occur is where two waterholes are both within the overlap zone of two neighboring bands. This pair of percentage columns may look so alike that they will appear as a distinct cluster, separate from the true core clusters on either side of it.

Thus far, we have proceeded entirely on the naive assumption that the territorial organization of our imaginary landscape is static—boundaries do not change with time. Hodder and Orton (1976:197) have already pointed out that this is a built-in problem of boundary detection because it will inevitably blur the pattern. Actualistic studies have yet to demonstrate what happens during a boundary change, and there are no good ethnohistoric accounts of territorial shifts. However, there is a large body of theory drawn from various disciplines that predicts that boundary changes are inevitable.

Demographic theory predicts that, in the long run, territories shrink, become more closely packed, and firm up their boundaries as population density increases. Ecological theory predicts the same when resources become more abundant and predictable (thus increasing population density) in the shorter haul. Culture theory predicts the same when hunter-foragers shift to herding and semisedentism, on a still shorter time-scale. Logically, the reverse must also hold—territories swell and boundaries become diffuse and overlap when population density decreases, or when resources dwindle, or when herders revert to hunter-foragers again. All three sets of predictions can be welded into one comprehensive model (fig. 1-11).

The *Demographic* option has long been a favorite of archaeologists (Cohen 1977, Gramly 1977, Hassan 1981). It is invoked increasingly by those studying hunter-forager societies—especially Holocene ones (Price and Brown 1985, and many others). It is a handy and simple "explanation" for the increased diversity and patchiness of style observed in so many Holocene lithic industries around the world, including South Africa.

Here, population growth during the Holocene is taken as a given, but is only really documented in the ZVAP area (Sampson 1985:104-5) where site counts increase steeply through time. However, J. Deacon (1984) has repeatedly invoked a mid-Holocene de-

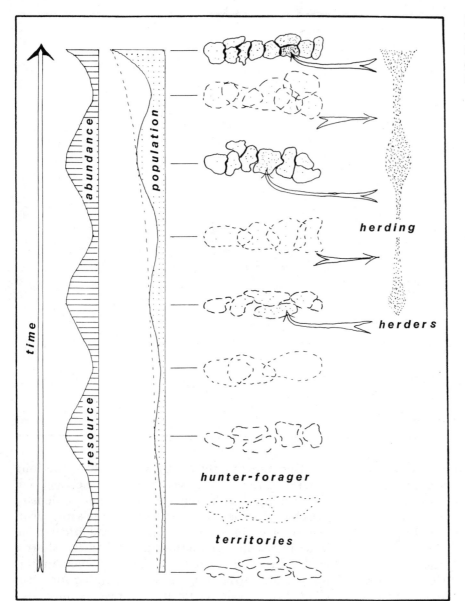

Figure 1-11. Summary diagram of the relationship between resource fluctuations *(left)*, population increase, territorial size/packing/fuzziness, and herder penetration.

population of the central plateau, with a specifically late Holocene population growth after 2000 B.C. If so, then the threefold increase in Smithfield sites over the preceding Interior Wilton (IW) site count bespeaks a very rapid population increase in the ZVAP area over the last 500 years. Any longer chronology for the IW (Humphreys and Thackeray 1983) makes the Smithfield site increase look like a population explosion! Humphreys (1979) has also suggested that population growth may have been an important driving force behind the stylistic changes that I have used to distinguish IW from Smithfield.

A rival scenario deduced from normative, culture-history models would be that the population increase was caused by in-migration of refugee San (with Smithfield technology) from north of the Orange River, where they were being displaced at approximately A.D. 1300 by the invading Iron Age

agripastoralists (Maggs 1976). Either way, population increases, and the predicted changes in territorial layout (more packed, smaller, firmer edged) must now be matched by the field data.

Ecological theory of territorial change is more factually grounded because it can be observed in both animals and humans. Animal ethology supplies the most important ecological components of the model. Territorial behavior in animals has several functions (Davies 1978), but the relevant one here is its role as a spacing mechanism, because it is clearly adaptive—it offers many alternative ways of mapping animals onto resources (Brown and Orians 1970). A cluster of formal, rigorously tested models explains how *resource abundance* and *patchiness (in time and space)* influence *feeding strategies* (Orians and Pearson 1979) which in turn influence *group size* (Caraco and Wolf 1975), *territory size* (Schoener 1971, Harvey and Mace 1983), and *perimeter defense* (Hamilton *et al.* 1976).

These same components are used to build limited models of hunter-forager spatial organization, but human models require extra components to help explain why humans are so often found outside their own territories (Yellen and Harpending 1972). Two components with obvious adaptive advantages are *social boundary defense* (Peterson 1975, Cashdan 1983), and *reciprocity* (Wiessner 1977). Other components with more subtle and distant adaptive relevance are *ritual/mythology* (Blundell 1980, 1982), *kinship* (Turner 1978), and *political structure* (Woodburn 1972, Layton 1986).

A small but important set of comparative studies (especially Cashdan 1983) ranks living or recently recorded forager societies along a habitat richness cline. The several components of territoriality (Guenther 1981) are each examined in the same rank order to discover at what point they change. From the rainforest (dense and predictable resources) end of the spectrum to desert (scarce and unpredictable resources) opposite extreme (fig. 1-12), territories become larger, more thinly populated, with less sharply defined boundaries that overlap more frequently and more extensively (Berndt and Berndt 1964, Tindale 1974, Jochim 1981, Hassan 1981, Madden 1983). Along this same gradient, perimeter defense (boundary patrol) gives way to social boundary defense (exclusion from information) as the most economic way of maintaining territories. Reciprocity increases along the cline, both in frequency and distance from home-territory. Visiting by individuals to adjacent territories also increases in duration, frequency, and distance from home-territory. Also hunter-forager bands may be placed on a gradient in Turner's (1978)

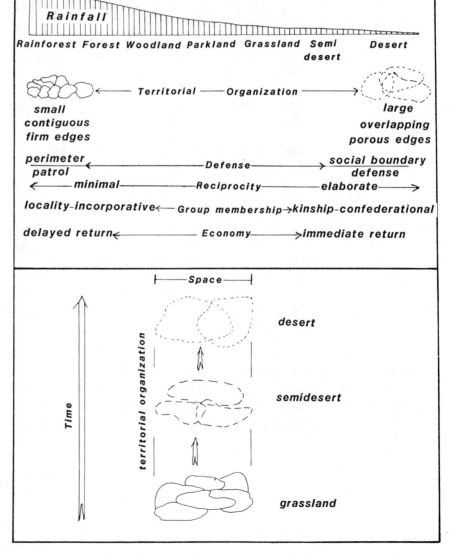

Figure 1-12. Summary diagram of the relationship between habitat cline *(top)*, territorial size/packing/ fuzziness, and four behavioral components of territoriality.

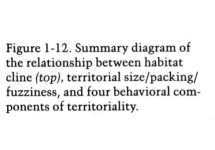

Figure 1-13. Summary diagram showing the relationship between habitat change through time and changes in territorial organization. Only the grassland-to-desert end of the habitat cline is shown.

terms, from "locality incorporative" (belong to the territory) to "kinship confederational" (belong to the family), with fictive kinship more easily obtainable in the former type of band, and temporary non-kin "visitors" more common in the latter. Along this same cline most economies shift from "delayed-return" to "immediate-return" (Woodburn 1982), and shift from relatively nonegalitarian to egalitarian political structures.

Note, however, that ecological theory explains only living and recent spatial behavior, and lacks substantial time-depth. It must be modified to a space-time framework (fig. 1-13) to become applicable to the ZVAP study, where only the grassland-to-desert part of the habitat gradient is relevant. For ecological theory to "work" in the ZVAP case, there must be extensive enough climatic change to cause the Karoo landscape to alter to grassland or to full desert between A.D. 1300 and 1800. At present we have not one scrap of evidence to suggest either scenario, but we have only just started to look. Also, the construct in figure 1-13 does not allow for the area to become totally abandoned during desertification. Silberbauer (1981) suggests that the G/wi band's collective "mental map" of its territory's resources is wiped out in such crises, when people die or migrate. They have to be relearned when the area becomes habitable again. Under such conditions, territorial configurations may be totally rearranged, and the marker-object maps of the two episodes (now mixed on surface sites) will produce nothing but random noise in the isopleth maps.

The *Cultural* (herding) option for modifying territories is less tractable because theory is still weakly developed. Models of hunter-to-herder cultural change are still in the making (Brooks *et al.* 1984), and a comprehensive (unified?) body of theory has yet to emerge. At the heart of the matter is the shift from high-mobility to semisedentism and all its ramifications (camp layout, storage, and so forth). Although it seems intuitively reasonable on ecological grounds that territories should become smaller and more sharply defined (Baxter 1975), it has also been pointed out (Lewis 1975) that there are *political* advantages for cattle keepers who expand their territorial range. In our case, the most relevant ethnographic data probably come from the stock-keeping Basarwa who clearly have smaller territories than their central Kalahari neighbors (Hitchcock 1982: table 11.5), and who evidently had boundary disputes as well (Hodson 1912).

Livestock was already present in the ZVAP area by the time that bowl decorations first appeared (see chapter 4). If there was increased herding activity leading up to that event at approximately A.D. 1300, style theory might "explain" the appearance of decorations as a response to increased social stress. Note that this model makes no attempt to distinguish between *adoption* of herding by San hunter-foragers, versus *space-sharing* by resident San and immigrating herders. Increased stylistic signaling between groups will be the result in both cases.

Thus far, none of these bodies of theory have taken into account the potentially disruptive forces of trekboer *colonizing* of waterholes, beginning in the mid-1700s, and escalating through the early 1800s. Generalized models of what happens to hunter-foragers when their space is invaded by western elements—missions, trading posts, farmers, game managers, government settlements, police, even armies—are slow to emerge, although the descriptive literature is growing rapidly (Leacock and Lee 1982, Schrire 1984). Territorial organization will be just one of many casualties, for example, the Nharo reorganization around boreholes (Barnard 1979); the emergence of Ojibwa family hunting territories as a response to the fur trade (Bishop 1974); or the decrease in Aboriginal range size after station-based settlement (White 1977).

One nearly universal response is that foragers' settlement patterns start to refocus around the farm, village, mission, or store as they map onto the newcomers as an additional (and focal) resource. People spend less and less time in their own territories, and the various group signatures (motifs) become concentrated and overlap in places where the intruders set up bases.

From all the foregoing, it will now be abundantly and depressingly clear that territorial boundaries can be expected to change through time. This in turn raises doubts about the prospects for field testing the model outlined in figures 1-9 to 1-11. But these are doubts, not certainties—and no existing body of theory can predict whether territories will change so radically in four to five centuries that the marker-object maps will be obliterated. What is more, these configurations of jumbled marker-distributions may yet be unraveled if the markers themselves changed with time. All is not necessarily lost, and further discussion will not resolve these doubts. It is time to reenter the real world.

TWO

The Upper Seacow River Valley

The "real world" in this case study is an archaeological map of surface sites (mainly lithics and pottery) left by parahistoric Bushmen and their prehistoric forebears. This map is probably the largest of its kind—roughly the size of the state of Delaware—and was deliberately constructed as a test-bed for boundary-detection methods. Before discussing the superabundant surface archaeology, however, it might be as well to describe its environmental setting. I have elected to review this at some length, not because environmental details have much to do with the problem at hand, but mainly because I want to expunge any preconceived images of a Kalahari-type setting, acquired by readers already well steeped in the Kalahari San literature. Consequently, readers anxious to get down to the business of boundary-detection may want to skim this chapter and pass on to the next, which deals with the archaeological trace itself.

The name Zeekoe (meaning Hippopotamus in the Dutch language) was given to a minor tributary draining the southern flank of the Orange River basin (fig. 2-1a) in the central plateau of South Africa. In ensuing centuries, the name has been anglicized to Seacow, and "Afrikaansed" to Seekoei. All three names are in use, but the Dutch is now virtually restricted to the early literature on the region. Road signs and official documents now use the other two interchangeably. I will use the English Seacow when referring to the drainage as a whole, and the Afrikaans Seekoei when referring to tributaries of the system (Bo-Seekoei, and so forth).

The first stage of ZVAP was a foot survey that mapped approximately 5,000 square kilometers of the upper and central valley (fig. 2-1b), and these results are described elsewhere (Sampson 1985). This volume will concentrate entirely on the upper valley (fig. 2-1c). The source tributaries of the Seacow rise on the rim of the Great Escarpment on the watershed of the Sneeuberg Mountains (fig. 2-2) at an average altitude of about 6,500 feet (2,000m). From here they cut steeply through valleys in the range's northern flanks, converging into four major arms: the Klein Seekoei, Elandskloof, Zoetvlei, and Bo-Seekoei (fig. 2-3). These debouch abruptly onto the plains of the Upper Karoo at around 5,250 feet (1,600m), where the impeded drainage at each exit has formed marshy areas called *vleis*. From here the streams drop more gradually for about fifteen miles (40km) across the flats to a point in the central valley where they merge into the Groot Seekoei channel at 4,500 feet (1,400m). The Klein Seekoei in the east and the Elandskloof in the center of the upper valley have failed to incise deep channels into the flats, so that in places they become little more than braided streams, occasionally disappearing completely. The Zoetvlei and Bo-Seekoei have cut deeper into the plains and have more obvious channels.

The Sneeuberg range, the Agter-Renosterberg range on the upper valley's eastern flank, and the valley floor are all composed of horizontally bedded, fossiliferous shales and mudstones of the Beaufort Series in the Karoo System. These are intersected at many places by intrusive dolerite dikes and sills that are generally more resistant to erosion than the surrounding sedimentary rocks. One massive sill complex forms the crest of the Sneeuberg range (Wellington 1955), with its most complete exposure visible in the flanks of the Compassberg—a sharp peak dominating the range at 8,200 feet (2,500m). Another massive dolerite complex makes up the Meiringsberg section of the range, and a third (the Winterhoekberge) occurs in the southwest corner of the valley. The latter area was not mapped during the ZVAP survey, and falls outside this study area. Relatively thin lenses of discontinuous siltstone are intercalated with the shales and mudstones, becoming both thicker and more continuous as one trends eastward across the area to the Agter-Renosterberg. Small

Figure 2-1a. Location of the Seacow River drainage (stippled) in relation to the central Orange River, nearby towns, and main dams of the Orange River scheme.

Figure 2-1b. About 5,000 square kilometers of the central and upper Seacow Valley (shaded) were searched for archaeological surface sites. Approximately 16,000 sites have been recorded in this area.

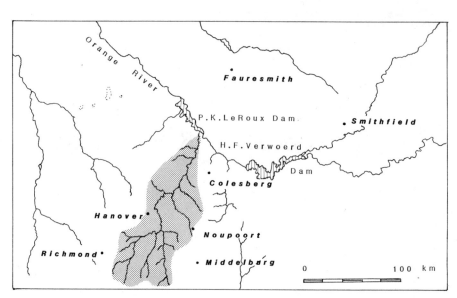

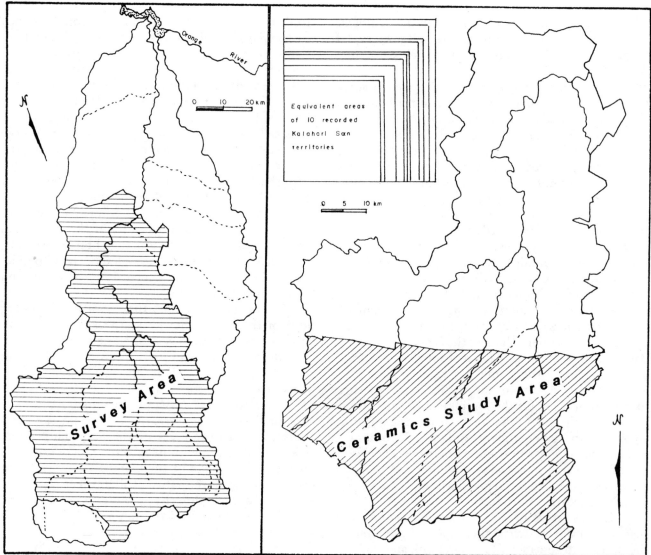

Figure 2-1c. Potsherds from all the known Bushman camps in approximately 2,000 square kilometers of the upper valley (shaded) were collected. The equivalent areas for San territories include both !Kung and G/wi examples.

overhangs and rockshelters occur under lintels of this siltstone, but they are extremely rare. The western rim is a dolerite dike dividing the Seacow drainage from that of the adjacent Ongersrivier Valley.

The floor of the upper valley is divided into flat basins by randomly oriented dolerite dikes that form rubble-strewn ridges. Where these intersect, or have spawned horizontal sills, swarms of low rocky hills and knolls occur. The classic flat-topped *koppies* considered so typical of Karoo landscapes are all but absent here, since thin horizontal sill cappings are rare. Drainage has been partly superimposed in this network of vertical intrusive rocks, and has been partly shaped by them. At points where dikes are cut through by stream channels, narrow steep-sided gaps in the ridges have formed. These *poorts* are invariably associated with spring-eyes, locally called "fountains" *(fonteine)*, where groundwater in the channel fill has been forced to surface. The country rock has excellent water-retention properties and groundwater is close to the surface in many places. The dikes serve as subsurface barriers to groundwater movement and are everywhere associated with fountains (fig. 2-3).

The flanks of dolerite ridges and hills retain protected remnants of the mudstones and shales, usually covered with large dolerite scree that obscures the shattered and partly altered nature of the contact zone. In places where surrounding shales have been baked by the intrusion, patches of high quality hornfels may occur. Because this is more durable than either the dolerite or the surrounding rock, it tends to form a slight protrusion in the flank scree slope. Hornfels outcrops are small and patchy, usually no more than a few meters long. Massive hornfels bodies only occur below horizontal sills, and are best exposed on hilltops where the overlying dolerite has been removed by erosion. Occasionally, the hot contact on either side of a ridge may have become so indurated that a double ridge has formed where the dolerite spine has eroded down faster than either flank. Sandy corridors may then form between these parallel crests of the ridge. Similar level sandy patches occur on the shoulders, saddles, and footslopes of dolerite ridges where rates of dolerite erosion have been uneven and localized.

The sediment cover of Karoo bedrock is generally very thin, and the upper Seacow Valley is no excep-

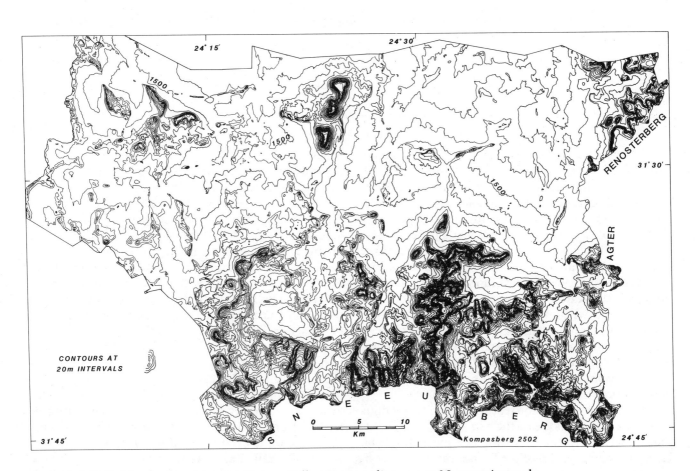

Figure 2-2. Relief features in the upper Seacow Valley. Contour lines are at 20-meter intervals.

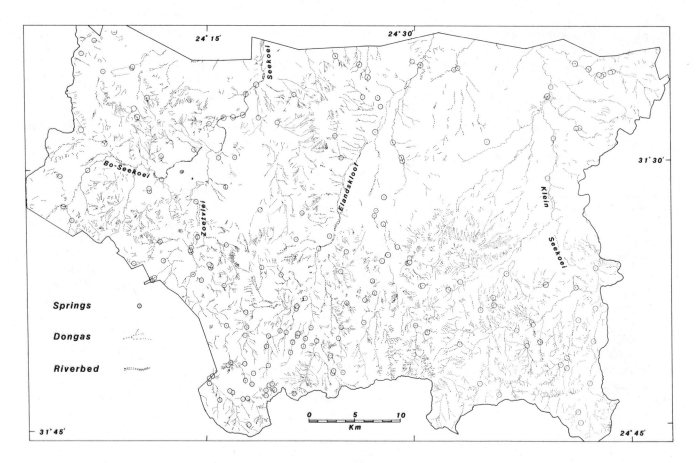

Figure 2-3. Drainage patterns and major spring eyes in the upper Seacow Valley. The five principal drainage channels are named.

tion. Soil type distribution is dictated almost entirely by bedrock type (van Rooyen and Burger 1974). Dolerite hill and ridge flanks have thin mantles of lithosols and reddish brown apedal sandy soils. Banked against north-trending ridges are rare patches of calcareous sandy soils that are clearly of aeolian origin. These have usually formed massive calcretes at depth. The flats are only patchily covered with thin, yellowish brown, weakly developed, sandy soils, sedentary on the Karoo sediments. There is also much stony ground without any sediment cover. Alluvial strips along stream banks are the only appreciable depths of sediment. These old channel fills are generally stratified, and the recent floodplain deposits have weakly developed sandy gray soils. Massive calcification is common in the old sediment bodies.

Another typical Karoo feature made conspicuous by its absence in this area is the *pan*—a playa blowout, usually with a fringe of sediments and colluvium. These are more typical of the Ecca Series to the west, and are not common in the region of Beaufort Series exposures. Only one atypical (nonblowout) pan at the Bo-Seekoei/Zoetvlei confluence has acted as a significant sediment trap, with subsequent deep calcrete formation (Partridge and Dalbey, 1986).

Vegetation cover in the upper Seacow is a typical Karoo *veld* of low, semidesert scrub, with varying amounts of seasonal grasses that disappear altogether during the dry winter season. Taller shrubs grow on the hill and mountain flanks, and there are no trees. No systematic veld-type mapping has been done in the upper valley, although detailed maps of some individual farms exist on government files. Karoo bushes dominate the landscape; these are woody plants and some mesembs—almost all lower than one meter in height. Scores of different species make up the community (Werger 1978), but any given area is usually dominated by one or two types. Their palatability varies greatly, and the best have outstanding nutritional properties, with record protein and phosphate contents even in the dry season (du Toit *et al.* 1940). Overall, Karoo vegetation has a remarkable carrying capacity, which belies its appearance. Among the better known highly palatable species are

Pentzia spp., *Salsola* spp., *Walafrida* and *Felicia* spp., but this in no way exhausts the list. In most places, however, less palatable species dominate.

Grasses are equally varied, and contribute significantly to the grazing only when they are available. Among the better known climax grasses are species of *Cymbopogon, Digitaria, Festuca, Fingerhuthia, Heteropogon, Panicum, Setaria,* and *Sporobolus,* but these are quite rare. There are also dozens of less palatable subclimax annual grasses. After good rains, grass stands may come to temporarily obscure the Karoo bushes, especially on dolerite soil covers. The crests of the Sneeuberg and Agter-Renosterberg are covered by a montane sourveld dominated by *Merxmuellera,* a thoroughly unpalatable tussock grass that replaces the Karoo bushes as the predominant type.

Vegetation cover on this landscape is typically thin. On the flats it is generally around five percent in winter and seven to eight percent after the rains when the annual grasses emerge. Typical tussock-grass cover on the mountains is around twelve to fifteen percent. Overgrazing coupled with repeated drought episodes can rapidly destabilize so vulnerable a cover, leading to huge areas dominated by subclimax communities, plus scores of different pioneer species together with invading ephemerals called *opslag,* comprising many varieties of thorny weeds and small unpalatable shrubs. Carrying capacity inevitably drops off, and overstressed areas become subject to sheet erosion. The more resilient Karoo bushes surviving in such areas display increasing amounts of dead woody stems with no leaf cover. When rested, the veld recovers extremely slowly, and seldom to its exact former species composition. Damage to heavily stressed patches seems to be irreversible. Acocks (1975) argued that this part of the Karoo had been a grassveld before the arrival of pioneer European stockfarmers, after which it was massively invaded by Karoo bushes. The observations that led him to these conclusions were "relic" patches of grassveld (including some in the upper Seacow Valley), which he believed had escaped overgrazing in the past. This led him inevitably to the conclusion that the plant community was no longer in its pristine state, and caused him to create the veld-type label of Upper False Karoo. His position is still held as an article of faith by many scholars, but opinions are becoming more sharply divided as the impact of quasi-cyclic droughts, longer-term climatic changes, and prehistoric stockherders are contemplated. Much detailed research is still needed, however, before we can be sure that the term "False" Karoo is, indeed, a misnomer.

Among the taller shrubs most commonly found on the ridges and mountain slopes of the upper Seacow are *Rhus erosa, Rhus lucida* and *Diospyrus australis,* with occasional invaders such as *Lycium austrinum.* These are widely scattered and seldom grow taller than two meters, with smaller, more stunted specimens in the high mountains. Note that the thorn bushes so common in the Orange River Valley and to the south of the Sneeuberg are entirely absent here. Other sporadic features of the ridge plant cover are aloes, a few bulbous plants, and other succulents. On the flats, the most visible bulbous plants are *Homeria pallida* and *Moraea polystacha,* which produce huge and colorful stands after good rains. The stream banks, mainly near the elongated pools surrounding spring eyes, support dense patches of reeds, dominated by *Cyperus marginatus* and *Phragmites australis.*

Like much of the Karoo today, the upper Seacow Valley is given over entirely to stock farming, wholly dominated by Merino sheep. Pastures are systematically and elaborately fenced, with a variety of rotational grazing systems in practice. Inevitably, indigenous large game herds are massively reduced (Bigalke and Bateman 1962) and must be reconstructed from early travelers' reports (Ellerman *et al.* 1953). By all accounts the flats were inhabited by enormous, dense herds of herbivores in the late 1700s and early 1800s. Typically, these were dominated by black wildebeest (*Connochaetes gnou*), red hartebeest (*Alcelaphus buselaphus*), zebra (*Equus burchelli*), quagga (*E. quagga*), springbok (*Antidorcas marsupialis*), and blesbok (*Damaliscus dorcas*). Only small herds of the latter two species survive today. Less frequently mentioned, but nevertheless present in numbers, were Cape buffalo (*Syncerus caffer*), eland (*Taurotragus oryx*), southern reedbuck (*Redunca arundinum*), bontebok (*Damaliscus pygargus*), and steenbok (*Raphicerus campestris*). Only the steenbok has survived and remains plentiful in the area today. Other lesser game sighted on the flats were warthog (*Phacochoerus aethiopicus*), and sundry carnivores, especially Cape lion (*Leo capensis*), leopard (*Panthera pardus*), cheetah (*Acinonyx* sp.), spotted hyena (*Crocuta crocuta*), hunting dog (*Lycaon picta*), caracal (*Felis caracal*), serval (*F. serval*), wildcat (*F. libyca*), jackals (*Canis* spp.), and silver fox (*Vulpes chama*). The modern sheep flocks are preyed on by the smaller cats and jackals today, but their numbers are dwindling rapidly. Still very numerous are colonies of Egyptian mongoose (*Herpestes ichneumon*), yellow mongoose (*Cynictis penicillata*), and rock hyrax (*Procavia capensis*). A wide variety of smaller nocturnal creatures are also mentioned in the early accounts: aardvark (*Orycteropus afer*), hares (*Leporidae* spp.), springhare (*Pedetes capensis*), porcupine (*Hystrix africae-australis*), Honey badger (*Melivora capensis*), and pangolin (*Manis temmincki*), all of which are under intense pressure today, but survive nonetheless. Another creature likely to survive because of its periodic commercial value is the ostrich (*Struthio* sp.).

Other prominent species with more restricted niches included hippo *(Hippopotomus amphibius)* in the river channels, none of which survive today. Montane species have a far better survival record: chacma baboon *(Papio ursinus)*, mountain reedbuck *(Redunca fulvorufula)*, and vaalribbok *(Pelea capreolus)*. All are under pressure, and the baboons are likely to be exterminated before much longer. The klipspringer *(Oreotragus oreotragus)* has virtually disappeared.

Reptiles have fared somewhat better than the mammals under the onslaught of modern farming practices. Prominent among these are large aquatic iguanas quite frequently sighted near waterholes, and Cape cobras, which are by far the most frequently encountered snakes. Still surprisingly abundant are tortoises, some of which grow to huge dimensions since they are not eaten by the modern populace.

Prominent among the most frequently sighted birds are the secretary bird, blue crane, and several birds of prey. Migrant waterfowl may be more frequent today than in former centuries when there were no dams and, therefore, fewer bodies of standing water. The larger species most commonly sighted are Egyptian goose, sacred ibis, and flamingo.

Insect life is varied, and the most significant ones from the Bushman's viewpoint are termites that build low mounds in relatively rare clusters and locusts that swarm episodically with sometimes devastating results (see below).

Fluctuations in the carrying capacity of the veld, and consequently in the abundance of game, is now and has been controlled almost entirely by rainfall. This is best characterized as a semiarid, summer rainfall regime with an average annual rainfall of about twelve inches (305mm). The bulk of this falls in thundershower patterns, leading to very high runoff rates, and soft penetrating showers are relatively infrequent. Rains most crucial to annual veld regeneration are the few unreliable showers occurring in spring, usually October and November. Karoo bushes respond especially well to these as temperatures start to rise, and patches of veld that have received spring rain are notably greener and leafier by midsummer. Spring rains do not fall every year, however. The summer or "general" rains begin normally in late December and last until March. Individual falls are widespread, unlike the patchier spring showers. Odd showers may occur well into the winter months (occasionally turning to snow), but it is not uncommon to go three months without a drop of rain. Summer droughts are common, pernicious, and unpredictable. A quasi-cyclic pattern of drought is beginning to emerge as good records accumulate, but these are not yet refined (Tyson 1978). Runs of several years of low rainfall are the norm, with as little as three to five inches (80–130mm) for the worst annual totals on some farms. The episodes are interspersed with runs of good years. At the opposite extreme are rare and localized cloudbursts capable of delivering six inches (150mm) in a few hours and causing extensive flooding. Annual total precipitation in the mountains is almost certainly higher than on the flats, although good records are not available. Snowfalls occur two or three times each winter, with occasional drifts accumulating to three feet (1m) or more. Snow flurries on the flats are less common, and build to only a few inches in depth.

Subzero night temperatures begin in April and may last as late as October. The starting date of first frosts is highly unpredictable, as is the length of the frost season. Winter night temperatures drop to their lowest points (usually around 15°F (−6°C) just before dawn, and daytime highs are generally in the lower sixties, cooling very rapidly at sunset. Summer highs only rarely go above ninety degrees (26°C) and nights are pleasantly cool.

High winds in the daytime are a characteristic feature of the Karoo. In the upper Seacow Valley they alternate every few days between strong west-northwesterlies and moderate east-southeasterlies. The northwesterlies increase during late winter and early spring, with peak gusts of over thirty-five miles per hour (3.5m per sec.) in midafternoon. At the end of the winter drought, these usually generate huge dust clouds. The southeasterlies are generally cooler, bringing some relief in summer, but chilling the days in winter and creating misery at night. Very light northerly nighttime breezes also increase the wind-chill factor considerably. Rains are not very clearly associated with any particular wind direction, although local opinion is sharply divided on the subject. Still days occur most frequently in summer, but also occur while the wind system is veering around from one habitual direction to the other. High, undulating dust devils are a common sight on such days. They also occur around the edges and fronts of convection storms, usually leading to full-blown electrical storms later in the day. Lightning strikes are very common during these episodes, particularly on dolerite ridges and hills.

Two other climate-related events must be mentioned. Soon after the first good rains following a prolonged drought episode, locusts hatch in the drier country to the west of the Seacow Valley. Devastating swarms move through the Upper Karoo (and many other parts of the country), stripping the veld cover as they go. The short-term effects are impressive, but locusts are endemic, and the vegetation is clearly adapted to such punishment once every several years or so. Modern control strategies have no doubt reduced their impact so that swarms like those reported in the nineteenth century are no longer witnessed. The second phenomenon has now entirely disappeared—devastating herds of springbok, known as *trekbokken*, were forced by severe droughts out of the arid western Cape into the Upper Karoo and elsewhere in quest of grazing. They, too, stripped the vegetation which, once again, seems to have had the capacity to recover. The last recorded *trekbokken* herd in the Seacow Valley was in 1872 (Gutsche 1968).

Seen from the viewpoint of the resident Bushmen, this habitat contrasts quite markedly with that of the northern Kalahari. Both regions share a common mean annual rainfall, but the similarity stops there. The Karoo bedrock is structured such that reliable waterholes are superabundant, in sharp contrast to the Kalahari sands that absorb rainfall to great depths, thus rendering surface water extremely scarce. There are 113 fountains in the study area treated in this volume, as well as scores of seasonal seeps that could yield water with a little digging. The upshot of this is that it is virtually impossible to stand at any point in the upper valley without there being a waterpoint within an hour's walk. Unfortunately, the relative reliability of each of these springs cannot now be assessed because all but a few are now surrounded by windpumps set over boreholes drilled into the surrounding shales. The watertable around each eye is thus held below surface, and the flow rate can no longer be monitored. Those few not so affected continue to flow right through the winter months, and it is assumed that most of the others did as well. There are no clear grounds for suspecting that the upper valley suffered the seasonal water shortages that dominate the lives of the Kalahari San.

During very severe droughts, many waterholes used to fail in the valley, and in 1862 "... all the springs dried up" (Gutsche 1968:133) around Colesberg. I suspect that even in these crises a few of the strongest eyes would have continued to yield. Indeed a few of these, such as Droogefontein and Sterkfontein, may have been named by the Dutch trekboers for their durability. It is reasonable to assume that waterpoints varied in usefulness from year to year, but not by very much.

The next most notable contrast with the Kalahari habitat is that the upper Seacow is chronically short of firewood. Although the modern San suffer terribly from cold on winter nights, there can be no comparison with the suffering caused by freezing conditions of the Upper Karoo. Although there are no long-term temperature records for the Seacow, it is credibly claimed that some of the Sneeuberg valleys are among the coldest places in South Africa. Although the Karoo bushes provide small dead limbs for firewood, as do the taller shrubs, these flare rapidly and ash rather than form good coals. There are grounds for believing that the quest for firewood in winter would promote frequent campsite moves, and it was wood, rather than water, that formed the central anxiety of daily life.

Another notable contrast with the Kalahari is the openness of the terrain and the huge vistas of the surrounding plains afforded from the ridges and hills. Monitoring the movements of game (and other Bushmen) was a relatively simple matter. On the other hand, stalking game would have been considerably more difficult, although the possibilities for game drives were far greater because of the superb visual control. Given these conditions, it is reasonable to speculate that hunting provided a substantially greater proportion of the Seacow Valley Bushman's diet. A steadier meat supply would have been supplemented by the usual foraged smaller animals, plus the additional features of freshwater mussels *(Unio caffer)* and several species of fish from the river channels.

Foodplants of the Seacow Valley have yet to be studied for their nutritional values and their seasonal abundance. There are about a dozen different tuberous plants and two edible seeds presently known to us, and no doubt the list will grow with further work. At present there seem to be no superabundant species equal in importance to the mongongo nut or tsin bean in the diet of the Kalahari San. One possible exception is the Boesmanuintjie *(Cyperus usitatus)*, but little is known yet of its natural history. Nothing we have encountered thus far would suggest, however, that the Seacow Valley Bushmen were heavily dependent on plantfoods as a staple.

If game animals were the dominant focus of their adaptation, then herd fluctuations would have been another central concern of their daily lives. Most gregarious herbivores are known to travel great distances to acquire adequate grazing, and there is little reason to doubt that the Seacow Valley herds did the same. The chief difficulty with this assumption is that there is no very clear documentation on historical changes in game abundance during drought episodes, or following locust or *trekbokken* devastations, or both. Gutsche (1968:128) makes the interesting point that during the drought of 1861 "... even the wildebeest came within a few miles of the dorp" (the town of Colesberg), suggesting that they were *not* inclined to trek out of the valley to other pastures. A great deal more information of this kind may be buried in archival sources yet to be winnowed for clues.

The impact of the modern cultural landscape has been alluded to repeatedly. The study area treated in this volume, measuring forty-four miles (71km) cross-valley by twenty-seven miles (44km) down-valley, covers a total of 798 square miles (2,065 sq km). Today it is divided into fifty-nine sheep farms (fig. 2-4), each bounded by a jackal fence and subdivided into sheep camps. Stock tanks supplied by boreholes occur in each camp, and a network of vehicle

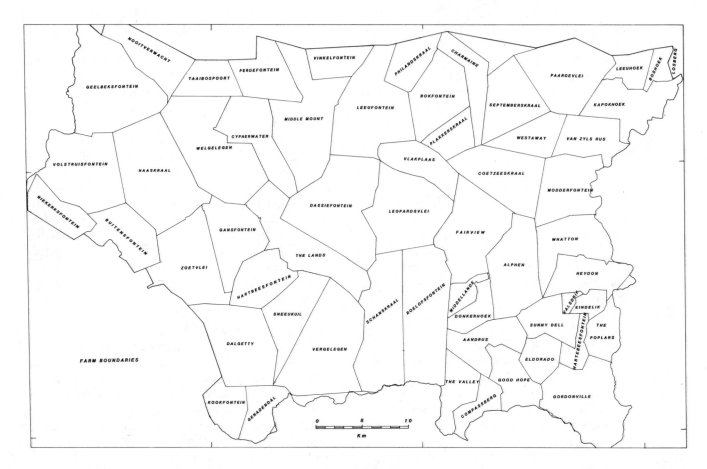

Figure 2-4. Sheep farm boundaries (with jackal-proof fences) in the upper Seacow Valley during the early 1980s. Farm names are used in the text to refer to specific parts of the study area.

tracks connects the camps. A farmhouse and yard with outbuildings and staff houses is usually centered in each property, some of which are now abandoned. Individual farms are connected by a system of permanent dirt roads maintained by machinery. The only other major feature in the area is a main gravel-topped road running east-west across the center of the study area and connecting the towns of Richmond and Middelburg. Another physical alteration to the landscape is plowing of patches of streambank floodplain, mainly for lucerne lands. Some of these (rare) lands are pump-irrigated, with consequent large-scale lowering of the watertable. There are also strings of dams thrown across the major and many minor drainages. All but the largest of these were breached by flash floods in 1974 and 1976. There are no other visible scars on the landscape, and damage to the archaeological residues of the former Bushman inhabitants is minimal. Now that their setting has been reviewed, we may turn to the residues themselves.

THREE

Archaeology of the Upper Seacow River Bushmen

The term *Bushman* will be used hereafter to denote those parahistoric hunter-foragers of the northern Cape and their prehistoric forebears. This will serve to distinguish the (living) Kalahari *San* from the (defunct) Karoo populations in space and time, and will help reduce ambiguities when comparing the two groups of people. *Bushman* has been used quite consistently in historical accounts (Wilson 1986:257-9), and this includes the Seacow Valley population. I find the arguments of Silberbauer (1981:3-6) and Cashdan (1983:64) in favor of this term more compelling than the objections to it raised by those who would promote the universal adoption of *San*.

An ethnohistory of the Seacow River Bushmen has yet to be written. Indeed, this may prove to be an impossible task given that they are seldom mentioned and never discussed in any detail in the journals of the few early travelers who passed this way in the late 1700s and early 1800s (Barrow 1806, Campbell 1815, De Kock 1965, Godée-Molsbergen 1916, Hutton 1887, Stow 1905, van der Merwe 1937). The only journal of any real worth—that of Erasmus Smits who ran a Bushman Mission at Colesberg from 1814 to 1816—is lost (Schoon 1972). Much unpublished archival material will have to be combed for chance references, and the amount and value of these are at present unknown. If the Seacow River Bushmen can be brought into historical perspective at all, such work lies in the future. This chapter will make no attempt, therefore, to pick through the published fragments of Bushman sightings, most of which describe the pitiful remnants of a rapidly disintegrating society on the expanding colonial border. Their relevance to the archaeological record has yet to be evaluated—a project that may eventually have relevance for stylistic boundary interpretation (chapter 13).

For the moment, then, the Seacow River Bushmen are better known as an archaeological en-

tity than a historical one. The purpose of this chapter will be to introduce the reader to what is known of their archaeological traces in the upper Seacow drainage, and to outline the interpretations already imposed on these remains. The archaeological residues of Bushman hunter-foragers who formerly inhabited the semiarid interior plateau of South Africa are referred to as the Smithfield Industry. The term is used here to mean specifically the Smithfield "B" of van Riet Lowe (1929). These residues are traceable back to the eighth century A.D. in the western Orange Free State (Horowitz *et al.* 1978) and to the late fourteenth century A.D. in the northern Cape Province (Beaumont and Vogel 1984).

Typical Smithfield assemblages contain flaked lithics (most commonly on unpatinated, blue-black hornfels), grinding and pounding equipment, bored stones, and sherds of a highly characteristic bowl-shaped pot decorated with a wide variety of stamp-impressed motifs. Endscrapers dominate the flaked lithics, the only other formal tools being reamers, single-platform cores recycled as trimming hammers, and rare convex scrapers. Otherwise flakes and flake fragments were used and jettisoned without formal shaping of the edge. Although rare backed microliths have been recorded on Smithfield sites (Sampson 1967a,b, 1970) and have been repeatedly included in the type list (Sampson 1972, 1974), more recent field experience has led me to doubt this association. It may be further noted that the definition used here excludes all earlier microlithic assemblages from the same region, which some authors (Butzer *et al.* 1979; Humphreys 1979) have lumped with the Smithfield Industry.

Assemblages dating to the late eighteenth and early nineteenth centuries A.D. usually contain rare items of European manufacture as well (Sampson 1967a). This contact association between resident Bushmen and early Dutch trekboer colonists is now particularly well documented for the upper Seacow Valley (Hart in prep.). Stratified deposits in Haaskraal and Volstruisfontein rockshelters have yielded rare fragments of European porcelain, glass, and metals a few centimeters below the surface of the fifteen inches (38cm) deep accumulation of Smithfield material. Their first appearance at these levels denotes the earliest contact between the two cultures. The density of European items increases erratically towards the surface of two of the deposits that mark the point at which occupation abruptly ceased. Some levels contain lead balls and firecaps, and there are scars on the back wall of Haaskraal shelter that look ominously like bullet marks. Both sequences provide an eloquent document of the fluctuating relationships of trekboer versus Bushman, and serve to demonstrate beyond any reasonable doubt that the Smithfield assemblage is indeed the archaeological trace of the Seacow River Bushmen mentioned in the written accounts of early travelers.

Near the base of both accumulations there is a layer containing stone tools and sherds of a completely different ceramic tradition, often referred to as Hottentot pottery (Laidler 1929; Schofield 1928; Rudner 1968, 1979). Hart (in prep.) has been at pains to demonstrate how this layer might be stratigraphically tied in to the base of two dry-stone walls in the talus slope of Haaskraal shelter. Because one of these is of a typical low-walled stock enclosure found elsewhere in the upper valley (Sampson 1984a, 1985), there are now grounds for believing that the Smithfield occupation *followed* a brief penetration of prehistoric herders into the upper valley. It is no longer certain that Bushman hunter-foragers shared the upper valley with prehistoric herders for any length of time, as I formerly proposed (Sampson 1984a, 1986a). Instead, they seem to have replaced the herders. It cannot be denied, however, that typical Bushman sherds are also directly associated in the herder levels in the excavated sequences. The material changes that took place at the interface between the top of the herder layer and the base of the Smithfield accumulation may reflect one of three possible scenarios:

(1) Bushmen from north of the Orange River were shunted southward into the valley by Late Iron Age incursions into what is now the Orange Free State. They either overwhelmed, absorbed, or displaced the herders to below the escarpment.

(2) On first arriving in the upper valley, the herders already practiced both the Smithfield and Khoi (Hottentot) ceramic traditions. They subsequently abandoned the Khoi tradition in favor of the other. This scenario would imply that the historical Bushmen were the descendants of earlier herder people, and may, in fact, have been part-time herders themselves—as Schrire (1980) has suggested.

(3) The Smithfield Bushmen were descendants of an earlier hunter-forager population represented by preherder levels called the Ceramic Phase of the Interior Wilton Industry (Sampson 1974:328-30). For reasons that are not clear, they opted to abandon their microlithic technology and to replace their ceramic tradition. Under this scenario, the Smithfield is just another phase of the Interior Wilton, rather than a separate industry, as Humphreys has proposed (Humphreys and Thackeray 1983:281). These resident hunter-foragers underwent this change at around the time that they received the herders into their midst, shared space with them for a brief spell, then ejected them.

No doubt other optional (still less plausible) scenarios could be concocted in our present state of ignorance about the origins of the Smithfield Industry. It is equally possible that the truth lies in some awkward and variable mix of all three of the above models. Excavation planned for many more shallow rockshelter deposits in the upper valley will no doubt help to refine the appropriate mix.

To date, most research effort has been invested in reaching some understanding of the Smithfield settlement pattern in the upper and central valley. This study area is now known to contain approximately six thousand Smithfield sites, and the published maps (Sampson 1985:87-93) are already out of date as more are added with each field season. The reason for this spectacular density is that high-grade hornfels outcrops are ubiquitous here as elsewhere in the valley. A total of 1,309 outcrops, each with highly characteristic Smithfield quarry debris close by, has been mapped thus far. The Bushman stone knappers could afford to be extremely wasteful, and little effort seems to have been made to conserve stone. Their prodigious output of flaked debris makes this one of the world's most spectacular archaeological records of any prehistoric hunter-forager society.

Although our map does not aim at 100 percent coverage, the available distributions are certainly complete enough that they are readily amenable to spatial analysis. The most obvious feature of Smithfield distribution is that sites occur in dense clusters (Sampson 1984b). In the field, it is a relatively easy matter to distinguish between the actual campsites and the minor chipping stations that were created through briefer tasks of the moment (*pace* Thomas 1986). Most site clusters contain a node of camps embedded in a wider scatter of minor chipping stations. The only parsimonious interpretation of this pattern is that it resulted from a radiating foraging pattern in which individuals set forth from a camp each few days to secure plants and animals from the surrounding countryside. These were partly processed in the field (small chipping stations, grindstones, and so forth) and returned to a nodal campsite that tended to accumulate much larger amounts of debris, including potsherds and foodwaste. The nodal camps are concentrated on the flat sandy patches on the footslopes and crests of dolerite hills and ridges, and most camps are within a half-hour walk (1km radius) of a fountain eye. Camps are nearly always carefully positioned so that the waterhole is visible from a position near the camp rim, but the camp is invisible to game drinking there. Other good reasons given by Kalahari San for camping some distance from a waterhole are to avoid predators and blood-sucking flies (Brooks 1984). Both would also have been valid reasons in the upper Seacow.

The distribution of camp nodes and their surrounding site swarms in the central and upper valley also reveal a marked increase in the number, size, and packing of camp nodes in the southwest corner of the survey. Although several factors may be responsible for this, carrying capacity seems at present to be the closest correlate:

The South African Department of Agriculture allocates to each sheep farm a Restocking Insurance Number, quoted in Small Livestock Units (SLU) per hectare. The SLU's for farms in this corner are three to four units higher than elsewhere in the upper valley. Computation methods are heatedly disputed by farmers, who feel that the number is too generalized for an entire farm. Officials responsible for the calculations are understandably vague about their methods! All parties agree, however, that the southwest corner of the study area has, within living memory, had a higher carrying capacity.

If we assume that it was also consistently higher during the last five hundred years or so, then it may be that Bushman population density reflected this, hence the higher camp density here also. Another potential contributor to the site distribution imbalance is that the Klein-Seekoei headwaters of the Sneeuberg are widely recognized by those who live in the upper valley to be colder in winter than the headwaters of the Elandskloof and Zoetvlei drainages. There are no temperature records to document this, however. There is rather better documentation for the widely held claim that the eastern rim of the valley (particularly Noupoort) is the coldest place in South Africa. It is intuitively reasonable, therefore, to predict that the plantfood growing season would have been much shorter on the east side of the valley because of earlier frosts, and this would also have reduced Bushman carrying capacity. Obviously, much more field research is needed before this can be verified.

Finally there is not the remotest possibility that the imbalance was caused by amateur collectors prior to the start of this project. Unlike North America, amateur pot-hunters are extremely rare in South Africa, and almost all residents of the upper valley knew nothing of Bushman sites before our arrival. Eventually, some minor holes in our data-set were caused on Zoetvlei by amaetur predations, but no damage was done elsewhere.

Certain springs were either avoided (no site cluster), or used exclusively for stalking game (chipping site cluster without nodal camps). There may have been a loose system of "tandem" spring use in which one eye was for drinking water while its nearest neighbor was reserved for game, but this was not invariably the pattern.

Camp nodes tend to contain multiple camps rather than a single large base camp. If Kalahari San camp residues could survive for any length of time (they do not), then they would probably show the same pattern. The period of residence at a San camp is limited to a few months at the very most, and usually for much shorter periods of a few weeks. The resources around the waterhole become so reduced by hunting and foraging that the game begins to avoid the place, and the future growth of the foodplant patches becomes threatened. The daily trip to and from rich enough patches becomes so long that the camp spot is no longer viable and the group is forced to move to another waterhole. This provides a sound analog for the Seacow Bushmen, who suffered the additional hazards of a very unstable and easily damaged plant community, and a perennial firewood shortage. Brooks (1984) indicates that it is a widespread custom that San do not return to previously occupied campsites when returning to a waterhole, until the campsites are "dried out" and overgrown. Instead they camp somewhere in the same general area. Under these conditions it is easy to see how a "favoured area," to use Silberbauer's (1981) term, might become littered with abandoned campsites. The upper valley Bushmen were no doubt compelled by identical constraints, and were obliged to take seasonal wind-direction shifts into consideration as well, when settling back in. If the site was last used at a different time of year, it might have been prudent to shelter from some other wind direction. If the prevailing wind shifted during this visit, it would be no great task to move camp to one of several other sheltered spots on the same ridge. Repeated occupation of Smithfield camps is demonstrated by radiocarbon dates (Beaumont and Vogel 1984) and by the fact that the vegetation on most camps has never recovered (Sampson 1986b).

Thus it emerges that the upper valley Bushmen must have been highly mobile on the landscape, as are modern Kalahari San, whose mobility patterns serve as valuable analogs. The latter allow us to project a crude mobility pattern onto the observed settlement pattern, and the fit is fairly credible. It is reasonable to assume, therefore, that the upper valley Bushmen undertook periodic (band?) movements between waterholes and shorter-term family or individual movements in and out of camp.

The seasonal scheduling of their mobility pattern (cf. Kelley 1983) is still under investigation. The preferred season of periodic reoccupation of an individual camp can be inferred from the direction(s) of the prevailing wind from which it is sheltered (Sampson, in press). Almost half of the 1,000 camps analyzed thus far are protected from wind by low ridges, boulders, bushes, or by combinations of these. The other half are in conspicuously unsheltered spots, seemingly calculated to catch whatever breeze is available. As described in chapter 2, prevailing winds are strong, warm northwesterlies and weaker, cold southeasterlies. The latter make for more comfortable conditions in summer, but unpleasant (sometimes lethal) conditions in winter. Overnight campers would do well to shelter from the E-SSE in winter to assure that the wind does not veer round to these directions, increasing the wind-chill factor dramatically. It is reasonable to infer that Smithfield camps in such localities were most frequently used in winter. Similar arguments can be constructed for mainly spring occupations of NNW-W protected sites, and for mainly summer occupations of unprotected sites.

Patterns of band dispersal and aggregation can be inferred by measuring Smithfield camp areas. The area of camp surface litter left by a modern Kalahari San band has a narrow range, and it differs clearly from that left by an extended family. Very similar measurements are obtained from Smithfield sites so that it may be possible to infer a dispersal (family) camp from an aggregation (whole band) camp (Sampson and Bousman 1985). Most small Smithfield camps are in unsheltered positions, suggesting that the prevailing pattern was summer dispersal and winter and spring aggregation. This model is to be tested by study of the diet and subsistence strategies reflected in excavated samples of foodwaste from small rockshelter deposits.

At present, our understanding of the Bushman diet, and indeed of their entire adaptation, is still very limited. The prediction made in chapter 2 that they were more dependent than the Kalahari San on game (and less so on plantfoods) has very little support from the field evidence. Faunal remains do not survive well on surface sites, and plant remains are not well preserved in rockshelter deposits. However, ostrich eggshell fragments and tortoise carapace fragments occur on almost all Smithfield campsites, and mussel shell fragments occur on most camps near the riverbanks. These fragments hint at a significant foraging component in the adaptation, repeated in the better preserved evidence from rockshelter deposits. Both local species of hare, springhare, porcupine, jackal, yellow mongoose, cerval, aardvark, and hyrax came from the Smithfield levels of Glen Elliott rockshelter, in a small valley not far to the east of the ZVAP area (Klein 1979:43). Most of these are nocturnal or burrowing animals, or both, caught with traps, snares, or hooked rods. They are available year-round and do not leave the area during droughts. This also applies to the fish, crabs, mussels, toads, frogs, and leguan remains from the same levels, and also to the tortoise, snakes, lizards, field mice, shrews, and moles (Sampson 1967b). The presence of these smaller creatures is rather more difficult to interpret, however, as they can also be introduced into the deposit by owls. My own hunch is that the bulk of this material was introduced by the Bushmen themselves, as much of it is in a fragmentary condition. This certainly gives the impression that foraging took up a considerable amount of their time, but they certainly hunted as well.

The hunted component of the Glen Elliott fauna includes zebra/quagga, warthog, eland, wildebeest/hartebeest, springbok (most numerous), and steenbok. Obviously the meatweights represented by this list far outstrip those of the foraged species listed above. The real contribution made by hunting to the Bushman diet remains uncertain, however, because shelter deposits probably accumulated far from the actual kill locations. Consequently, few really large skeletal parts would have been carried back to the shelter or base camp from the kill or butchery site out on the plains. Most shelter faunas will continue to present this rather biased picture, with the additional contamination of natural bone accumulation by owls, jackals, and porcupines, who might have periodically used the shelter between Bushman occupations. One final observation on this topic is that there is absolutely no indication of any adaptational shift from the underlying Interior Wilton levels to the Smithfield. Although this lends some slight support to scenario (3) discussed earlier in this chapter, there are too few data as yet, and the taphonomic biases may mask actual differences. The purported similarity between the two adaptations cannot be considered firm.

Another aspect of upper valley Bushman culture to be considered is the rock art (Sampson 1985:99-100). Not all these paintings and engravings can be firmly ascribed to the Smithfield, but there is a tight association between one painted rock face at Glen Elliott and the Smithfield deposits there. I suspect that the bulk of the upper valley rock art is of Smithfield date, but cannot yet specify which sites should be so ascribed. Many painted images are, I suspect, of "form constants" or elementary trance visions. These include vertical lines or rows of dots, zigzags, crosses, and grids. Images of animals are rarer and executed throughout in a relatively crude and rigid manner. Recognizable are eland (most common), felids, ostrich, zebrids, wildebeest, birds, and baboons. Livestock include a cow, plus a few horses and a dog. Human figures are extremely rare, and usually depict Europeans rather than Bushmen. Perhaps the most important aspect of the paintings is that most of them are far removed from areas of settlement, the bulk of them occurring on small siltstone overhangs on the steep slopes of the mountains. I favor the position of Lewis-Williams (1986) that such paintings are mainly the work of trance healers, who recorded elements of their trance visions in an effort to conserve healing powers acquired during trance for later use. If we allow that trance states were induced at "private" crevices in the mountain flanks in preparation for out-of-body travel in the power quest (Harner 1980), then the anticorrelation between settlement pattern and painting distribution begins to make some sense.

Finally, we may turn to that one aspect of the material culture of the upper Seacow River Bushmen that will concern the rest of this study—their pottery. The typical Smithfield vessel is a grass-tempered, slab-built, thick-walled, vertical-sided, flat-bottomed cooking bowl, the sides of which are decorated with poorly controlled lines and/or networks of stamp impressions (fig. 3-1) produced with several different styluses and by several different methods.

It is of interest to note that fiber-tempered cooking pots are used by foragers and pastoralists in the Americas, Asia, and Africa, where each group has found the same technical answer to the shared problem of moving possessions from camp to camp. There are clear similarities between the porous fabric of Late Archaic midwestern potsherds from North America and vessels currently or recently made by Siriono, Turkana, Eskimo, and Smithfield Bushmen (Reid 1984a). By making and using vessels of this design, three advantages accrue to their highly mobile users. First, the voids in the fabric allow the vessel to absorb a fair amount of shock during transport, so that it will withstand rougher treatment than other voidless wares. Second, it can also absorb a great deal of *repeated* heating (thermal shock) without spalling or bursting in the cooking fire (Reid 1984b). Third, the airspaces in the fabric make the vessel lighter to carry.

Nothing is yet known of the clays or clay sources used in the upper valley (fig. 2-1c). Numerous exposures are to be found along the stream banks, but these are extremely hard and sometimes poorly sorted. According to Bleek's (Bleek and Lloyd 1911) informant—the /Xam Bushman named ‖Kabo, also called Klein Jantjie—women potters of the Kaaienveld in the Kenhardt district of Bushmanland (fig. 3-2) used digging sticks to clear the overburden from a red clay (with glittering particles). This was

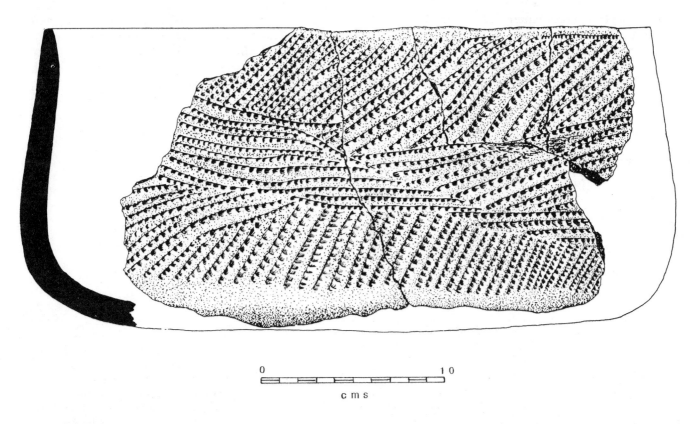

0   1 0

c m s

Figure 3-1. Reconstructed Bushman bowl from a Smithfield surface site at Jouberts Gif (see figure 3-2).

41

then scooped out of the hole into a bag and carried back to camp. There, it was pounded while dry, and then winnowed, the harder particles being removed for later pounding (presumably for temper). The refined clay, pounded down to sand-size particles, was then poured onto a good springbok skin ready for wetting and tempering (Bleek and Lloyd 1911:343). In the upper Seacow Valley, the most easily procured sources of clay occur on the meander bends of dried-up stream beds, where one to two-inch (2.5–5cm) crusts form after minor channel flows. When the mud-laden water dries up, a clay layer forms over the sandy channel bed. This cracks up into hand-sized fragments of well-sorted clean clay, which can be gathered without much effort, and the sandy bases brushed off.

The particle inclusions in the fabric are crushed dolerite and chopped grass, in varying proportions. Crushed potsherd or grog is difficult to distinguish from the doleritic inclusions without thin-sectioning. Although grog was most probably used, this has yet to be verified. The dolerite particles are very easily obtained from the soil cover of any dolerite outcrop. Nothing is yet known of species used in the fiber tempering, but there is a clear dominance of chopped grass. Two readily available sources would have been the dung of large herbivores and the chopped grass stored in termite mounds. Dung usually contains seeds that may explode during firing, so this source would require more cleaning. The termite-derived grass would have been less readily available, but could be used without further cleaning. Furthermore, termite-cut grass is of very even length, mostly in the range of four to nine millimeters, which appears to fit well with the range of grass stem impressions seen in freshly broken sherds. Kannemeyer (1890) describes Bushmen using grindstones for breaking down the grass stalks and working them into the clay. The /Xam account describes how the women gathered stems of "male" grass that they bound up and took home to be pounded with the clay, adding water until it was soft and workable (Bleek and Lloyd 1911:343). The grass tempering is relatively abundant in the fabric—so much so that radiocarbon dates can be derived directly from sherds (Beaumont and Vogel 1984). The inner and outer surfaces of the sherd also display numerous fiber impressions of variable thickness, orientation, and contortion, which belies the evenly bedded appearance of the internal structure seen in a fresh break. This obviously produces a marked "channel" porosity in the fabric (Reid 1984b:64).

The bowl was slab built. The /Xam account has the woman making the lower part of the pot first (Bleek and Lloyd 1911:344). The base plate must have been pinched out from a single large ball of prepared clay to a circle up to about one foot (30cm) in diameter and up to one-half inch (13mm) thick. Two or three other rectangular slabs of similar thickness must have been prepared for the sides, each about six inches (15cm) wide and of varying length, depending on the number of panels to be applied. These were pinched together and joined to form a cylinder that was then placed onto the circular base plate. Again, the /Xam account: "They put the clay down (in a circle)" (Bleek and Lloyd 1911:345). The two units were then pinched together and shaped to form a tightly curved but very thick join around the basal edge.

The vertical sides were then drawn and thinned towards the upper rim to produce a tapering wall:

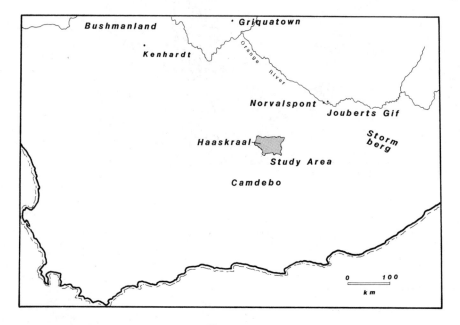

Figure 3-2. Locations of complete or near-complete Bushman bowls, and of ethnohistoric accounts of bowl making. The locations of decorative motifs described by Dunn (1931) are also plotted. The motifs discussed in this volume come from the study area (stippled).

"And they smooth the clay very nicely indeed; they moulding, raise (the sides of) the pot" (ibid:345). This was done with a shaped rib fragment also used as an eating ladle (ibid:facing 212). The sides of the bowl were also made to belly out slightly to form a sub-convex surface. This was done by pinching rather than scraping so that the height of the cylinder side-walls lost during their fixing to the base was regained. Little attention was paid to the rim, although rare vessels have flat-topped rims. Many have a slight bevel on the inside, with just the faintest hint of rim eversion, but it is not always clear that this was intentional.

Very few complete or near-complete Smithfield bowls have survivied, and not many have been published. Lichtenstein, while in Bushmanland in 1804, saw Bushmen with "a kind of clay pot, but very squat and even in the circumference" (1928-30) but he did not illustrate it. Burchell's (1822,2:32) drawing of a bowl made in 1811 is too small and crude to be of much use, and its provenience is unrecorded. Dunn (1931:84-5) was able to rebuild most of a seven-inch (18cm) diameter bag-shaped bowl from sherds found in 1876 on a shelter deposit surface in the Stormberg (fig. 3-2 for localities). Schofield (1948:53) mentions "a shallow dish about a foot in diameter and three inches deep ... decorated with impressions made with a grass belt to give the general idea of a basket, found at Norval's Pont on the Orange River." This is only thirty-seven miles (60km) upstream from the Seacow/Orange confluence and only five miles (8 km) downstream from the other nearly complete specimen (fig. 3-2) found at Jouberts Gif (Sampson 1970:166). Another is being assembled from the Smithfield deposits at Haaskraal shelter (Hart pers. comm). These very few specimens (fig. 3-2) must serve for the moment as an indication of the range in Smithfield vessel sizes and forms. Nothing in the vast sherd collection from the upper Seacow, including several partly reconstructed bowls, suggests any other variations, but this cannot be taken as the last word on the subject without investing in a very large refitting program.

In the /Xam account, the bowl was then left to sun/air-dry to a leather hardness before firing, and it was anointed with fat to keep it from splitting (Bleek and Lloyd 1911:345). In the Seacow Valley, potters could have applied their stamp-impressed decorations at any stage during this drying period. Some potters preferred to start immediately, so that the stylus penetrated deeper into the soft clay, which in turn clung to the stylus, thus producing ragged edges characteristic of sticky work. Others left the decoration until the clay was quite dry and a very clean-edged, shallow impression resulted. Most potters strove for some compromise between these two extremes. The details of the decorative techniques will be described in later chapters. Unfortunately there is no mention

of decoration in the /Xam description, and decorated sherds have not been recorded from Bushmanland (Schofield 1948; Rudner 1979). Note, however, that Dunn (1931:85) recalls that in Bushmanland pots had "little or no decoration on them" in 1872, implying that some minimal decoration was possible.

The /Xam narrative details a "little pot" set down to air-dry next to the "large pot," then another little pot is made; then a little pot that is "grown," that is, larger (Bleek and Lloyd 1911:345). It is a pity that this part of the narrative is somewhat ambiguous, as it is the only clue to how many vessels might be made in a single batch. Depending on one's reading of it, the batch was anywhere between two and five bowls. Note that throughout, the description refers to "they" (meaning the women) suggesting that this was a group task, with the intent of sharing the batch among them. There is also a note (ibid: 347) that one informant's wife had been taught potmaking by her mother's older sister and by another older cousin on her mother's side. The implications of the note are very important for this study because it would seem that potmaking was a routine wifely chore, taught to the young in each family. It also implies there were no professional potters who mass-produced bowls for a wider market.

Once properly air-dried, the vessel was fired in an open bonfire. It must have been routine practice to place the bowl rim-down in a modest blaze, then to pile wood around it. The vessel sank into the ashes as the fire settled, leading to a characteristic reduction firing in the air-starved interior, while the outer surface fired in a typical oxidation environment. As a general rule the interior was fired to the buff-brown range (typically Munsell 7.5YR6/4), while the outside produced a dark brown-to-black color range (Munsell 7.5YR3/2). Typical of such methods, the colors are very uneven from one place to another on the bowl surface. The effects of repeated use in cooking fires probably served to mottle the surfaces still further.

||Kabo's account makes no mention of the firing, and Schofield (1948:53) suggests that this omission was simply caused by his own absence while looking for a springbok—needed to complete the potmaking process. He was never present when his wife conducted the firing. Evidently a pounded acacia gum (either from the berries or sap) was mixed with water and boiled in the (fired?) bowl, presumably to seal its interior. Some of the mixture was ladled over the outside with a springbok horn spoon. Following this, the freshly slaughtered springbok blood might also be boiled in the bowl. This was then ladled out and the residue was allowed to dry on the inside surface. It was then ready for use.

That Smithfield bowls were used for cooking there can be little doubt. ||Kabo states that it was used for boiling meat (Bleek and Lloyd 1911:347), and

Dunn (1931:84) stated that they held between a pint and a quart, and were used for cooking meat, broth, and "a kind of porridge of ground grass seed." Dozens of rimsherds in the upper Seacow Valley collection still retain a greasy, carbonized soot—undoubtedly a burned food residue—on the outer surface. A particularly thick example from Haaskraal rockshelter is currently being examined for its amino-acid content (Hart pers. comm). This completes the review of what is known of Bushman potmaking. Before turning to the decorative techniques used by Seacow Valley potters, some introductory remarks about the sherd collection and sorting procedures are in order.

FOUR

Sherd Collection and Classification

The intent of this chapter is to describe the field collecting procedures and the laboratory sorting of sherds from the upper Seacow Valley (fig. 2-1c). It also reviews some gross characteristics of the sherd collection itself. The narrative will then pass on to the chronological ordering of the collection, which dictated how it was first sorted into the two major classes.

During the original survey of the upper and central valley (fig. 2-1b), field notes were routinely taken on the presence of potsherds at Smithfield "camps" (chapter 3). In the upper valley, such sites were relocated, and their sherds were collected during two seasons in 1982 and 1984. At the same time, selected areas in hills around waterholes were more intensively resurveyed, and substantial numbers of camps were added to the inventory. These, too, were collected. Published maps (Sampson 1985:90-91) include the results of the 1982 resurvey program, but do not reflect the additions from the 1984 work. The presently known distribution of all sherd-yielding sites in the upper valley is given in figure 4-1. Surface sherds from all 987 localities have been collected.

Eight archaeologists participated in the original survey, which totaled fifteen months. A standardized recording procedure was maintained throughout. All sites, including Smithfield camps, were field-documented on file cards, then marked and numbered on air photos. Their locations were later transferred onto 1:50,000 scale maps (20m contour intervals). During the resurvey, it was found that an experienced scout could relocate a camp from its map point only, but the air photo was needed on some occasions. All camps were successfully relocated and flagged. An experienced scout could relocate sites at roughly twice the rate that two collecting teams could process them, so that the remainder of the scout's working day was taken up with intensive resurvey of areas judged to be inadequately mapped during the

first survey. New camps were also flagged, recorded, and added to the inventory. The scout operated from a trail bike equipped with a quiver to hold about twenty flags for the day's work.

As figure 4-1 shows, there are more camps on the west (Bo-Seekoei/Zoetvlei) side of the upper valley than on the east (Klein Seekoei) side. This reflects the actual distribution (fig. 3-1), and is not a spurious product of the relative amounts of survey and resurvey work. One exception is the very thin distribution in the Klein Seekoei headwaters, particularly the farms Whatton, Heydon, and Sunny Dell, and The Poplars (fig. 2-4), which could not be reached for double-checking by the close of the 1984 season. I am reasonably certain that the camp inventories around these fountains could be increased further. Reasons for the overall east-west imbalance in site distribution need not be sought in our survey design, however. The real causes in the discrepancy are linked to carrying capacity (chapter 3).

Sherd collection procedures were as follows: two teams, each composed of one archaeologist and three staff, collected the sherds; each laborer carried beribboned wire pegs with which to flag the sherds dispersed among the lithic debris; a piece of tape was attached to each identified sherd, which was then pegged. The archaeologist followed the laborers with the following task-sequence—write a consecutive number on the taped sherd, score with a steel stylus the same number on a twenty-four millimeter in diameter by two millimeter thick aluminum disc, replace the sherd with the disc, bag the sherd, and pull the peg. Searching was seldom exhaustive, except on very thin sites. A halt was called when the pegging rate dropped so low that nothing new was found after a timed spell of five minutes. Extra time was spent on sites where it seemed likely that the sherd total could be pushed to thirty. The first six aluminum discs laid out on the site were prepunched (with a steel die

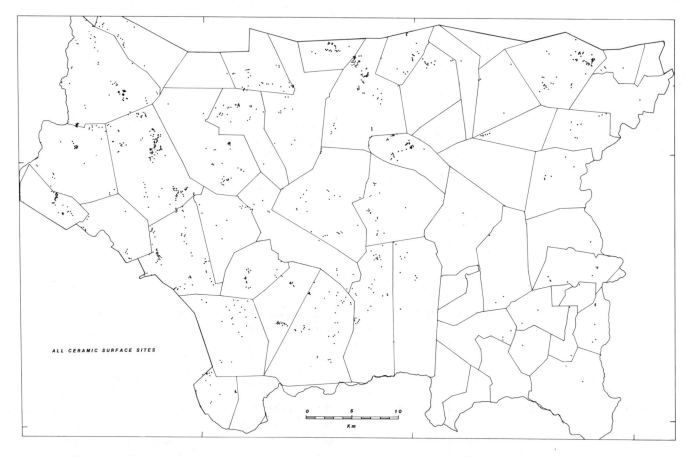

ALL CERAMIC SURFACE SITES

Figure 4-1. Map of the upper Seacow Valley study area showing farm boundaries and locations of 987 surface sites from which ceramics were collected.

stamp) with site's permanent field number to aid future relocations. The two teams operated from pickup trucks.

A few discs have undoubtedly been removed from sites by the children of farm laborers, especially when the site is near a modern farm *werf*. I dare say that a few have been swallowed by pet ostriches, also. These losses are too trivial, however, to cause even mild concern. More serious was the drying up of my disc supply (scrap metal dealers in Port Elizabeth) early in the 1984 season. This forced me to change to a much smaller and thinner disc that tends to blow around in high winds if it is not lying flat on the ground. The proveniences that we have been trying to preserve will be somewhat more suspect at sites on the east side of the valley because of this.

One positive aspect of the disc method is that it allows us to monitor the turnover of sherds in the soil. Casual revisits to previously collected sites have yielded potentially interesting patterns of disc movement caused by stock trampling, rain, and burrowing animals. New sherds have also come to the surface, but have not been collected. Sampling (of any design)

was consciously rejected as a collecting strategy because the goal was to build a large enough sherd population that individual design distributions could be plotted. The validity of this decision will become apparent in later chapters and need not be defended further here. The morality of total sherd stripping from so many sites should also be addressed, as the field record for posterity has been massively altered by this action. The decision is defensible on the grounds that: (1) the sherds are being destroyed in the field by natural agencies; (2) only a portion of the sherds at most sites were on the surface at the time of collection; (3) the discs are a more durable replacement, albeit slightly more at risk from human interference; and (4) the upper valley collection, huge as it may seem, is but a minuscule sample of the total Smithfield camp population of the Karoo. The charge that we have made the resident population more familiar with the appearance and whereabouts of Bushman pottery should also be answered. It cannot be denied that this has occurred, but the key to the defense is in the population's attitude. Sheep farm staff have been known on two occasions to bring in handfuls of sherds from the field. When the farmers told them to replace them and it became apparent that they were not going to be paid, all interest ceased. As long as a large-scale market in illicit artifact trafficking does not evolve in South Africa, no future hazards are foreseeable.

Routine field laboratory processing of the collection proceeded as follows: the content of each site bag was laid out, with each sherd placed on its numbered pressure-tape label (now removed from the sherd and stuck to the bench). Every sherd was white-marked and then labeled as follows: (1) farm name code letters, for example, ZOE for Zoetvlei; (2) the permanent field number of the site, also on the bag, the basemap, inventory card, and die-stamped discs at the site; (3) the sherd number, copied from the pressure-tape label and also scored on the disc lying on the site surface. The goal of this labeling system is to assure that the position of every sherd in the collection can be relocated, should future intrasite patterning studies ever require such information.

Preliminary sorting of the collection followed a standard procedure. Inevitably, the sherds collected from larger sites are a mixture of three occupation periods—Interior Wilton, Khoi (herder), and Smithfield (see chapter 3). At first the intent was that each site collection be first sorted by period. As we are still ignorant of the finer points that distinguish Interior Wilton from Khoi sherds, the preliminary sorting soon devolved to three categories: (1) decorated Smithfield sherds; (2) obvious Khoi sherds (slipped, lugs, rims, and so forth) and; (3) a residue of undecorated Smithfield mixed with smaller amounts of Interior Wilton, and probably some damaged (spalled slip surface) Khoi sherds. Only category (1) is treated in this volume, while the Khoi collection will be described elsewhere (Hart in prep.). The entire collection is presently in live storage at the field laboratory on the farm Zoetvlei.

The distribution of total sherds (all categories) per site in the collection is given in figure 4-2, with a few excessively large totals enumerated in the caption. About one quarter of all the sites yielded fewer than five sherds, with a rapid drop-off in site counts to thirty to thirty-five sherds, after which the drop-off curve begins to level out. The J-shape of the curve is typical of random-yield patterning, from which no behavioral or taphonomic inferences can be drawn. Some basic statistics of the collection may now be presented. It contains 65,800 sherds representing a minimum vessel count of 3,947 vessels of all kinds and periods. The Khoi (herder) component includes 9,600 sherds representing at least 707 vessels. There are 7,043 decorated Smithfield sherds, representing a minimum total of 2,815 Smithfield bowls. The balance of the collection is a mixture of Interior Wilton, probably some Khoi, and some undecorated Smithfield vessels.

Hereafter, the decorated Smithfield sherds are considered in isolation from the rest of the collection. Throughout, the sorting was done only by myself, in an attempt to reduce between-analyst variations, but one built-in disadvantage of this approach is that there is no independent cross-check and verification of my matching. In the first round of sorting, every effort was made to match decorated sherds from the same site so that a minimum vessel count per site could be obtained. The sherds deemed to be from a single vessel were assigned to a labeled, styrofoam tray for easier manipulation. Before describing the basic subdivision of the vessels, some problems arising from the "minimum vessel" sorting need to be discussed.

It has been mentioned already that decorations were applied to most of the vertical outer sidewalls of the bowl. The lines of impressions usually stop just short of the rim at the top, and also stop about one inch (2.5cm) from the curved join with the base-plate. Very rare rimsherds display decoration right to the rim itself. Only one vessel in the entire collection has stamp impressions onto the top of the rim itself. The size of decorated sherds vary widely from (rare) large hand-sized panels to (common) crumbs with surfaces

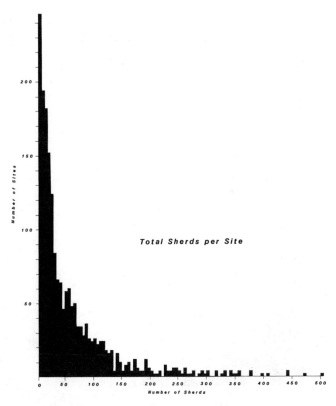

Figure 4-2. Distribution of sherds recovered per site. Not included in this diagram are eleven sites that yielded more than 500 sherds.

no bigger than a thumbnail. The bulk of the collection falls between these extremes. Refitting was done wherever possible, but it was inevitably the larger panels rather than the smaller pieces that refitted most frequently. The number of sherds per vessel (fig. 4-3) varies widely, with very few vessels indeed represented by more than ten sherds. This graph raises interesting questions about the fate or present whereabouts of the rest of these vessels. Two postdepositional pathways may have led to a vessel's particular sherd-count in the collection—burial or destruction. At present, I suspect that the answer will be more often destruction than burial. Having visited many hundreds of Smithfield camps, it is clear that repeated occupations have so disrupted the plant cover that sheet erosion on camps is normal (Sampson 1986b). This leads me to predict that very little will be found underground in the normally thin soil cover. The exceptions will be those few larger, richer sites that have not been rilled or gullied because of bedrock configurations. Here I expect that bioturbation periodically buries and reexposes sherds.

There are no grounds for believing that Smithfield sherds dissolve, like those described for the much older midwest Archaic vessels (Reid 1984b). Half-dissolved sherds are not encountered on surface sites,

nor in excavated sequences, where they remain firm and intact down to the lowest levels of their occurrence. I do not believe that the archaeological record of the Karoo is being "deceramicized," to use Reid's awkward term, because grass-tempered ware was not introduced that long ago [tenth century A.D. in the Interior Wilton levels at Zaayfontein (Beaumont and Vogel 1984)]. The usual destruction pathway does not seem to be dissolution but rather progressive fragmentation at the surface. Breadcrumb-sized pieces may eventually dissolve, but anything larger is more vulnerable to treadage—today mainly by sheep, but in the past by game animals that no doubt visited abandoned camps, causing the kind of havoc described by Yellen (1976) on recent Kalahari campsites. The upshot of this is that burial is a preservative, while reexposure is a threat. I believe that the survival rate of a vessel is entirely tied to its history of burial and reemergence. It is tempting to suppose that the better represented vessels are younger than the poorly represented ones, and there is some circumstantial evidence to support such a claim (see below). However, too many processual factors interfere with this simplistic equation, so that it cannot necessarily be applied to individual vessels, but only to whole (decorative) classes of vessel.

The next question to be addressed is this: can one vessel be decorated with two or more completely different motifs? This has obvious ramifications for the validity of the minimum vessel count. I sorted on the assumption that this never occurred, because I never found two different motifs on a single sherd. My reading of rocker-stamp subclasses has proved to be faulty (chapter 12), but my non-rocker sorting has withstood blind testing for several motifs. Unfortunately, the ethnohistoric record affords no clues to the validity of my assumption. Note, however, that the Bleek and Lloyd text on Bushman potmaking (1911:343-47) implies that potmaking was a collaborative task among a group of women. It is not unreasonable to suppose that the decorating stage might sometimes have been collaborative as well, with the result that two or more hands are present in patterns of a single pot. Nevertheless, it remains impossible to state categorically that more than one technique and one stylus tip shape was used on an individual vessel.

At present, my assertion is based on the limited set of observations on the largest panels available in the collection, plus the Jouberts Gif bowl mentioned in chapter 3. There is not a single sherd in the entire collection that unambiguously displays two different motifs. Furthermore, sherd matching was not based exclusively on the decorations, but also on surface texture, color, temper scars, and thickness. Admittedly, Smithfield bowls may vary in any one or all of these features from one side panel to the next, so the multiple-attribute comparison is not entirely foolproof. Ultimately, I was forced to decide whether to

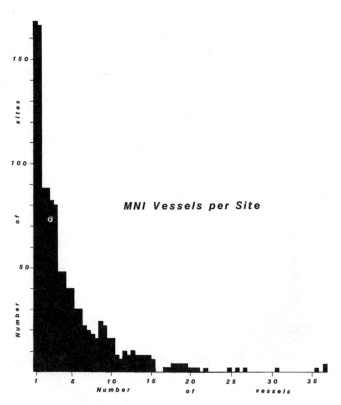

Figure 4-3. Distribution of minimum numbers of individual decorated bowls per site in the upper Seacow Valley.

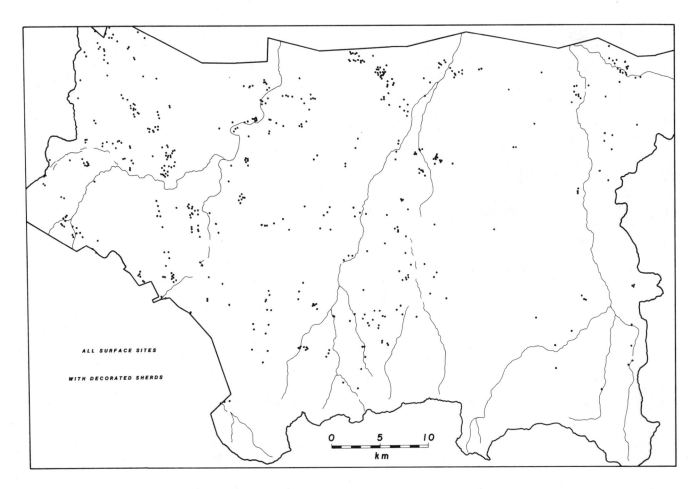

ALL SURFACE SITES

WITH DECORATED SHERDS

0   5   10

k m

Figure 4-4. Map of the upper Seacow Valley showing the distribution of 592 sites that yielded decorated sherds.

present the trays of matching sherds within a more conservative framework of "panels" or to take a calculated risk and present them as "vessels." I decided to stand by my original assumption and to trust my own accumulated experience of the collection, while accepting that I have probably divided a few bowls into separate and spurious "vessels" (chapter 12). I nevertheless believe such errors are confined entirely to the rocker-stamp wares, where it has occurred rarely enough that it will make no significant difference to the overall results. The basis of my confidence in this judgment is that decorations are so varied, and individual idiosyncratic features are so common, that sherd matching is quite easy. With enough experience, one decorator's hand can be distinguished from another's.

Altogether 592 (60%) of the collected sites yielded Smithfield decorated sherds. Their locations are plotted in figure 4-4, where it emerges that the same east-west imbalance seen in site distribution density (fig. 4-1) persists. Sites that failed to yield fragments of decorated vessels were mainly those with very low sherd counts, and there were a few that turned out to be herder sites with virtually no reoccupation by Bushmen.

The minimum vessel count per site for decorated Smithfield bowls is mapped in figure 4-5, which reveals that a few sites have very large vessel counts. This pattern raises a question touched on briefly at the end of chapter 3. Could there have been mass production and trade of bowls by a few potters centered at various points around the valley? Certainly the figure 4-5 pattern would fit such a scenario, if it is assumed that the high-yield sites were the points of production in the upper valley. However, other explanations are far more likely. Two of the high-yield sites were rockshelter taluses, and shelters are so scarce in this area that any accessible overhang exerted a "gravitational pull" as strong as the waterholes on the settlement pattern (Sampson 1984b). Thus the high vessel yield reflects more intensive occupation, not the presence of a bowl manufactory. The same could apply to the open sites with high yields, although the reasons for intense occupation at these is less obvious. Another point that refutes the manufactory model is that these sites produced none of the typical signs of such industry—no concentrations of wasters, showing heat-spalling, firecracking, rim squatting, dunting, or bloating (Rye 1981). Another feature arguing against manufactories is that the

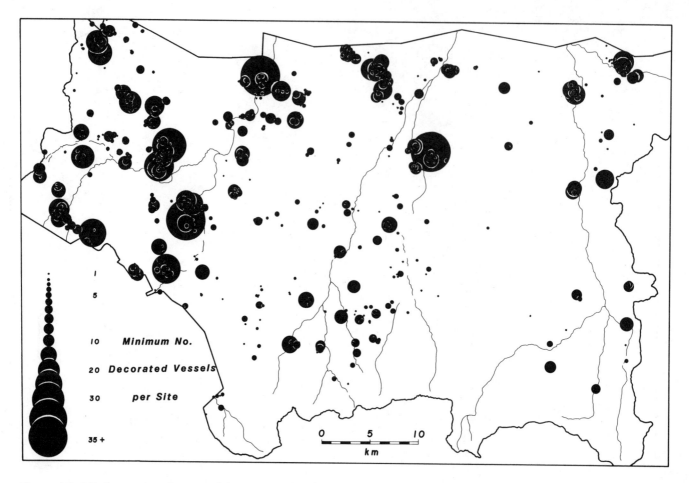

Figure 4-5. Minimum vessel count of decorated Smithfield bowls at each of the sites shown in figure 4-4.

high-yield sites are distributed on the landscape (fig. 4-6) in apparently irrational patterns that would not fit any very obvious preconceived notion of how pots would be distributed from manufacturing centers (Hodder 1977). On the contrary, the case for there having been hundreds of individual potters— probably one to each extended family—is rather compelling, given the tremendous variability in the decorative motifs.

This completes the discussion of questions raised by the minimum vessel count, and we come at last to the problem of how best to classify the decorations—so that the styrofoam trays, each containing the remains of one vessel, could be grouped into shared motifs. As already noted, absolutely nothing is available in the ethnohistoric fragments on Bushman potmaking about decorative techniques, except a suspect reference by Dunn (1931), which will be discussed in detail in chapter 8. Thus, I was obliged to learn to replicate them all myself on a trial-and-error basis on commercial clay, using various items picked up in the veld. In the course of this exercise, I tried out hundreds of different objects that I thought might have served as a *stylus*. Nearly all could be

safely rejected as candidates, and I feel reasonably confident that this tiresome process of elimination has left a residue of items that come so close to replicating the actual patterns that they were indeed used as such. Small residual doubts here and there will be discussed as they arise in the following chapters, each dealing with a different family of stylus tips and the ways in which they were handled.

As a first step in the classification, the entire collection of decorated bowls was divided into two gross categories, namely rocker-stamp motifs and non-rocker motifs. This decision was based on some preliminary stratigraphic evidence that separates them in time. The implications of this decision are important enough to justify a closer look at the sequences in question.

Two shallow rockshelters on the west side of the study area were excavated (fig. 4-7). As mentioned in chapter 3, Haaskraal rockshelter has provided a shallow but undisturbed, stratified sequence (Hart, in prep.) inside the dripline. There are two reasonably clear breaks in deposition (fig. 4-8, top), each marked by color and textural changes. Undecorated potsherds appear immediately above the first sedimentary break (estimated at A.D. 900) and the first non-rocker motifs appear several centimeters above (estimated at A.D. 1300). The sherd sample is still rather small, so the stratigraphic order of appearance of the various non-rocker decorations remains uncertain. However, *the first rocker-stamp sherds appear above the second sedimentary break* (estimated after A.D. 1500). Although numerous, the sherds belong to only four bowls.

Although the scree-filled talus outside the shelter yielded far more pottery, the sediment is leached and lacks stratification. Both lithics and radiocarbon dates indicate stratigraphic inversion, possibly brought about by mass wasting of the upslope deposits, which dammed up behind a low stone wall built as a stock enclosure (see chapter 3). Consequently, the sequence of sherd decorations is inverted and mixed. There is a residual doubt that the second sedimentary break inside the shelter could have resulted from occupants scooping out deposit and throwing it down the talus.

Deposits inside Volstruisfontein shelter (fig. 4-9) are also leached because of periodic seepage from the rear wall. Consequently, there is no visible stratification, and the sediment can be excavated only in thin, arbitrary spits. So far, only fifteen decorated sherds from seven vessels have been recovered, but the stratigraphic sequence, *non-rocker followed by rocker, is repeated here also.*

Thus, pilot excavations have suggested that rocker-stamp ware may be younger than non-rocker ware. This hypothesis is not refuted by dates run on three decorated vessels (C-14 on the grass temper) taken from surface sites. Unfortunately, no impres-

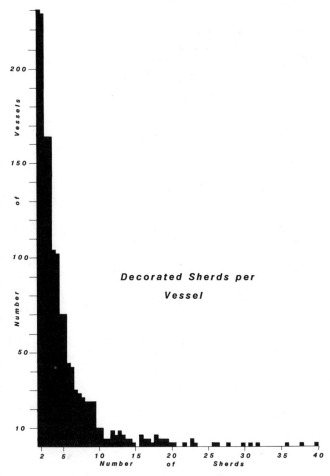

Figure 4-6. Distribution of decorated sherds per vessel recovered from the upper Seacow Valley. Not included in this diagram are two vessels represented by 44 sherds and by 328 sherds, respectively.

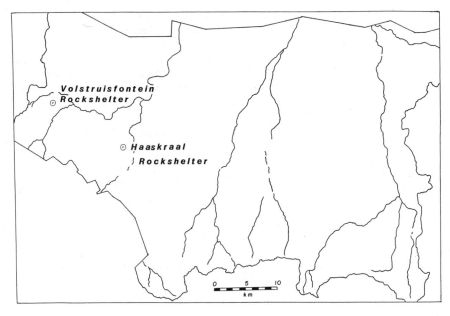

Figure 4-7. Locations of excavations at Haaskraal and Volstruisfontein rockshelters in the upper Seacow Valley study area.

51

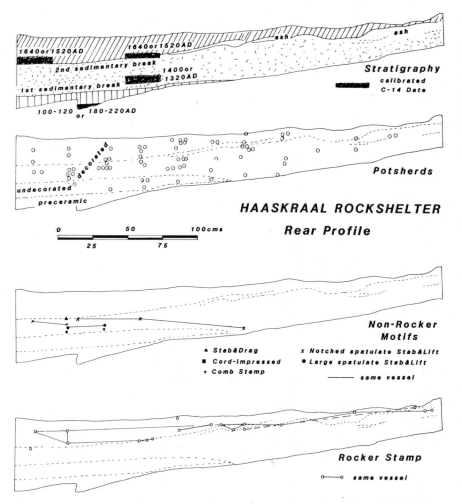

Figure 4-8. Rear profile of the excavation inside Haaskraal rockshelter, showing stratigraphy, dates, and sherd contexts. The positions of potsherds have been projected onto the rear section. Depth is accurate, and lateral position is within 25 centimeters according to Hart (in prep.). Note that rocker-stamp decorations overlie non-rocker motifs.

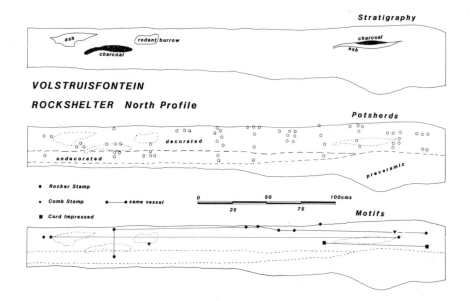

Figure 4-9. North profile of the test trench at Volstruifontein rockshelter. The rock wall is to the left of the section, and the steep talus slope is to the right. The positions of sherds have been projected onto the section. Depth is accurate and lateral position is within 25 centimeters according to Hart (in prep.). Note that rocker-stamp decorations overlie non-rocker motifs.

sions were made of these sherds before they were mailed for dating, but the color slides made by Dr. John Vogel before they were destroyed suggest the following results. The calibrated date from a rocker-stamp bowl was A.D. 1500 or A.D. 1620 (± 40). A non-rocker(?) sherd from Middle Mount (fig. 2-4) yielded A.D. 1440 (± 45), and another non-rocker vessel from the same site yielded A.D. 1370 (± 50) (Beaumont and Vogel 1984). Note that overlapping sigmas prevent a definite statement that all three are of different ages. However, it is probably safe to state that one of the two non-rocker specimens is older than rocker—a result duplicated in the pilot excavations.

This basic sequence may also account for the overwhelming abundance of rocker-stamp sherds in the surface collections. As discussed above, there are reasons to suppose that the (younger) rocker ware has not yet disintegrated (Reid 1984a,b) to the same extent as the (older) non-rocker wares. It seems more likely that the non-rocker has been worked farther into the underlying soil, so that less of it is now visible, but this cannot possibly apply at all sites. Other options for explaining this discrepancy will be discussed in the final chapter.

The intent of the following analyses will be to develop types and subtypes of non-rocker and rocker-stamp decorations. Point-plots of their distributions will help to isolate those few motifs expected to have restricted distributions on the landscape. Types and subtypes that do not display the density distributions characterized in chapter 1 will be dismissed as background noise. Only by these laborious means can appropriate "marker objects" be selected for further consideration in the quest for territorial boundaries.

Throughout this exercise, the underlying assumption will be that marker motifs represent the handiwork of bowl-decorating "lineages"; that is, generations of potters who learned and passed on a particular combination of attributes. A further assumption [derived from the solitary analog of the Bleek and Lloyd (1911) text] is that the "lineage" was loosely connected by kinship and would be more vigorously practiced by women of the same band. A rider to this assumption is that a young potter, who was taught a particular decorative motif by older women of her band, would, when marrying into a neighboring band, adopt the motif of the area to which she had moved—as documented by Herbich (1986) for the Luo. With this in mind, we can now pass on to a general consideration of the non-rocker decorative motifs.

FIVE

Introduction to the Non-Rocker Motifs

It is the earlier set of motifs underlying the rocker-stamp levels in both excavations that provide the most valuable information on stylistic boundaries. They will be referred to here collectively as the non-rocker motifs. They cover a wide array of patterns made with several different stylus tips. Thus, the non-rocker group has absolutely no typological coherence, but serves merely as a context within which to develop a framework for further analysis. The only attribute they have in common is that they (apparently) all predate the rocker-stamp wares, and were all made within the same two or three centuries. Almost nothing is known yet about the sequence in which they appeared, nor is it certain which were exact contemporaries. A few rather obvious connections will emerge, however, during the course of analysis.

The purpose of this chapter is to introduce the range of non-rocker styluses and techniques, without dwelling at length on typological systematics—later chapters will show why specific attributes were selected and combined to form the typology of motifs. Instead, this narrative will pass on to the question of how best to cluster the available sites into non-rocker cells with large enough vessel counts to allow the percentage calculations needed to conduct the testing proposed in chapter 1. Finally, it will review some preliminary results derived from two such tests. This done, it should hopefully become clear that the study area has captured four major spatial-stylistic units. These same units dictate the sequence and layout of analytical chapters that follow, each concerning a different family of motifs dominant in a particular unit.

It is tedious to belabor the systematics of Bushman pottery decoration, but a few basics will have to be treated here before passing on to more interesting matters. Two variables come into play when decorating a Bushman bowl—stylus and technique. Stylus here means the nature, shape, and alterations of the stylus tip. Technique means the angle of entry of the tip into

the clay surface, the depth of penetration, manipulations while in the clay and during withdrawal, and spacing between insertions. Note that "design" in the conventional sense of punctate-row layout, spacing between rows, and patterning of rows, will not be treated at all in this work. Like the study of form, decorative design analysis requires whole or nearly intact pots, and these are virtually absent. A few passing comments will appear in later detailed chapters on the position of punctate rows, but that is all. This work is about the mechanics of decoration, not about decorative design structure. Thus the term "motif," as used in this chapter heading and henceforth, means the *visual effect* achieved by wielding a certain stylus in a certain way along the single row of punctates. The term specifically excludes patterning of the rows themselves.

Replication experiments (detailed in later chapters) and other rare historic sources suggest that at least sixteen different stylus tips were used. These were: (1a) bevel-cut stick forming a large spatulate tip; (1b) the same with a V-notch cut in outer edge of the tip; (1c) the same with a U-notch in the outer edge of the tip; (1d) the same with very small multiple notches cut around the edge; (1e) the same with a shallow groove cut in the bevel face; (1f) pointed bevel-cut stick with a sharp spatulate end; (2) bevel-cut reed shaft or bone splinter forming a small spatulate tip; (3) condyle of the mandible of a small mammal; (4) humerus distal of a small mammal; (5a) porcupine quill tip; (5b) porcupine quill root or base; (6) cord of grass twine; (7) ostrich eggshell bead necklace; (8) miscellaneous stick ends; (9a) plain mussel shell edge; (9b) mussel shell edge with multiple notches. Variations in the comb notching of the latter allow for several different subtypes, which can be dealt with later.

The techniques are rather easier to identify through replication, once the stylus tip is known. These include: stab-and-lift (the tip parts from the clay between marks); stab-and-drag (tip is not removed between marks); gash; channel; twine-impress; and comb-stamp. The latter is not really a distinct technique, but is retained here to mean stab-and-lift with a mussel shell. To avoid tiresome repetition, it will suffice here to point out that not every technique is used with every stylus. The most common imprints and the stylus tips that make them are illustrated in figure 5-1. These are discussed, along with the nuances of interpretation in the relevant chapters on individual styluses.

The point-plot of all non-rocker vessels is given in figure 5-2. Like the distribution map of total vessels (fig. 4-4), high-yield sites are more densely packed into the parcel of land west of the Zoetvlei-Seekoei line, also along a narrow cross-valley fringe on the north rim of the study area. The center and southeast portions of the map are dominated by more scattered, low-yield sites. A brief inspection of this map will confirm that almost none of the high-yield sites has a vessel count large enough to produce reliable percentage calculations of the individual motifs at that site. Thus, individual sites cannot be used as data-points for the framework needed to conduct the analysis outlined in chapter 1. In that hypothetical

case, such hazards were to be circumvented by grouping the vessel contents of all the sites clustered around single waterpoints into "cells," thus raising the sample size to a level where percentage calculations become more reliable. In the real world, however, even this maneuver fails to produce the desired sample sizes in all parts of the map. Scattered single-vessel sites must be either sacrificed or grouped into huge cells covering wide tracts of landscape. Clusters from adjacent waterpoints must sometimes be combined, and still further compromises are called for.

Literally every analytical result to follow will be influenced by the way in which the sites have been clustered. If a site-cluster (cell) is created such that it turns out later to straddle a stylistic boundary, then the percentage values attached to that cell will be a mix of two dominant motifs from contiguous areas. When such a result emerges, the offending cell must be stripped down again to its component sites and recombined with sites stripped out of adjacent cells to develop a new cell configuration that does not straddle the boundary. Even this manipulation is not always successful. One or both of the newly formed pair of cells on either side of the boundary can produce

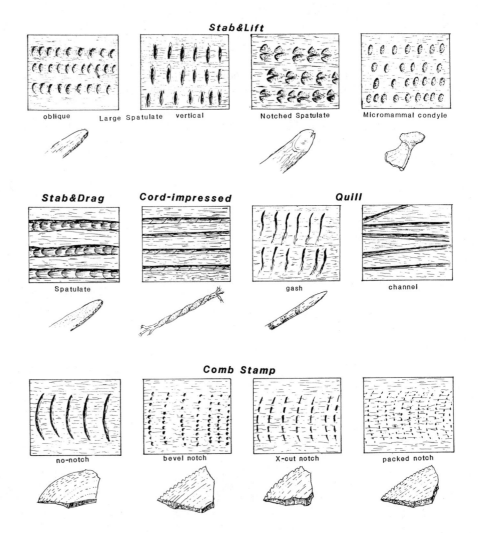

Figure 5-1. Some common non-rocker motifs. The stylus tips used in replication experiments are shown below the panels of typical impressions made with these tips. The bottom-row styluses are fresh-water mussel shell fragments.

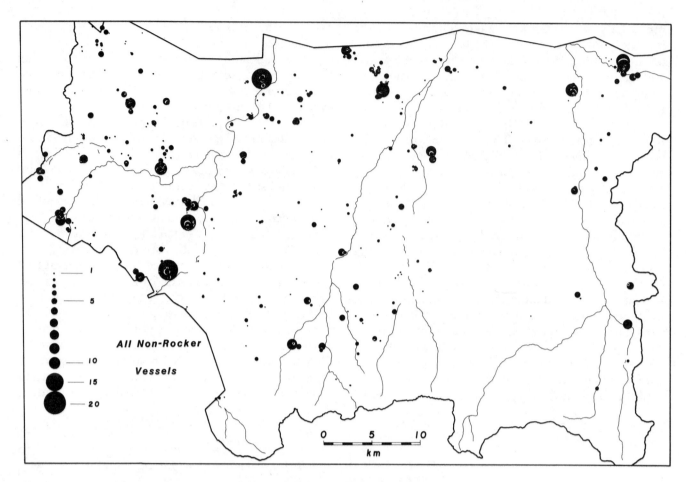

All Non-Rocker

Vessels

Figure 5-2. Map of the upper Seacow Valley study area showing the minimum
vessel count per site for bowls decorated with non-rocker motifs.

Figure 5-3 *(above right)*. The distribution of cells (clusters of adjacent
sites) showing the total non-rocker
decorated bowls within each cell.

Figure 5-4 *(right)*. The non-rocker
cells (as defined in figure 5-3) are referred to in the text by the labels
shown here.

Non-Rocker Vessel

Counts per Cell

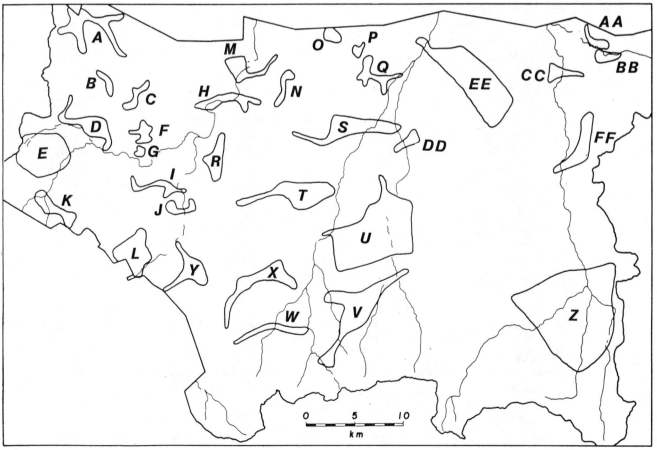

flaws—either a sample size becomes too small, or a cell covers so much ground (for example, a wide scatter of single-vessel sites) that its value as a data-point is greatly diminished. There is no "optimal" clustering, and a viable working arrangement emerges only after several trial manipulations, in which low sample sizes must be accepted in some places, and large cell areas must be accepted in others. The result is thus a patchwork of compromises, with only the richest areas containing the desired small cells with large samples.

The cellular arrangement shown in figure 5-3 is thus the end-product of trial-and-error testing, and should not for a moment be construed as a framework on which to conduct a "blind" test to discover where the stylistic boundaries were. Only my first test-shot was truly blind. The cells shown here were literally hand-fitted to the results obtained by several tests, and the clustering is thus heavily loaded with the foreknowledge of where the boundaries will emerge. After some reflection, I elected not to drag readers through the detailed history of this testing, but to summarize the principles and assumptions used. First, it was assumed that closely packed sites were more likely to be used by the same stylistic group than by two or more adjacent groups. Thus, nearest-neighbor was throughout a guiding principle for grouping sites. Second, a target sample size per cell was set at approximately thirty vessels. Third, sacrifice of single-vessel sites was avoided except where an addition would cause a cell to billow out to enormous and implausible dimensions on account of a single vessel. Fourth, all cells conform to mountainous barriers—no cell will straddle a mountain range. A fifth related principle had to be abandoned as unworkable in the real world—no cell will straddle a river channel. Just one example of this laborious test cycle will be given later in the chapter to illustrate the reason that I was forced to abandon this principle, and this will hopefully suffice to reassure the reader that there is nothing gained in detailing here how every test-shot was modified!

The end-result (fig. 5-3) retains some glaring flaws that I was unable to eradicate. Henceforth, each cell will be labeled according to the lettering system shown in figure 5-4, to which the reader is asked to refer in this and later discussions. Cell Y has the lowest sample count (ten vessels) but was nevertheless retained because it cannot be joined with sites from cell L across the Zoetvlei channel, which turns out to be a major stylistic boundary. Also, cell Y cannot be joined to sites from cell X because a mountain range intervenes. Actually cell Y is artificially diminished because it contains a large site that was systematically looted before we could collect from it—the only such case of vandalism in the entire survey region, but damaging to the analysis, nonetheless. Other cells

with low sample sizes are S and T, which had to be enlarged to encompass every available single-vessel site in the rather empty country just west of the Elandskloof. A third low-sample cell is BB which I have retained separate from AA on the other side of the stream channel because its motif composition is definitely the same as AA, in spite of sampling doubts. In contrast, the small samples in cells X, T, and S will doggedly return to haunt the analysis.

The other main compromises are cells I and J, which straddle the Zoetvlei boundary, plus the excessively expanded cells EE, U, V, and Z, which were necessary to accommodate widely scattered sites. Although somewhat damaging to the results, they are compromises that can be lived with, because they form data-points in important parts of the study area, which cannot otherwise be represented. It should also be noted here that I have not had time to double-check the quality of the original survey of cell Z and also of the gap between Z and FF. There are grounds for suspecting that only a few of the camps in this stretch of the Klein Seekoei were found. Further fieldwork may well improve the data quality in this corner of the map. Finally, I was forced to sacrifice a couple of single-site outliers, shown in figure 5-3.

What follows is an example of just one of the tests, towards the end of the cycle, used to arrive at the clustering chosen in figure 5-3. I had in fact already arrived at this configuration and was exploring the possibilities for splitting cells that straddled stream channels. The goal of this test was to explore to what extent river channels coincided with stylistic boundaries. The breakdown of each cell sample into motif types had already yielded the following dominant forms (fig. 5-5): comb-stamp wares yield the highest values west of the Zoetvlei-Groot Seekoei line; micromammal incisor impressions, when combined with small spatulate work, dominate between this line and the Elandskloof; large plain spatulate decorations prevail in the upper Elandskloof and the country to the east; quill decorations dominate in the far northeast corner of the map; the only other motif to dominate a cell is combined notched spatulates in cell CC. In the "river/boundary" test that followed, I downgraded the minimum cell sample size to fifteen, broke up any cell into smaller components of about this size, and attempted to rebuild minicells that were not cut through by any rivers. This proved feasible everywhere except in cell Z and the far eastern tip of cell S. The numerically dominant motif in each minicell was then identified and plotted on the minicell map (fig. 5-6).

Comb-stamp again dominates west of the Zoetvlei-Seekoei line, but the line does not coincide precisely with the stylistic boundary. Moving northwards along this line, it emerges that cell J is not a mixed cell and the stylistic boundary runs between

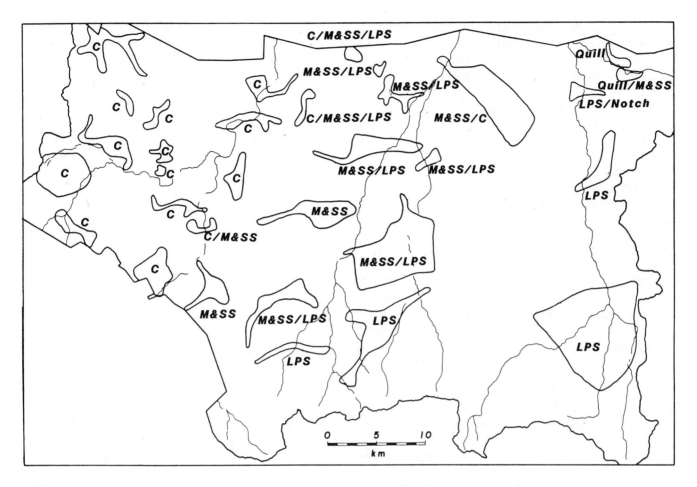

Figure 5-5. Each non-rocker cell contains more vessels with a particular motif. C = comb-stamp; M&SS = micromammal incisors and small spatulate; LPS = large plain spatulate; Quill = all porcupine quill motifs; and Notch = V-notched spatulate. Double entries mean that two motifs share numerical dominance in the cell.

cells I and J. Again at cell C farther north, comb-stamp does indeed dominate both banks of the river. Cell M on the other hand does seem to be a mix of two motifs, which become properly separated in the minicells on either riverbank. Moving to the center of the map, the west branch of the Elandskloof shows no obvious stylistic divisions on either side of the channel. Along its east branch, however, minicells positioned opposite each other on either bank are consistently characterized by different motifs. The pairing is not always between the same sets of motifs, however. Still farther east, no such separations occur on the Klein Seekoei, and the quill motif dominates on both banks of the (unnamed) tributary in the northeast corner.

Given the small sample sizes of each minicell, these results show remarkably strong patterning, leading to the provisional working hypothesis that there are fragments of four major stylistic units present in the study area, and that the boundaries between these units coincide only in a few places with major stream channels (fig. 5-7). The most extensive overlap between units occurs in the north central sector of the map, and the units that overlap most extensively are the large spatulate and micromammal/small spatulate.

If these propositions have any merit, then the same results should emerge no matter what angle of entry into the data-set is selected, and no matter what analytical procedures are applied. Unfortunately the minicell layout in figure 5-6, although near optimal for bringing out boundaries, presents too many sampling doubts when further testing is developed. Thus, I reluctantly fell back on the arrangement given in figures 5-3 and 5-4 as the best possible compromise between sampling needs for further analysis, and minimum boundary mixing. This is the analytical framework used for all further non-rocker spatial analysis, unless otherwise specified for individual tests.

The procedures outlined in chapter 1 were then applied to this framework, mainly to test the viability of the framework. In the first test run, the vessel content of each cell was sorted by *stylus* type only. Eleven categories were used: large plain spatulate-thin, ditto-thick, ditto-pointed, large notched and grooved spatulates combined, small spatulate, incisors, condyle and humerus combined, cord and bead combined, quill, blunt stick, and mussel. The count for each of these categories in each cell was converted to a percentage of the cell total. Next, accumulative percentage differences were computed between adjacent cells (fig. 5-8). Values above the 50 percent difference level were then plotted as lines of varying thickness between cells (fig. 5-9). When this is compared with the hypothesis summarized in figure 5-7, there is a reasonably good fit between the two maps along the east margin of the comb-stamp zone, and the overlap sector at its north end is also registered. Also, in the far northeast corner, the margin of the quill boundary is present but weakly developed. Elsewhere, the fit is poor.

These first results indicate that there is probably more to the spatial organization of style here than is provided for by the hypothesis. To explore that possibility further, accumulative percentage differences between each cell and all other cells were computed, following the procedures outlined in chapter 1. This time, linkages between cells at below the 60 percent difference level were plotted (fig. 5-10) in a four-level hierarchy reflecting the strength of each link. Again, there is absolutely clear separation of the comb-stamp zone to the west, which also yields the highest level of clustering, that is, cell linkages with the lowest percentage differences. The comb-stamp zone itself now hints at a division between north and south subzones, divided by the Bo-Seekoei channel. Some weaker north-south clustering occurs in the Elandskloof, but not between contiguous cells. Again, there may be some separation in the headwaters from the main group of Elandskloof linkages. Clustering farther east of this group is minimal, and the quill zone in the northeast corner fails to cluster out from the rest.

The second test run on this framework applied the same procedures, but the vessel content of each cell was classified according to *technique* rather than stylus. This time only five categories were used: stab-and-lift, stab-and-drag, channel or gash, cord or bead impressed, and comb-stamp. Here, several stylus types have been divided and different parts collapsed into new categories. Only the cord or bead and comb-stamp were the same values used in the previous stylus-based test. The smaller number of categories inevitably produces smaller accumulative percentage differences between cells (fig. 5-11), and is therefore less sensitive than tests using larger numbers of classes. First, any value higher than 30 percent difference was plotted as a line between cells with line thickness between cells reflecting increasing values (fig. 5-12). Here, the comb-stamp margin is very clearly delineated, with the north-south division of comb-stamp also beginning to emerge. Farther east, there is now a strong grouping of cells in the

Figure 5-6. The non-rocker cells have been divided into minicells in an attempt to avoid stream channels passing through cells. The numerically dominant motif is given for each minicell.

Figure 5-7. First approximation of non-rocker stylistic boundaries. Circles = comb-stamp; double bars = micromammal incisors and small spatulate; dark stipple = quill; and white/dashed line = large plain spatulate.

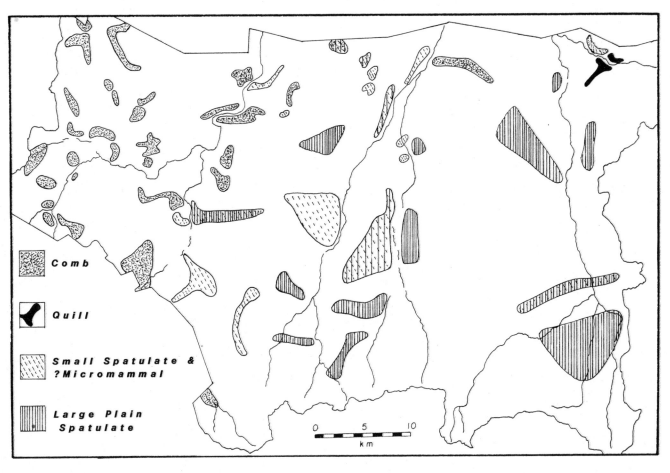

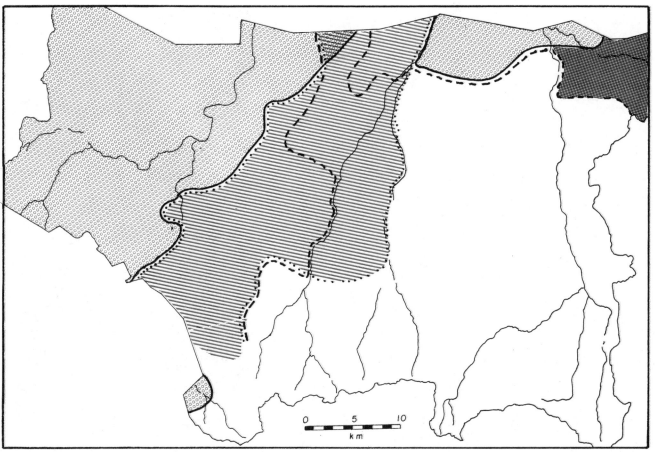

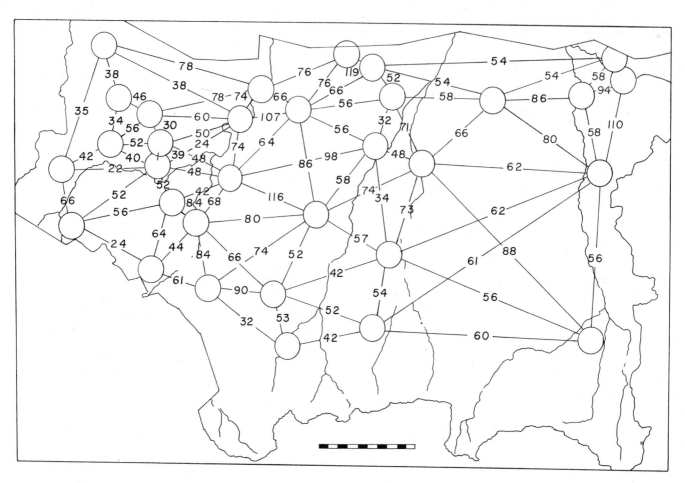

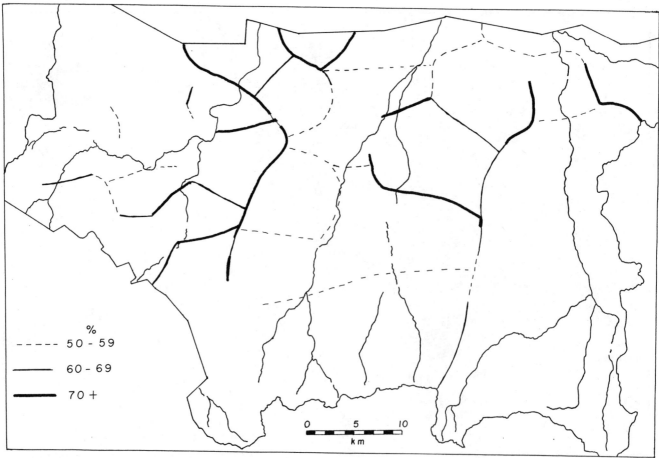

%
- - - - 50 - 59
———— 60 - 69
━━━━ 70 +

0   5   10
km

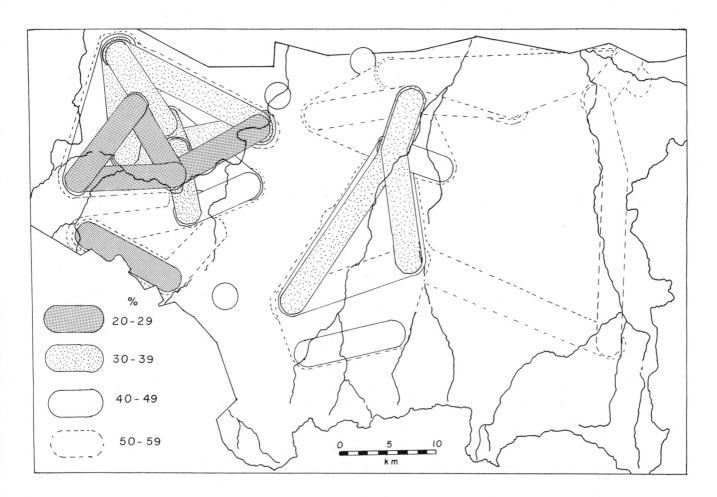

Figure 5-10. Accumulative percentage differences between all non-rocker cells arranged as a clustered hierarchy. Differences greater than 60 percent have been omitted. Computations are based on frequencies of eight stylus tips recovered from each cell.

Figure 5-8 *(above left)*. Accumulative percentage differences between contiguous cells. Computations are based on frequencies of eight stylus tips recovered from each cell.

Figure 5-9 *(left)*. Accumulative percentage differences between contiguous non-rocker cells, represented as lines of varying thickness, passing between cells. Differences less than 50 percent have been omitted. Computations are based on frequencies of eight stylus tips recovered from each cell.

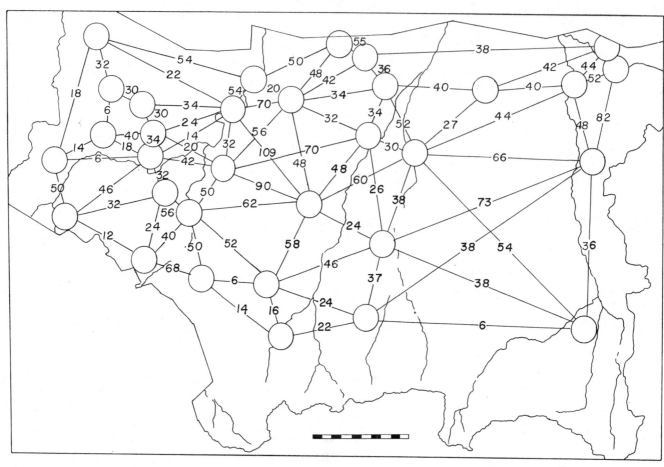

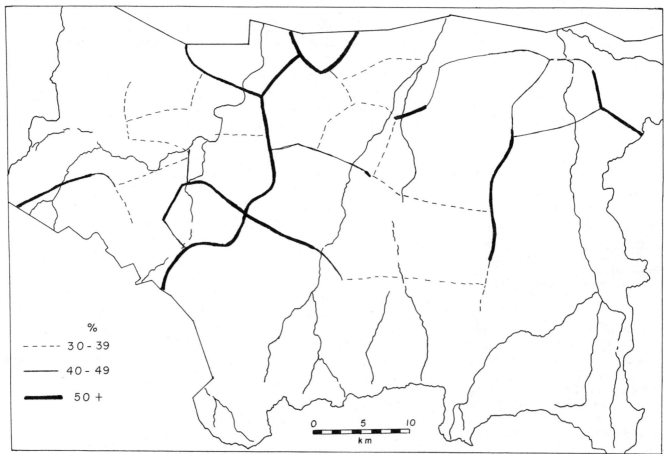

%
- - - - 30 - 39
———— 40 - 49
━━━━ 50 +

0   5   10
km

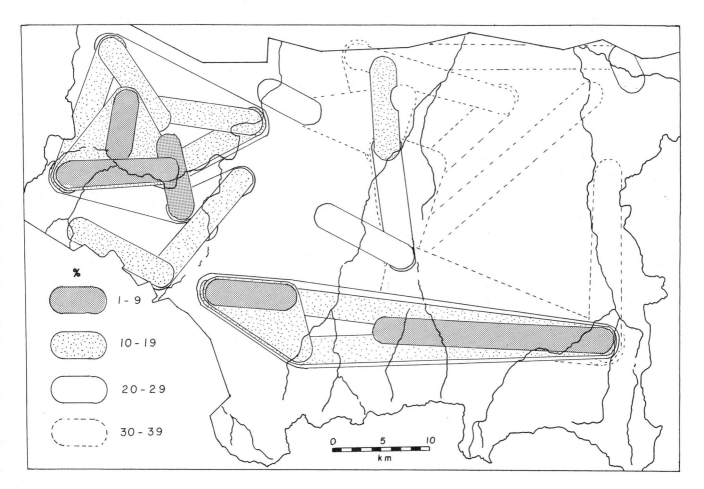

Figure 5-13. Accumulative percentage differences between all non-rocker cells, arranged as a clustered hierarchy. Differences greater than 40 percent have been omitted. Computations are based on frequencies of five decorative techniques recovered from each cell.

Figure 5-11 *(above left)*. Accumulative percentage differences between contiguous cells. Computations are based on frequencies of five decorative techniques recovered from each cell.

Figure 5-12 *(left)*. Accumulative percentage differences between contiguous non-rocker cells, represented as lines of various thickness, passing between cells. Differences less than 30 percent have been omitted. Computations are based on frequencies of five decorative techniques recovered from each cell.

Elandskloof headwaters with those in the Klein Seekoei—a far better fit with the figure 5-7 hypothesis. Also, the quill zone in the northeast is well demarcated. Obviously, the smaller number of categories in this test has dampened a great deal of statistical noise, present in the previous run, and there is consequently an even better fit with figure 5-7. The latter remains incomplete, however, because the second test confirms the need for subdivisions of the comb-stamp zone. Whether anything can be done to clarify the overlap area in the downstream reaches of the Elandskloof remains an open question, subject to detailed analysis later.

As a final check on this second, technique-based test run, differences between all cells were computed and the best linkages below the 45 percent difference level were plotted (fig. 5-13). Again, there are signs of clustering in the north and south divisions of the comb-stamp zone, with clear separation of this zone from the east. Separate clusters are also emerging in the upper and lower reaches of the Elandskloof, and there is very strong linkage between the two headwater systems of the Elandskloof and Klein Seekoei. Also, the quill zone cells cluster out together. Thus it emerges that spatial analysis of technique, rather than stylus type, gives the clearer signal, mainly because it contains fewer categories, and is therefore a more robust test.

The stage is now set for a sequence of more detailed analyses, organized in such a way that the ensuing chapters pass across the valley from west to east. Each chapter treats a specific group of related stylus tips that are dominant in a particular zone—comb-stamp, small spatulate, incisors or notches, large spatulates, and quills.

SIX

The Comb-Stamp Decorations

As mentioned in chapter 5, comb-stamp decorations are most easily replicated with the edge of a fragment of freshwater mussel shell, almost certainly *Unio caffer*. The shell edge is lightly notched, then pressed into the air-dried outer clay surface, to form a gentle arc of very small punctate impressions at right angles to the vessel rim. This is repeated in a stab-and-lift motion, thus creating a band of parallel arcs (for example, fig. 5-1, bottom row) running around the vessel a few centimeters below the rim. It is unusual to find a sherd with more than a single band. Sherds bearing this motif are normally thinner and smaller than those described elsewhere in this volume. Also, about one third of all comb-stamp sherds have very slightly convao-convex outer (decorated) surfaces, indicating a thin-walled, slightly necked vessel, with the comb-stamp band around the neck itself or on the upper shoulder. Matching sherds from single vessels never exceed four or five in number, and these are so small that reconstruction of vessel form is impossible. Overall, the available material hints at a small pot rather than a bowl.

A comb-stamp sherd was among the earliest decorations in Haaskraal rockshelter (fig. 4-8), and others were at intermediate depth in the Volstruisfontein deposit (fig. 4-9). This suggests that the motif may have been among the first to appear in the upper valley, and it probably fell from use before the time of European contact. Thus, the antiquity of this quite fragile vessel type would explain why only a few sherds from each vessel are to be found on surface sites today.

Comb-stamp vessels are highly concentrated in the west half of the upper valley, with a thinner distribution along the north rim of the study area (fig. 6-1). A small concentration also occurs south of the Meiringsberg on the southwest edge of the map. Isolated vessels were recovered from only a dozen sites elsewhere, and the motif is entirely absent from the upper reaches of the Elandskloof and Klein Seekoei.

This is the most restricted distribution displayed by any motif in the collection.

Ecological explanations of this pattern are easily refuted, since the overall distribution of the mussel shell used to create this motif fails to covary with the motif itself. Its natural distribution is riverbound: *Unio caffer* is still found sporadically in all local streambeds, and was much more prevalent before stone weirs were built at dozens of points along the major drainages. It decreases in abundance as one goes upstream, and is absent in the mountainous headwaters of the Klein Seekoei, Elandskloof, and Zoetvlei. However, it persists upstream along the larger channels of the Bo-Seekoei where the comb-stamp motif is also most abundant; thus, a correlation would seem possible. But mussel shell fragments occur on many of the larger Smithfield sites in the upper valley and on some smaller ones not yielding pottery (fig. 6-2). Many of these are several kilometers away from the nearest riverbank, indicating that mussel shell was commonly available and was carried about by Bushmen in all parts of the valley, including those where it was not readily available. This point is reinforced by the fact that mussel shell was used a few centuries later to make a rocker-stamp motif, found in literally every camp-cluster in the study area (chapter 12). Thus, any ecological model purporting to explain these distributions must invoke a restricted natural distribution for *Unio* in comb-stamp times, and a wider dispersal in rocker-stamp times. Although somewhat farfetched, this is at least a field-testable hypothesis. It is refuted, however, by the fact that mussel shells were carried far from their points of origin. A more reasonable explanation is that the makers of comb-stamp ware were constrained by socioterritorial considerations to the west half of the upper valley.

Further support for this rival hypothesis comes from the distribution of rare porcelainite flakes

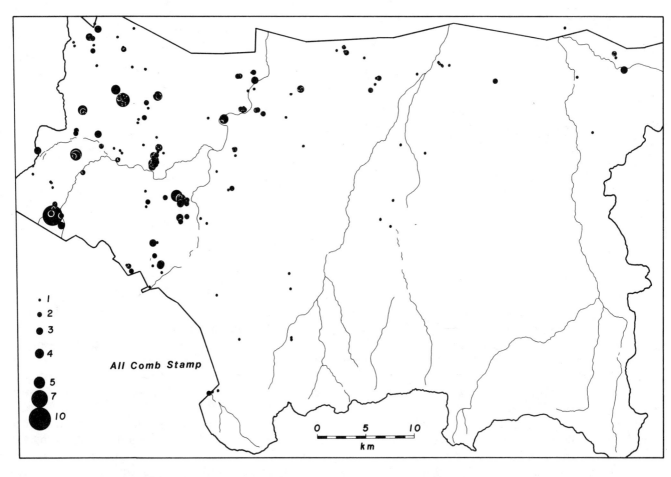

All Comb Stamp

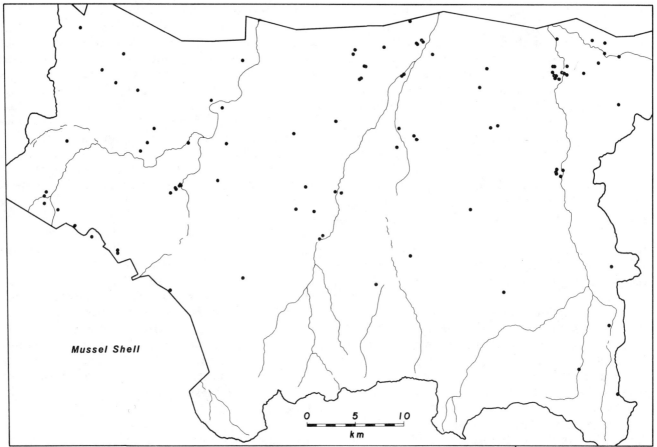

Mussel Shell

Figure 6-1. Map showing minimum numbers of comb-stamp decorated vessels per site in the upper Seacow Valley.

Figure 6-2. Map showing distribution of all Smithfield surface sites with mussel shell fragments.

found on numerous Smithfield camps and minor lithic scatters (fig. 6-3). This off-white, soapy-textured stone is an indurated siltstone known to outcrop only on the farm Nooitverwacht at the northwest rim of the study area, and well within the comb-stamp zone. It has no obvious flaking properties or edge-holding qualities that might make it more desirable than the locally abundant and widespread hornfels. Evidently the Bushmen also found this to be so—several lithic scatters of hornfels occur on the porcelainite outcrop itself, which was used sporadically as a lookout point from which to view the vast Ou Vlak plains to the north. There are no grounds, therefore, for suspecting that porcelainite was deliberately collected or distributed as an exchange item. Its distribution may be taken as a casual and unconscious trace of the limits of movements by its users. A remarkably good fit occurs between the porcelainite map and the distribution of minicells (fig. 5-6) dominated by comb-stamp vessels (fig. 6-4).

When the point-plot map is manipulated to portray the comb-stamp frequency in each non-rocker cell (figs. 5-3 and 5-4), the overall pattern holds (fig. 6-5), but two other patterns emerge—the relative frequency of rocker-stamp within its western concentration is uneven, and the strip along the north edge is not uniformly thin. When these plots are further manipulated to form an isopleth map (fig. 6-6), this unevenness becomes more apparent. Moving from west to east, there is a high plateau followed by a minor drop-off "shoulder" of 20 percent, then a narrow ledge followed by a second shoulder with a 25 percent drop-off. This double-shoulder pattern conforms closely with the expectations of the model outlined in chapter 1 (fig. 1-7), and suggests a provisional interpretation like that portrayed in figure 6-7. This is almost certainly too simplistic, however. Another variation on this hypothesis could assume that the recovery rate of sherds within the purported "lifetime range" is zero, so that this outer fringe merely reflects the limits of the "annual range." This arrangement would help to widen the implausibly narrow belt between cells I and J.

In either variant, the study area appears to have captured a substantial part of a single core area, no matter how one chooses to interpret the fringes. The size of this fragment suggests a territory very comparable in size to those at the smaller end of the Kalahari San size range (fig. 2-1c), a quite reasonable comparison given the Seacow Valley's higher carrying capacity. The comparison with Kalahari analogs breaks down, however, when the size of the "annual range" is compared with that of the Dobe !Kung (figs. 1-2ab), which extends out at least 50 kilometers from the edge of the territory. At least two alternative explanations for this discrepancy spring to mind. A purely taphonomic explanation would be that the recovery

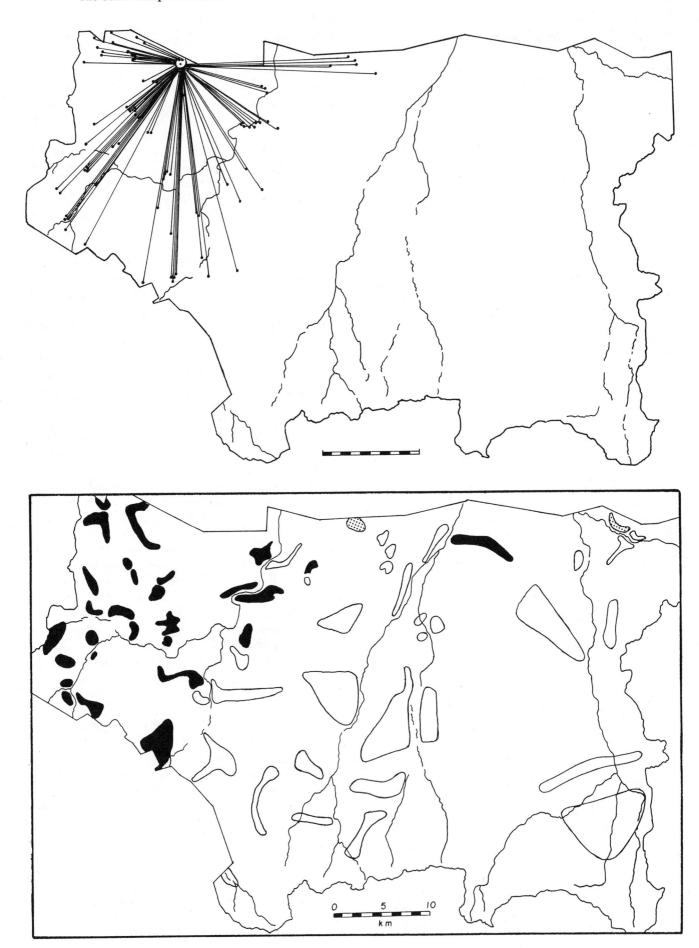

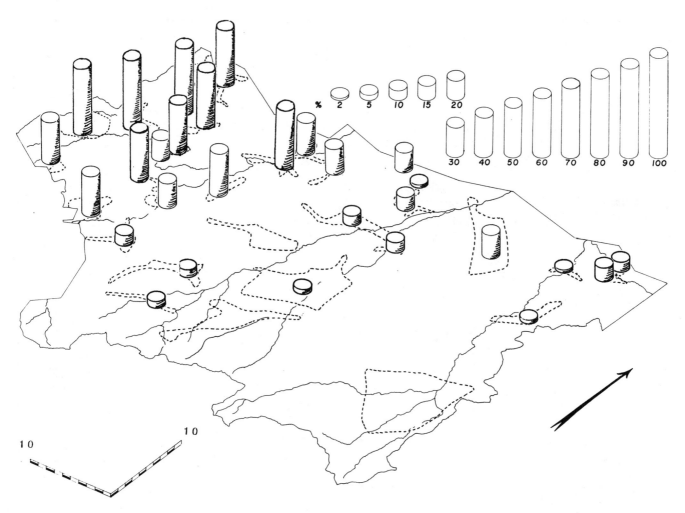

Figure 6-5. Isometric map showing comb-stamp vessels as percentages of total non-rocker vessels per cell.

Figure 6-3 *(above left).* Map showing location of the porcelainite source outcrop on the northwest rim of the study area, together with the locations of Smithfield surface sites on which porcelainite flakes have been observed.

Figure 6-4 *(left).* Minicells, as derived from figure 5-6. Black cells are numerically dominated by comb-stamp vessels. In stippled cells, comb-stamp vessels share dominance with another non-rocker motif.

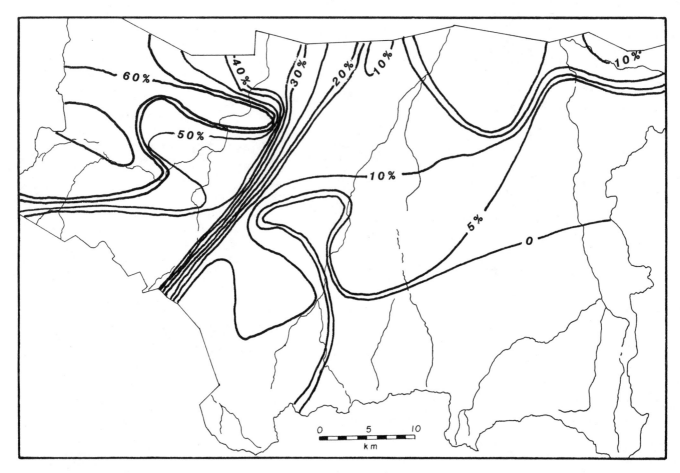

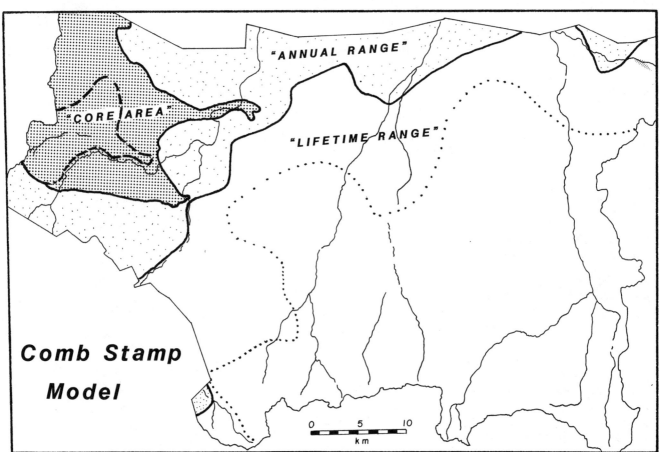

Comb Stamp
Model

Figure 6-6 *(left)*. Isopleth map showing the frequency of comb-stamp vessels, as a percentage of total non-rocker vessels per cell. Note the two separate frequency drop-off "shoulders," that is, clustered isopleth lines.

Figure 6-7 *(bottom left)*. Simplistic model of comb-stamp distribution, interpreted in terms of the model outlined in chapter 1 (see figure 1-3, *top)*. It makes no allowance for stylistic variability within the comb-stamp class.

Figure 6-8a. Example of comb-stamp with sharp, unnotched shell edge.

Figure 6-8b. Positive impression of figure 6-8a.

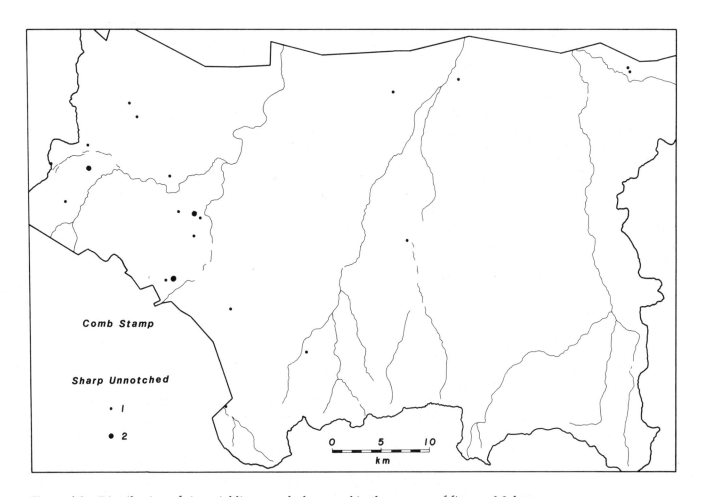

Figure 6-8c. Distribution of sites yielding vessels decorated in the manner of figures 6-8ab.

rate of sherds drops to zero well before one reaches the outer limits of the actual annual range. A purely behavioral explanation would be that territories in the Seacow Valley were more hard-edged than in the Kalahari, as predicted by the adaptive model of Cashdan and others (chapter 1). A combination of both is also a viable explanation, and their relative merits will be explored when other neighboring motif distributions have been described.

There are, however, additional complications besetting the simplistic model portrayed in figure 6-7. These stem from spatial variations in the several subtypes of comb-stamp decorations, some of which tend to cluster spatially themselves. Before this clustering can be discussed, however, the variants and their classification need to be reviewed.

The typology of this particular array of comb-stamp motifs is relatively straightforward. First, the decorations made with unnotched shell edges were separated. These are not, strictly speaking, comb-stamp decorations at all, since the arc of punctate impressions is replaced with a curved gash in the clay. Close inspection of the trough of individual gashes does sometimes reveal tiny ridges, which I first took to be microscopic notches on the shell edge, but later replication experiments revealed them to be natural irregularities along the shell edge formed by annual growth rings. The unnotched specimens were subdivided as follows. Three subclasses were arbitrarily created, based on the thickness of the shell edge used—that is, sharp, intermediate, and blunt.

The sharp-edge category was doubtless executed with extremely fresh shell, and seldom penetrated deep into the clay surface (fig. 6-8ab). Its distribution suggests a tendency to cluster along the west bank of the Zoetvlei, and it is also quite common in the outer fringes of the comb-stamp distribution (fig. 6-8c). The intermediate subclass was produced by either a slightly more mature shell edge, or one that had worn slightly through natural causes, handling, or deliberate grinding. In a blind test, I was unable to distinguish between replicated gashes made by worn or ground shell. Because this subclass was far more numerous, I thought it might be useful to distinguish between vertical-entry bands, in which the edge is pressed near-perpendicular into the clay (fig. 6-9ab) and oblique-entry bands where it is pressed in diagonally (fig. 6-10ab), but their distributions (figs. 6-9c, 6-10c) display no obvious differences. Taken together, they display a marked concentration in the adjacent cells F and G, but are not common in the north fringe. The blunt subclass is quite rare, and could conceivably have been made with the edge of a piece of ostrich eggshell, rather than mussel. However, beveled ostrich eggshell (OES) edges do not occur naturally and would have to be ground down. Mussel, being far softer, is quite commonly beveled by weath-

ering, and seems a more likely candidate (fig. 6-11ab). Its distribution shows no clustering, but it is relatively common along the northern fringe (fig. 6-11c).

The larger group of true comb-stamp was classified according to three variables: angle of entry (vertical or oblique), spacing of the notches (open or packed), and notch shape (beveled or rectangular). The systematics of this arrangement produce a total of eight subclasses, and the collection yielded specimens that fit into all of them. Only two of these arbitrary subclasses are poorly represented in the collection and may be invalid. They are briefly described with examples and point-plots, before passing on to the analysis of their relative frequencies.

Stamp arcs composed of small, packed rectangular notches (fig. 6-12ab) are easily replicated with a shell edge notched with a hornfels flake. A light sawing motion produced a sharp-edged U-bottomed notch with rectangular sides. Care must be taken not to press too hard or the edge will crumble. Also the flake must be held steady with each stroke running exactly parallel to the previous one. Whether the resulting comb is pressed into the clay at a vertical or oblique angle (fig. 6-13ab), the result is similar and only really noticeable in the positive impressions. Diagonal-entry specimens are much rarer (figs. 6-12c, 6-13c), and their combined distribution shows no obvious clustering within the general comb-stamp zone.

To produce an arc of rounded punctates (fig. 6-14ab), the comb must be notched by drawing a hornfels flake across the shell edge with a deliberate wobbling motion. This has the effect of crumbling the vertical sides of the U-bottomed notch, and the corners of the resulting comb teeth are thus rounded. With a little practice, quite close-packed teeth can be created, although they tend to break off if sawing is too vigorous. This design of comb was quite popular and ubiquitous (fig. 6-14c), and the diagonal-entry variation (fig. 6-15ab) is likewise widespread but again less abundant (fig. 6-15c).

To create an arc of elongated rectangular punctates (fig. 6-16ab), it is a simple matter to space the crosscut notches in the comb more widely apart. This makes for a less fragile toothrow and manufacturing breaks are less common. Again, there is nothing noteworthy in the point-plot of this subtype (fig. 6-16c), and the diagonal-entry variation (fig. 6-17ab) is again the scarcer of the two (fig. 6-17c). Spaced notches with beveled sides (fig. 6-18ab) appear to have a similarly bland point-plot (fig. 6-18c), and the diagonal-entry version (fig. 6-19ab) is again very scarce (fig. 6-19c).

We may now turn to the question of the relative frequencies per cell of the various subclasses. The first problem encountered is the rather small sample

Figure 6-9a *(right)*. Example of comb-stamp with shell edge of intermediate thickness and vertical entry.

Figure 6-9b *(far right)*. Positive impression of figure 6-9a.

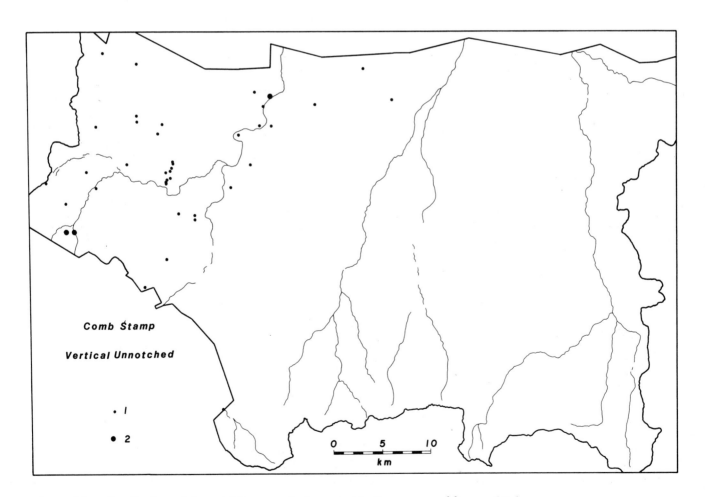

Figure 6-9c. Distribution of sites yielding vessels decorated in the manner of figures 6-9ab.

Figure 6-10a *(far left)*. Example of comb-stamp with shell edge of intermediate thickness and diagonal entry.

Figure 6-10b *(left)*. Positive impression of figure 6-10a.

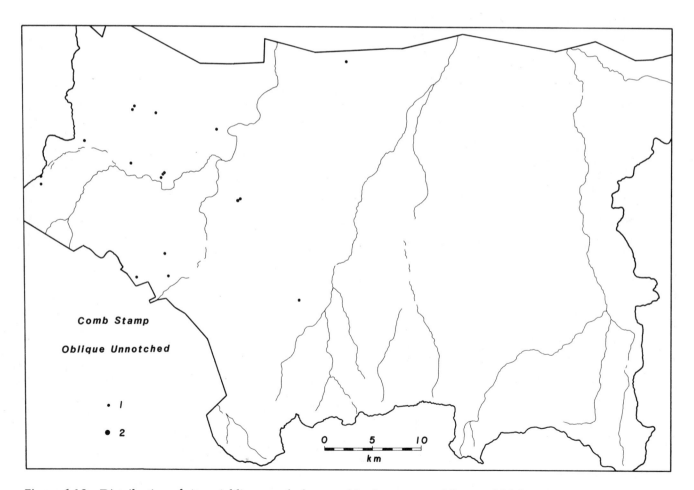

Figure 6-10c. Distribution of sites yielding vessels decorated in the manner of figures 6-10ab.

Figure 6-11a *(right)*. Example of comb-stamp with blunt shell edge.

Figure 6-11b *(far right)*. Positive impression of figure 6-11a.

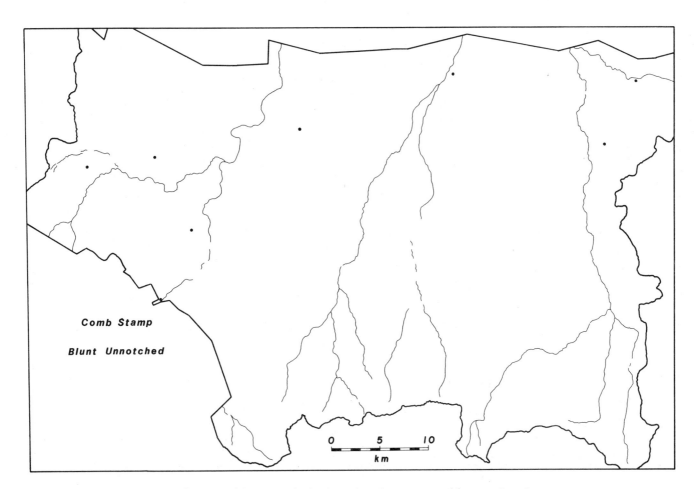

Comb Stamp

Blunt Unnotched

Figure 6-11c. Distribution of sites yielding vessels decorated in the manner of figures 6-11ab.

Figure 6-12a *(far left)*. Example of comb-stamp with packed rectangular teeth and vertical entry.

Figure 6-12b *(left)*. Positive impression of figure 6-12a.

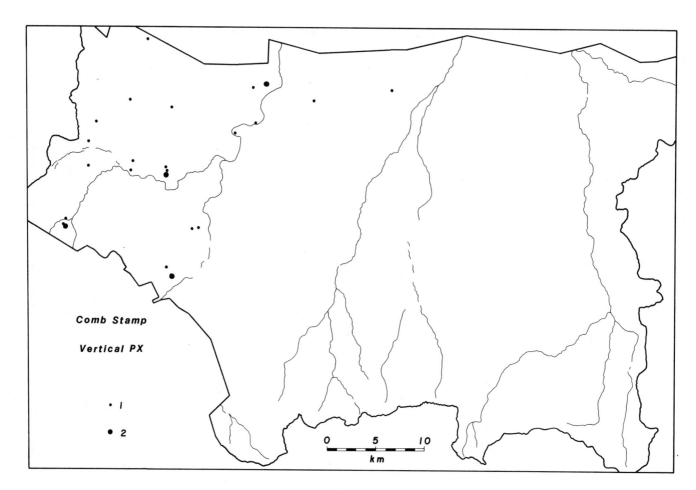

Comb Stamp

Vertical PX

• 1

• 2

Figure 6-12c. Distribution of sites yielding vessels decorated in the manner of figures 6-12ab.

size in each cell. When subclass-counts per cell are converted to percentages, the values are so small, that there is a real danger that apparent variations will be created by "noise" emanating from all the other vessels in each cell. As a very simple first attempt to circumvent this hazard, I plotted the numerically dominant subtype in each cell, without recourse to percentage values at all. The results of this elementary step were surprisingly encouraging (fig. 6-20). Vessels decorated with the packed, round-toothed comb (fig. 6-14 and 15) tend to dominate a belt of cells running from north of the Bo-Seekoei, and clear into the northern fringe. In the parcel of land bounded by the Bo-Seekoei and Zoetvlei, unnotched shells were used most frequently, with an overlap in cell E of the packed, round-tooth variant. Unnotched shell again dominates in a scatter of cells in the north fringe, notably between the Seekoei and Elandskloof. Crosscut, rectangular-tooth variations dominate a few cells, particularly in the south, where they overlap the unnotched cluster. The implications of this patterning hint that there may be stylistic subdivisions within the comb-stamp core area, and also in the fringe, which deserve closer inspection.

It seemed worthwhile, therefore, to apply the clustering procedure outlined in chapter 1 (for example, fig. 1-10), despite the hazards of low percentage values. To reduce this danger somewhat, I combined all four subclasses of unnotched comb, and the vertical, diagonal variations of all the others. The resulting classes were: unnotched, packed or square-tooth, packed or round-tooth, spaced rectangular-tooth, and spaced bevel-notch. Obviously, not all the cells could be included in the test, as sample sizes were too small, particularly at the eastern end of the north fringe. The combined percentage differences between all cell pairs were computed, and three quite clear-cut clusters emerge (fig. 6-21). The strongest is, of course, on the east side of the Groot Seekoei, where percentage values are smaller, and differences are consequently fewer. More encouraging is the cluster bounded by the Bo-Seekoei and Groot Seekoei channels, which contains the highest cell values, yet still displays strong clustering tendencies, particularly between nearest neighbors. The third cluster is bounded by the Bo-Seekoei and the Zoetvlei, but is relatively weakly bonded, even though cell values are relatively low.

This analysis only partly confirms the pattern produced by the first crude test shown in figure 6-20, and it was deemed advisable to try a third and independent analytical approach to determine which, if any, is to be preferred. The goals of the third test were: (a) to circumvent difficulties created by non-comb "noise" in the percentage frequencies of individual cells, and (b) to bypass the influence of cell percentage values on the strength of clustering. To do this it was necessary to combine nearest-neighbor cells until the sample-size of comb-stamp vessels was large enough to produce viable frequencies of subclasses expressed as percentages of total comb-stamp only. Conflation becomes increasingly drastic as one moves farther out to the fringes of the distribution (fig. 6-22) where sample size per conflated cell is still too low to be entirely safe.

Nonetheless, accumulative percentage differences between cells were computed and clustered with the result seen in figure 6-23. This conforms more closely with the first elementary test in that there is strong separation between north and south, along the line of the Bo-Seekoei, but substantial overlap between each and the northern fringe. Note, however, that there are strong bonds between conflated cells MN and OPQ in the northern fringe, hinting at the possibility of a third cluster.

To pursue this possibility, a fourth independent cross-check was devised, as an alternative to the clustering approach. Four ratios were computed from various complimentary attributes for each cell. These ratios were notched or unnotched, diagonal or vertical entry, cross-cut or bevel-notch, and spaced or packed notch. The ratio number is computed by simply dividing the number of one attribute in the cell into the number of its shadow-attribute. Thus a cell with twenty-four vessels having twelve unnotched and twelve notched will yield a notched or unnotched ratio of 1.0. Neighboring cells yielding similar ratios are then linked into pairs or groups.

The vertical or oblique entry ratio showed very little intercell difference. In each combination of notch shape and packing, the diagonal-entry version formed a smaller component. My guess is that it reflects only that the potter leaned over her vessel on the ground (diagonal) or held it up in the left hand (vertical) when executing the decorative band. When all diagonal-entry vessels are mapped as a group, they show no obvious clustering. It is reasonable to suppose, then, that the distinction between vertical and diagonal entry is of no further interest.

The best correlation was between the cross-cut or bevel notch ratio and the spaced or packed ratio that shared most linkages (fig. 6-24). The most extensive grouping is between the contiguous cells ABCD, all north of the Bo-Seekoei and west of the Groot Seekoei. Another three-way link is between E, LY, and HR, which are widely separated from each other in the southern half of the comb-stamp zone. Cells K and IJ also match ratios in this same area. Of most immediate interest, however, is the match between MN and OPQ in the northern fringe, thus confirming the strength of this bond.

A fifth and final cross-check was attempted, without much success. Its failure stems from the invalid assumption that individual attributes covary in space. In this test, I plotted individual attributes (all

Figure 6-13a *(far left)*. Example of comb-stamp with packed rectangular teeth and vertical entry.

Figure 6-13b *(left)*. Positive impression of figure 6-13a.

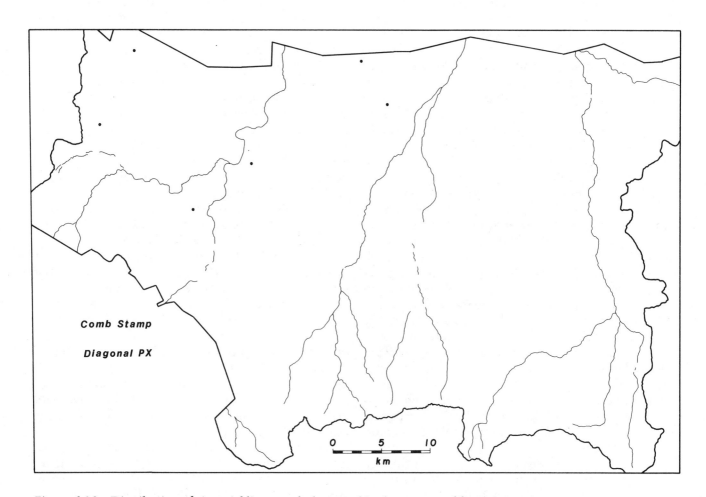

Comb Stamp

Diagonal PX

Figure 6-13c. Distribution of sites yielding vessels decorated in the manner of figures 6-13ab.

Figure 6-14a *(right)*. Example of comb-stamp with packed round teeth and vertical entry.

Figure 6-14b *(far right)*. Positive impression of figure 6-14a.

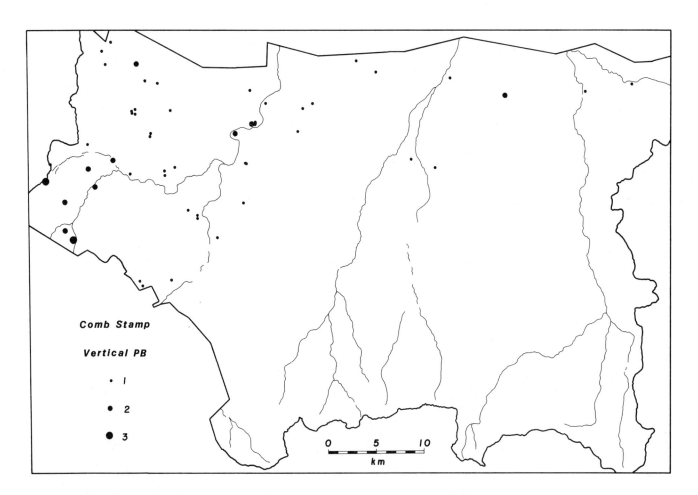

Figure 6-14c. Distribution of sites yielding vessels decorated in the manner of figures 6-14ab.

81

Figure 6-15a *(far left)*. Example of comb-stamp with packed round teeth and diagonal entry.

Figure 6-15b *(left)*. Positive impression of figure 6-15a.

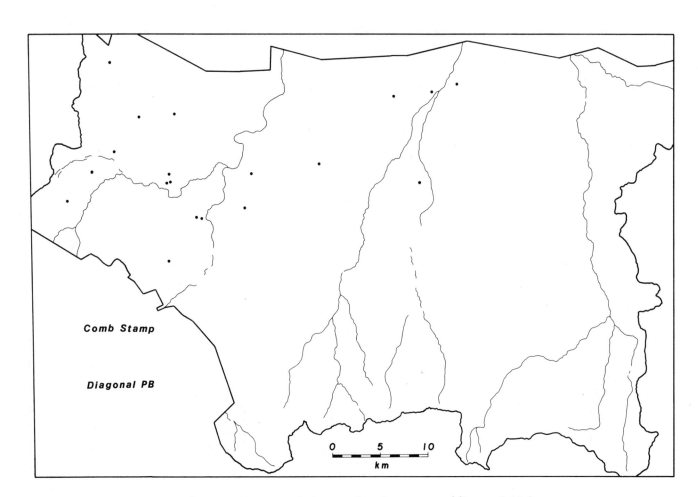

Comb Stamp

Diagonal PB

Figure 6-15c. Distribution of sites yielding vessels decorated in the manner of figures 6-15ab.

Figure 6-16a *(right)*. Example of comb-stamp with elongated rectangular teeth and vertical entry.

Figure 6-16b *(far right)*. Positive impression of figure 6-16a.

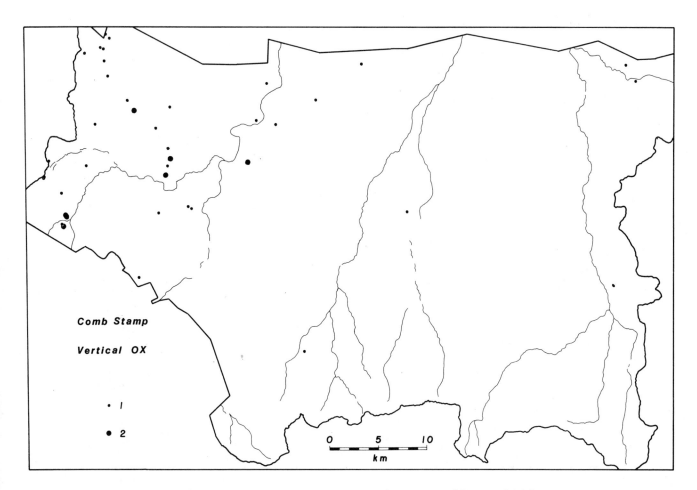

Figure 6-16c. Distribution of sites yielding vessels decorated in the manner of figures 6-16ab.

Figure 6-17a *(far left)*. Example of comb-stamp with elongated rectangular teeth and diagonal entry.

Figure 6-17b *(left)*. Positive impression of figure 6-17a.

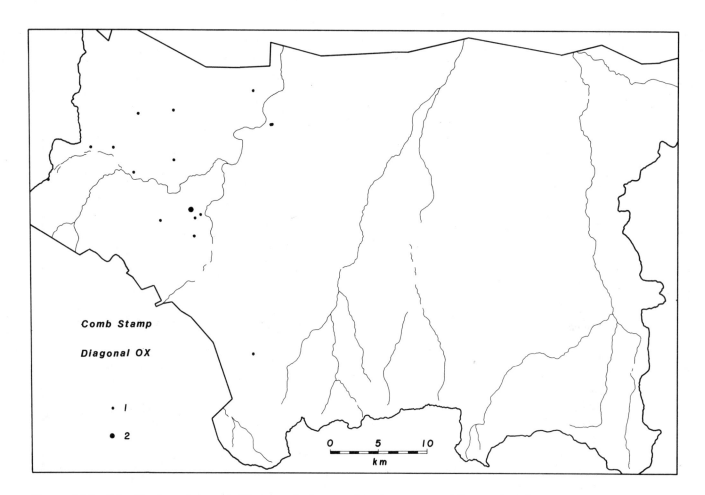

Comb Stamp

Diagonal OX

· 1

● 2

Figure 6-17c. Distribution of sites yielding vessels decorated in the manner of figures 6-17ab.

Figure 6-18a *(right)*. Example of comb-stamp with elongated rounded teeth and vertical entry.

Figure 6-18b *(far right)*. Positive impression of figure 6-18a.

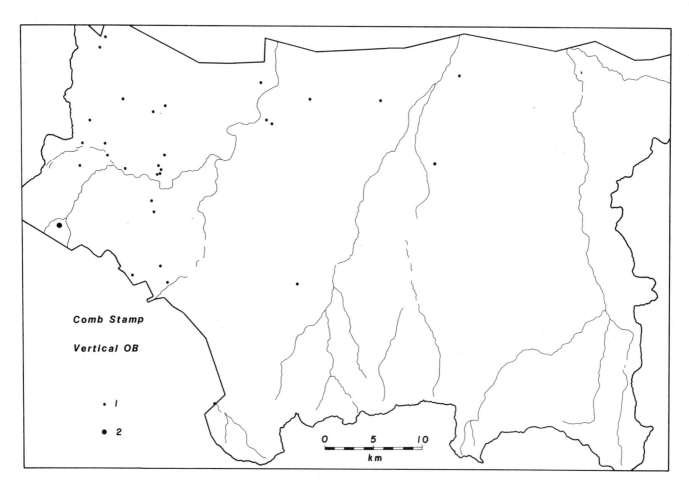

Comb Stamp

Vertical OB

• 1

● 2

0   5   10
km

Figure 6-18c. Distribution of sites yielding vessels decorated in the manner of figures 6-18ab.

Figure 6-19a *(far left)*. Example of comb-stamp with elongated rounded teeth and diagonal entry.

Figure 6-19b *(left)*. Positive impression of figure 6-19a.

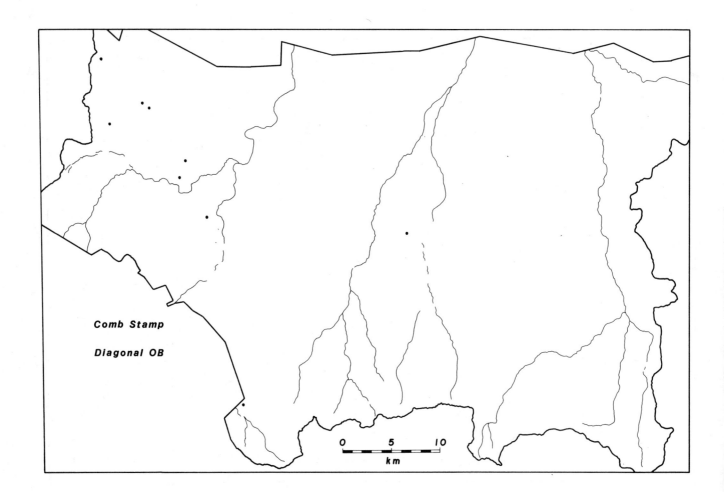

Comb Stamp

Diagonal OB

Figure 6-19c. Distribution of sites yielding vessels decorated in the manner of figures 6-19ab.

Figure 6-20. Cells dominated by packed round teeth comb-stamp (black); by unnotched shell comb-stamp (stippled); by packed square teeth comb-stamp (diagonal lines); and by elongated rectangular teeth comb-stamp (vertical lines).

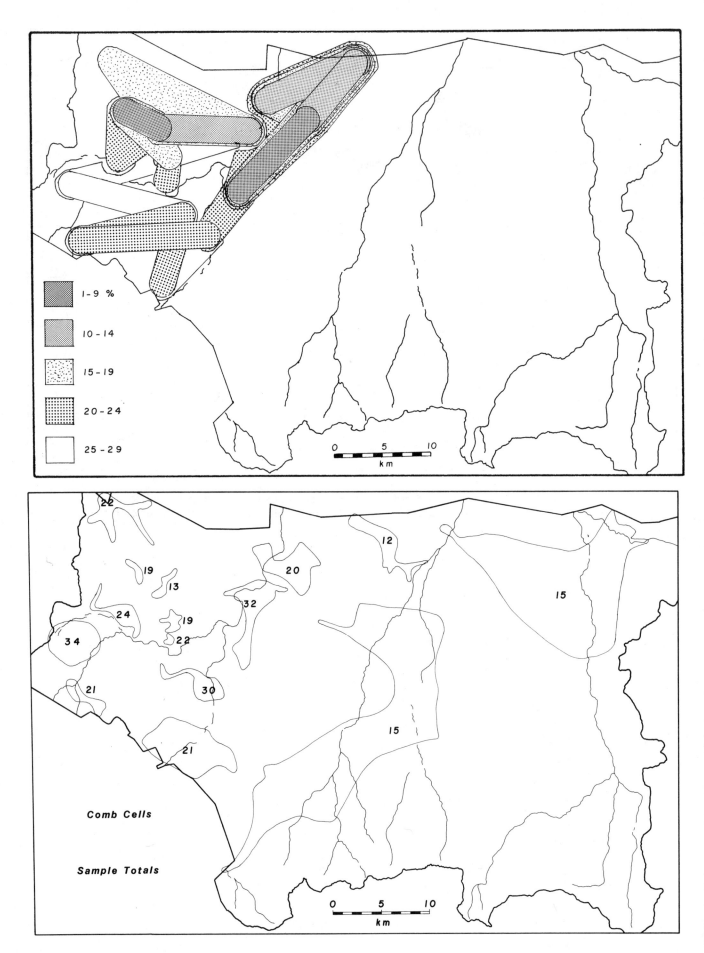

Comb Cells

Sample Totals

Figure 6-21. Accumulative percentage differences between all western cells, using four classes of comb-stamp. Each class was calculated as a percentage of total non-rocker vessels per cell. The cluster hierarchy omits differences greater than 30 percent. The five classes are: all unnotched; all packed square tooth comb; all packed round tooth comb; all elongated rectangular tooth comb; and all elongated rounded tooth comb.

Figure 6-22. Enlarged cells, showing total comb-stamp vessels per cell.

unnotched, all packed notches, all bevel notches, and so forth) as percentages of comb-stamp totals in each conflated cell. The results of each were plotted as isopleth maps, and frequency drop-off shoulders were isolated on these (appendix). When these various shoulders are plotted on the same sheet (fig. 6-25) there is again a tendency for cells MN and OPQ to cluster together, but without very strong separation from the other two. Separation between north and south is equally jumbled and ambiguous, so these results cannot be considered very convincing. Clearly, individual attributes do not constitute markers, whereas combinations of attributes do. No other insights are to be gained from this test.

No matter what angle of attack was used in the analysis, the following results tend to recur: (1) all but the last (theoretically flawed) test indicate a separation between cells to the north and south of the Bo-Seekoei channel; (2) all but the first elementary test indicate a cluster of cells on the east side of the Groot Seekoei channel, in the northern fringe; (3) all but the last test indicate some connections between cells south of the Bo-Seekoei and cells east of the Groot Seekoei; and (4) all but the second test suggest some connections between cells on the north side of the Bo-Seekoei and those east of the Groot Seekoei.

The most economical interpretation of these results is that the river channels were the stylistic boundaries containing at least two different groups, each characterized by its own subclass of comb-stamp decoration: (a) unnotched and crosscut in the south, contained by the Bo-Seekoei and Zoetvlei channels; (b) packed round-tooth in the north contained by the Bo-Seekoei and Groot Seekoei channels. The northern fringe east of the Groot Seekoei was a zone of overlap in the annual ranges of both (a) and (b).

An alternate, but riskier interpretation of this "overlap" area would be that it was occupied by a third group without its own distinctive subclass of decorations, but using the neighboring two substyles in similar proportions. At present, this option is intuitively unreasonable, but can be tested only by expanding the study area northwards.

Thus it emerges that the simplistic model portrayed in figure 6-7 requires some modification, but it should not be scrapped altogether. The "core area" must be split into a northern and southern half, divided by the Bo-Seekoei channel. Stylistic overlap between these two subcores is far more intense than that predicted for the original model, which predicts no such splits in any case. Further interpretations are called for.

Unfortunately the study area has captured only parts of each subcore, so that the true area of each remains unknown. It seems unlikely, however, that either will reach the size of even the smallest Kalahari San territory, and it is also unlikely that either area

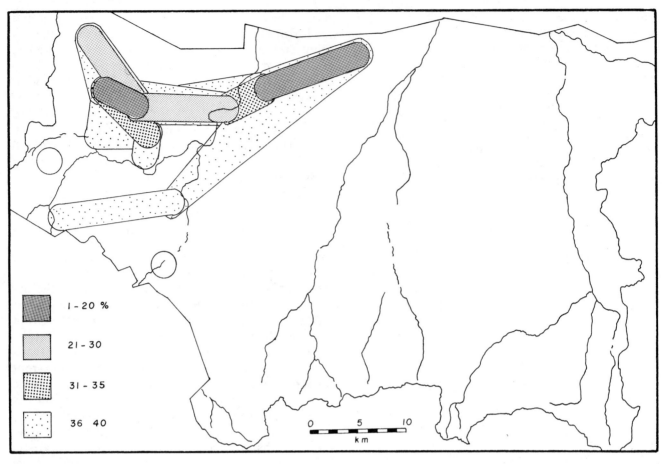

1 – 20 %

21 – 30

31 – 35

36 40

0   5   10

km

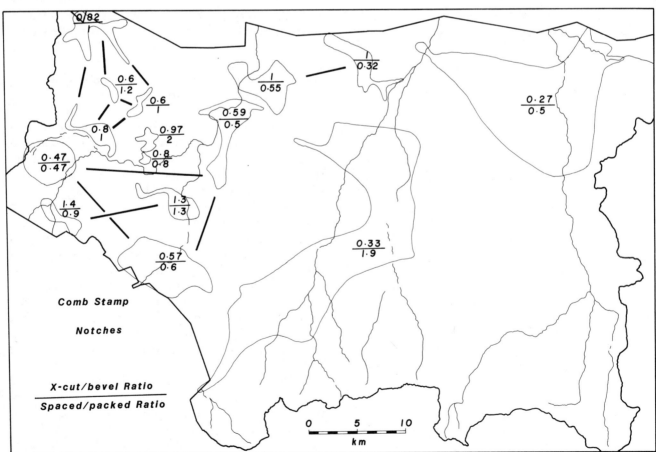

Q/82

0·6
1·2

0·6
1

1
0·55

1
0·32

0·27
0·5

0·8
1

0·97
2

0·59
0·5

0·47
0·47

0·8
0·8

1·4
0·9

1·3
1·3

0·33
1·9

0·57
0·6

Comb Stamp

Notches

X-cut/bevel Ratio

Spaced/packed Ratio

0   5   10

km

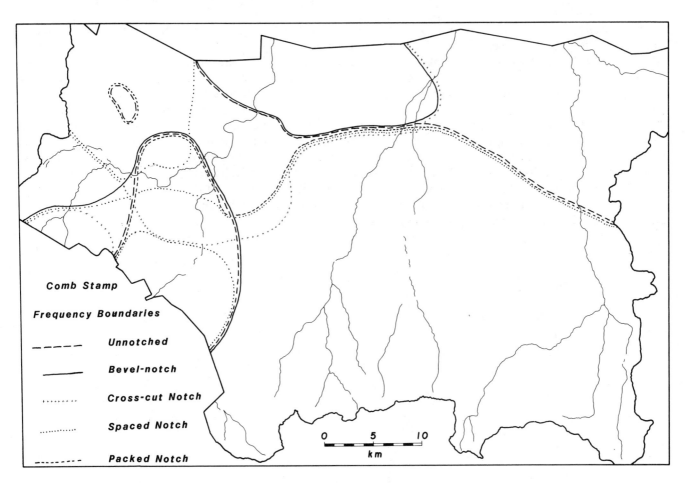

Comb Stamp

Frequency Boundaries

- - - - -   **Unnotched**

————   **Bevel-notch**

·········   **Cross-cut Notch**

············   **Spaced Notch**

- · - · - ·   **Packed Notch**

Figure 6-25. Summary map of frequency drop-off "shoulders" derived from isopleth maps of different attributes of the comb-stamp class. The original isopleth maps are shown in the appendix.

Figure 6-23 *(upper left)*. Accumulative percentage differences between enlarged cells (see figure 6-22) using four classes of comb-stamp. Each class was calculated as a percentage of total comb-stamp vessels per enlarged cell. The cluster hierarchy omits differences greater than 40 percent. The four classes are: all unnotched; all packed square tooth comb; all packed round tooth comb, all elongated rectangular tooth comb; and all elongated rounded tooth comb.

Figure 6-24 *(left)*. In each enlarged cell, the rectangular/round tooth ratio appears above the horizontal line, and the packed/elongated tooth ratio occurs below. Thick lines connecting cells draw attention to similarities between them.

could have supported a full band. Some other config-uration should be sought to explain (a) the absence of "dead ground" between the subcores, (b) the intensive overlap of substyles across their mutual boundary, and (c) the relatively subtle differences between the substyles characterizing each subcore.

The most parsimonious explanation would be that groups within the band, most probably extended families, had preferential foraging rights over specific areas within the band's territory. Boundaries between these subterritories would have been contiguous and very soft-edged, with a much heavier traffic flow (and pot exchange) than would occur between neighboring bands. The original model does not allow for such an arrangement to be visible in the archaeological record—hence the need for so many independent cross-checks. Unfortunately, there is no clear-cut ana-log for such organization among the Kalahari San, al-though the G/wi come closest with their family-based subterritories during the bad winter and spring months. There is no evidence, however, that families used the same subterritories year after year. Of course this dearth of Kalahari analogs does not necessarily preclude the possibility that the Seacow Valley Bushmen may have been so organized.

SEVEN

Small Spatulate Stylus and Related Types

The identity of this small spatulate-shaped stylus remains uncertain, and it may include several different objects made of different materials, but all producing similar-looking imprints. Stylus width varies between two and three millimeters and its track is readily distinguished from that of the large plain spatulate (see chapter 9), which does not grade into the small variety. Among numerous attempts to replicate the tracks to be described below, none was wholly satisfactory although those coming closest to the real thing were produced with an obliquely cut end of a bullrush stem. Various obliquely cut sticks and bone fragments were tried, as well as porcupine quills, but none produced the desired effect. There is a distinct possibility that some very shallow, sharp-ended imprints were produced with the small fingernail of a Bushman child—a notion which, obviously, I have not had the chance to test.

Whatever the stylus, it was applied in both stab-and-lift and stab-and-drag motions. These two techniques are almost never found together on the same sherd, although their use on the same bowl cannot be ruled out. They will be described and mapped separately, as their distributions do not exactly covary. Also included in this chapter is a small sample of tracks that closely resemble the deeper stab-and-drag pattern, but which may just have been created by cord-wrapping. Finally, a larger pointed spatulate imprint is compared with the regular small spatulate, and their two distributions are discussed.

Stab-and-lift is used here to mean the technique by which the stylus is thrust diagonally or nearly vertically into the clay surface (stab), then extracted entirely (lift) and moved to an adjacent point where the motion is repeated, thus forming a line of punctate marks with clear spaces between them (fig. 7-1ab). On most bowls these lines run parallel with the rim—that is, horizontally around the bowl exterior, but this is not invariably so because rare panels have near-

vertical or diagonal orientations. The gap between any two punctate lines is normally about equal to the gap between individual stab-marks, thus creating an overall mesh-like decoration down the side of the bowl. This effect is not of even quality, however, because no importance was attached to horizontal control. Evidently the bowl was rotated with the left hand while the decorator leaned over the rim and inserted the stylus at an angle roughly diagonal to the axis of the line. Individual lines of stab-marks are seldom straight, but bend and wave erratically. Groups of parallel lines follow the gentle curves, then break off where they intersect with the bends in lines already laid down (fig. 3-1). These parallel groups probably reflect single bursts of work, with the potter changing position periodically, or breaking off to rest.

Initial inspection of the stab-and-lift point-plot (fig. 7-1c) suggests a marked cluster in cells P and Q near the north rim of the study area, but attempts to subdivide this class on the basis of spacing and depth produce no very obvious patterning. When vessel counts per cell are converted to percentages, cells P and Q produce a modest spike (14%), but there are others at X, Y (21%), and Z (12%), also. Patterning like this (fig. 7-2) contrasts markedly with the expectations of the original model (fig. 1-7) and more closely resembles the sort of random variations to be expected from background noise rather than signal. This implies that the stab-and-lift category is, in fact, spurious, and was not recognized by the Bushmen themselves as an emblemic style.

Stab-and-drag differs from stab-and-lift only in that the stylus is not removed entirely from the clay before being reinserted, very close to the previous stab mark. This motion creates a U-bottomed channel in the clay, with low, close-spaced, lunate shaped ridges across the bottom itself (fig. 7-3ab). The spacing and orientation of the channel varies in much the same way as that described above for stab-and-lift

Figure 7-1a *(far left).* Example of small spatulate stab-and-lift decoration.

Figure 7-1b *(left).* Positive impression of figure 7-1a.

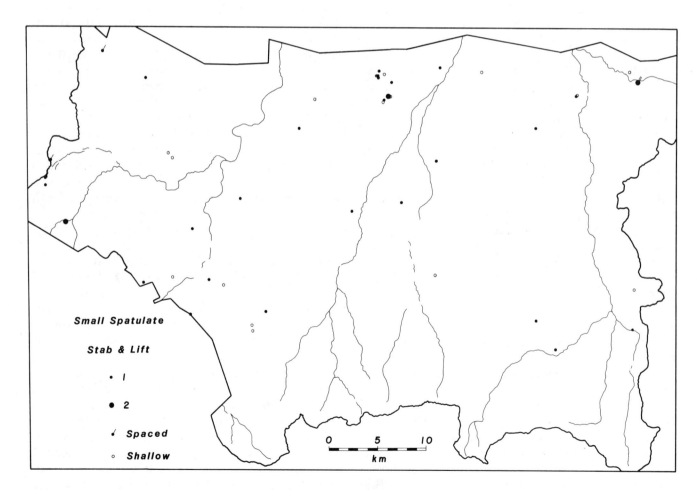

Small Spatulate

Stab & Lift

• 1

● 2

✓ Spaced

○ Shallow

Figure 7-1c. Distribution of sites yielding vessels decorated in the manner of figures 7-1ab.

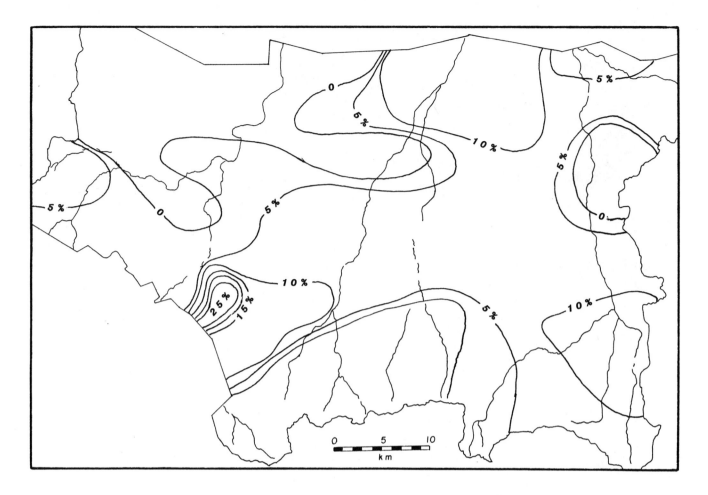

Figure 7-2. Isopleth map of percentage frequencies per non-rocker cell of small spatulate stab-and-lift.

rows. Stab-and-drag is far more time consuming, however, and it cannot be executed in a wet sticky clay without creating an unattractive mess (a quite frequent occurrence in the collection). Likewise, it cannot be done on air-dried clay that has been allowed to get too hard, unlike the stab-and-lift that works better on drier clays. Overall, stab-and-drag is a more demanding technique, but it has one advantage in that it requires much less care and attention to maintain a straight line and to hold even spacing between parallel channels.

The point-plot for stab-and-drag (fig. 7-3c) suggests a nearly ubiquitous pattern without obvious clustering, but there is a marked scarcity in the Klein Seekoei drainage to the east. When converted to percentages per non-rocker cell (fig. 7-4), however, the large, low-yield cells S and T in the Elandskloof drainage appear to have disproportionately high frequencies. This could be dismissed as noise created by sampling deficiencies, but the adjacent high-yield cells U and V in the upper Elandskloof also produce higher percentage values than their neighbors, albeit not high enough to create significant drop-off shoulders. Overall, the cell-cluster STU is not prominent enough to fit the expectations of a territorial model, nor does this cluster stand out in the point-plot. Parsimony dictates, therefore, that the pattern is a coinci-

95

Figure 7-3a *(far left).* Example of small spatulate stab-and-drag decoration.

Figure 7-3b *(left).* Positive impression of figure 7-3a.

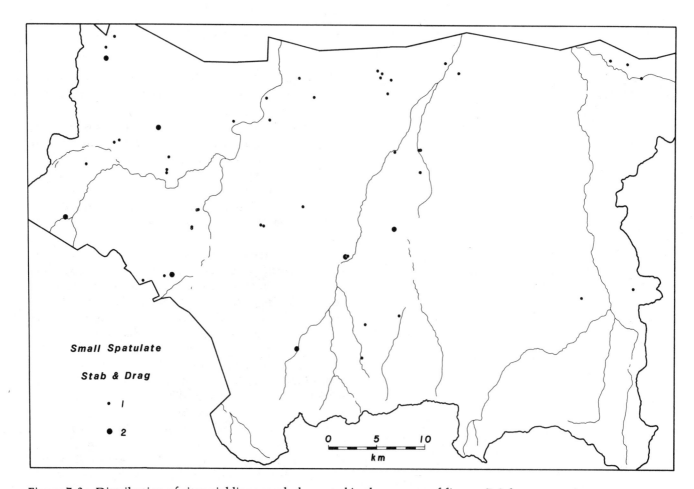

Small Spatulate

Stab & Drag

• 1

● 2

Figure 7-3c. Distribution of sites yielding vessels decorated in the manner of figures 7-3ab.

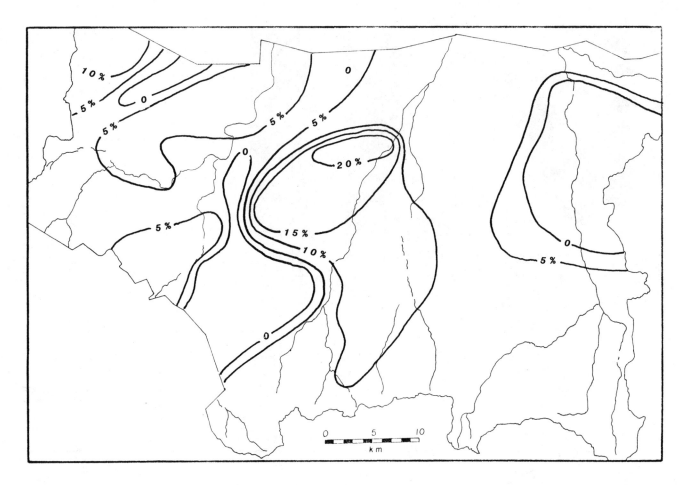

Figure 7-4. Isopleth map of frequencies per non-rocker cell of small spatulate stab-and-drag.

dental and, therefore, spurious by-product of sampling noise, and it follows that the technique was not an emblemic style, but merely background noise.

Before analyzing the combined distributions of these two variants, it is useful to include a third category that I may have artificially separated from the stab-and-drag category. This was labeled "cord-impressed" on my (very hesitant) reading of the orientation of the small lunate ridges in the channel bottoms of some stab-and-drag specimens. It seemed to me that they were diagonal to the long-axis of the channel, and they seemed to "wrap around" the positive impressions of the channel in such a way as to suggest a twine impression (fig. 7-5ab). I did not attempt to replicate such twine from local grasses, however, but used ordinary parcel string to produce what I thought was a convincing impression. For the following reasons, I now suspect that my interpretation was an error.

The "cord" point-plot (fig. 7-5c) is again ubiquitous, with a slight northeastern bias, and a hint of clustering in cell DD on the east branch of the Elandskloof. When this plot is combined with the stab-and-drag distribution, and the combination is computed as percentages per non-rocker cell, a high-frequency plateau of five contiguous cells emerges along the Elandskloof drainage (fig. 7-6). Moreover,

Figure 7-5a *(far left)*. Example of "cord-impressed" decoration. There are grounds for believing that this may be small spatulate stab-and-drag executed with unusual neatness.

Figure 7-5b *(left)*. Positive impression of figure 7-5a.

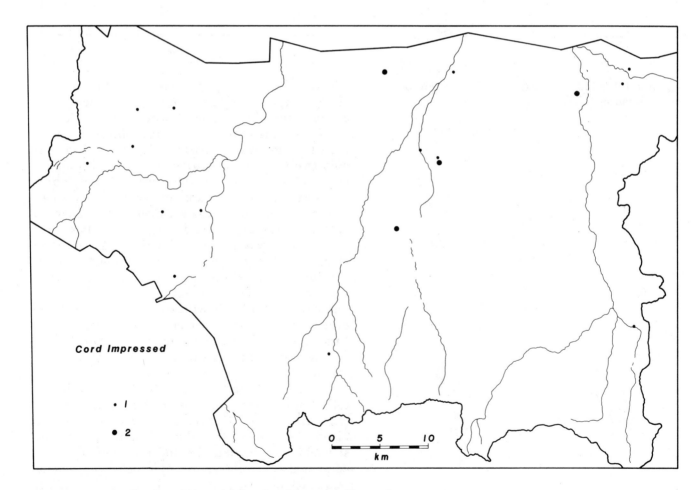

Cord Impressed

• *1*

• *2*

Figure 7-5c. Distribution of sites yielding "cord-impressed" vessels.

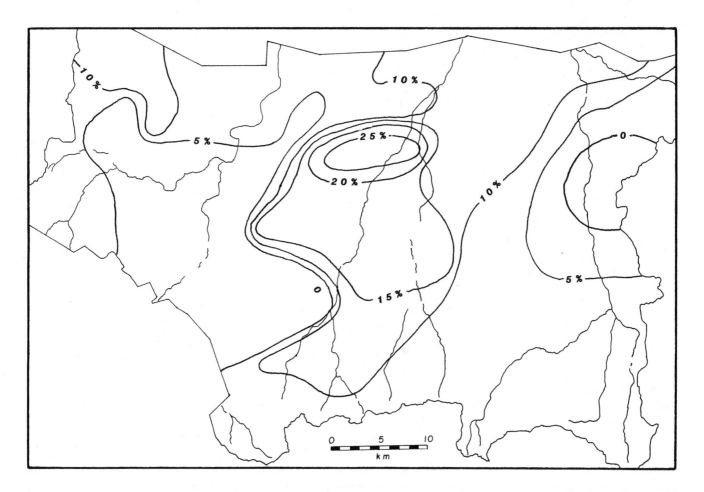

Figure 7-6. Isopleth map of frequencies per non-rocker cell of small spatulate stab-and-drag combined with "cord-impressed" vessels.

three of the included cells (P, DD, and U) have relatively large sample sizes, and a clear 15 percent drop-off shoulder appears between the Zoetvlei/Seekoei line and the Elandskloof west branch. Unfortunately, the east side of the cell-cluster remains ill-defined, as the drop-off rate is gradual, thus spoiling its fit with the standard territorial model. This pattern is suggestive enough, however, to lead me to suspect that I may have read too much into certain stab-and-drag patterns, thus artificially splitting up their true distribution.

We may now turn to the possibility that the stab-and-lift or drag dichotomy was also an artificial rift in the actual pattern. When all stab-and-lift, stab-and-drag, and "cord" are point-plotted together (fig. 7-7) there are marked signs of clustering along the northeast rim of the study area. When this map is converted to percentages per non-rocker cell (fig. 7-8) something approaching the expectations of the model (fig. 1-7) is achieved, although the southern rim is not all that it should be. The other anomaly is the 30 percent spike over cell Y, which can be safely dismissed as sampling noise, cell Y having the smallest sample on the map (fig. 5-3). There are now grounds for believing, therefore, that the small spatulate, used in either mode, is a vehicle for emblemic style.

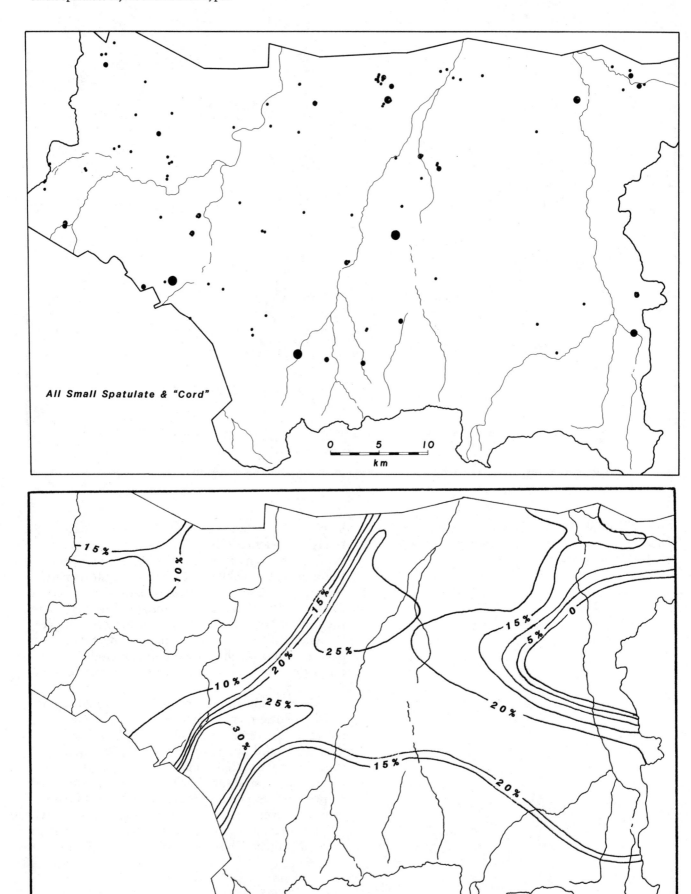

All Small Spatulate & "Cord"

Figure 7-7. Distribution of sites yielding vessels decorated in small spatulate stab-and-drag, small spatulate stab-and-lift, or with "cord-impressed" patterns.

Figure 7-8. Isopleth map of frequencies per non-rocker cell of small spatulate stab-and-drag combined with small spatulate stab-and-lift, and with "cord-impressed" vessels.

It is impossible to determine, however, whether the high-frequency plateau thus obtained reflects most of one "core area" or merely a fragment of an "annual range" of some core area just to the north of the study area's rim—which possibly nicked it at cell P. The latter interpretation has more appeal at present because of the very diffuse nature of the point-plot, and the localized increase in frequency in the far northwest at cell A. Obviously, no amount of analysis is going to solve this question, which can be answered only by extending the study area farther downstream.

Before leaving this topic, another pertinent decoration will be reviewed as it superficially resembles small spatulate, and has a quite comparable distribution—the pointed spatulate. The pointed spatulate was used in a stab-and-drag technique that, on casual inspection, looks quite like the pattern already discussed, except that the channel is normally a little wider and consistently deeper. The most notable difference, however, is that it displays a row of punctate marks along the floor of the channel instead of the thin lunate ridges. The cause of these becomes apparent in the positive impression of the channel, which reveals a flat-sectioned, pointed stylus (fig. 7-9ab). My early conviction that this could be replicated with an obliquely cut porcupine quill (rather in the manner of a quill pen) led nowhere, and I eventually managed a fair copy of this with a bone-shaft fragment.

The point-plot (fig. 7-9c) suggests another ubiquitous, bland distribution typical of background noise rather than signal. The conversion to percentages per non-rocker cell (fig. 7-10) does little to dispel this impression, and produces apparently randomly distributed spikes, including an overinflated figure for the poorly represented cell Y. There is a hint of a slightly higher-frequency ridge just east of the Zoetvlei-Seekoei line which runs, oddly enough, parallel with the west (downslope) shoulder of the small spatulate plateau seen in figure 7-8. Also, two of the random spikes (cells Y and Z) covary with spikes at the southern extremities of the same plateau. Can it be that the pointed spatulate is just another variation of the small spatulate array?

When the pointed spatulate figures were combined with those for small spatulate stab-and-drag (plus "cord") the resulting configuration suggested jumbled noise, indicating that the addition of the pointed spatulate had destroyed whatever patterning the others had produced. When the stab-and-lift figures were added to this concatenation so that all classes are included, the resulting frequency distribution (fig. 7-11) displays no improvement over the combined small spatulate pattern first achieved in figure 7-8. The addition of the pointed spatulate to the pool has tended to bring out multiple spikes that

 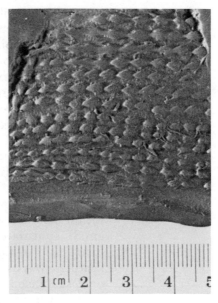

Figure 7-9a *(far left).* Example of large pointed spatulate stab-and-drag decoration.

Figure 7-9b *(left).* Positive impression of figure 7-9a.

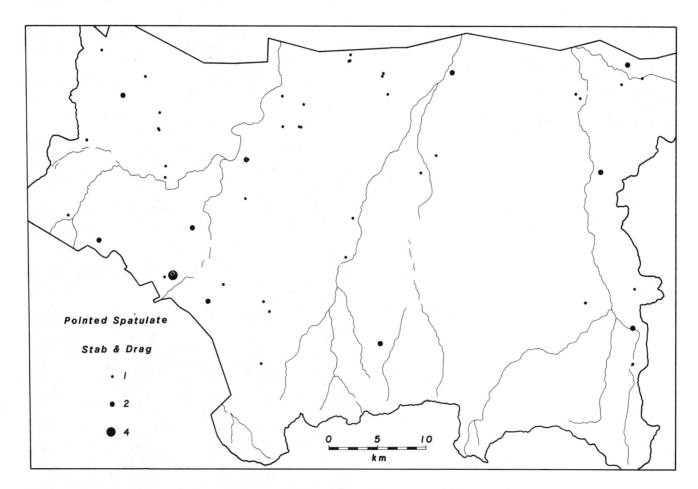

Pointed Spatulate

Stab & Drag

· 1

● 2

● 4

0   5   10

km

Figure 7-9c. Distribution of sites yielding vessels decorated in the manner of figures 7-9ab.

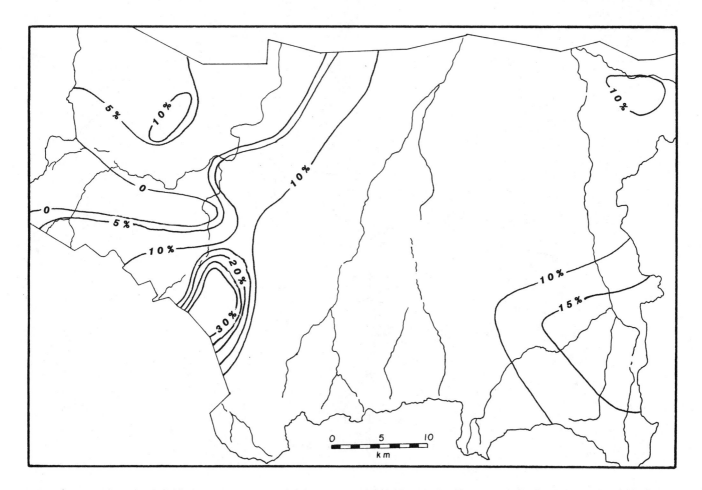

Figure 7-10. Isopleth map of the frequencies per non-rocker cell of large pointed spatulate stab-and-drag.

disrupt the relatively even surface of the small spatulate plateau. Two rival interpretations suggest themselves, each of equal merit:

(1) The pointed spatulate is a variation of the small spatulate theme, and all four subtypes (S and L, S and D, "Cord," Point) are just segments in a wide range of background noise, devoid of any signal. This implies that small sticks and bone fragments were sporadically used as stylus tips by potters in all parts of the valley, and the resulting decorations were nowhere regarded as emblemic style. The fact that there is a high-frequency ridge between the Zoetvlei-Seekoei line and the Elandskloof is a spurious by-product of the rapid drop-off in comb-stamp to the west (chapter 6) and the more gradual drop-off in large plain spatulate to the east (chapter 9). In this scenario, the ridge is nothing more than a statistical accident and does not represent a true plateau.

(2) Only the pointed spatulate is background noise. Bone fragments were used casually as stylus tips by potters in all parts of the valley, and the resulting decorations were nowhere regarded as emblemic style. Covariance with the small spatulate is spurious coincidence, but the small spatulate plateau is valid, reflecting an emblemic style.

Various attempts to conflate cells to sample sizes large enough to analyze this group on its own, as was

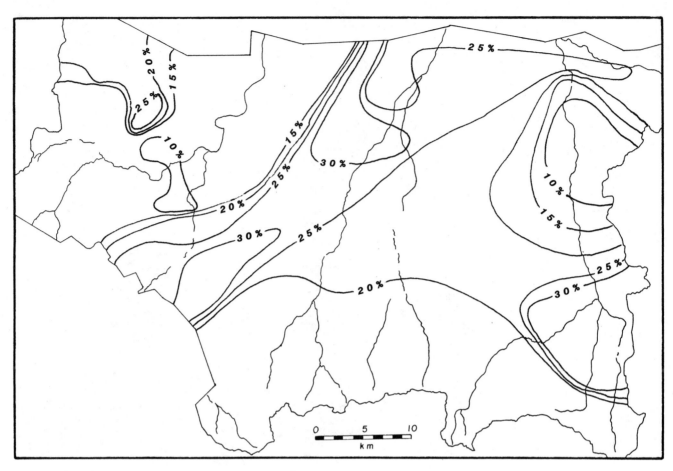

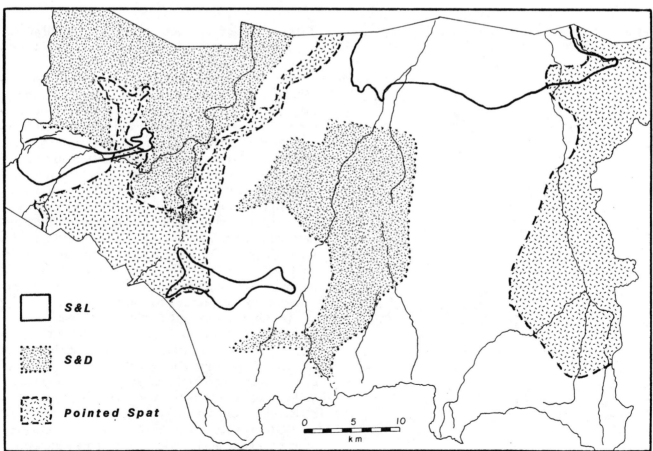

Figure 7-11. Isopleth map of frequencies per non-rocker cell of all small spatulate (including "cord"), plus large pointed spatulate stab-and-drag.

Figure 7-12. Summary distribution map showing cell clusters dominated by small spatulate stab-and-lift (S&L); small spatulate stab-and-drag plus "cord" (S&D); and pointed spatulate.

done with the comb-stamp sample, produced no meaningful results. The main source of trouble stems from the relatively small numbers of specimens in all but a few cells. So many must be conflated to bring sample totals to approximately twenty each, that the resulting comparisons have little or no meaning. Only the results of the first (elementary) test may be worth reproducing here. In this test the numerically dominant subtype is simply plotted, without recourse to percentages, and without considering cell sample size. Several contiguous cell-clusters emerge—a surprising enough result given the small numbers in many cells (fig. 7-12). Pointed spatulate prevails in the Klein Seekoei drainage, stab-and-drag in the Elandskloof *and* in the area east of the Groot Seekoei and north of the Bo-Seekoei. The parcel of land contained by the Bo-Seekoei and Zoetvlei channels is dominated again by pointed spatulate, which spills over to the north and east. Stab-and-lift has far more patchy dominance, but is most notable along the northeast rim of the study area.

The last three subdivisions echo those of the comb-stamp distributions already discussed in chapter 6. One obvious question arising from these plots is why this group is so much more diffusely distributed than the comb-stamp? The latter drops off quite rapidly to zero from the heart of its core area, and scarcely penetrates the small spatulate plateau. Time differences cannot (at present, anyway) be invoked to explain the difference—the two styles appear to be direct contemporaries. Both were found together at similar levels in the deposits of Haaskraal and Volstruisfontein rockshelters, where they appear to be among the earliest motifs in the valley. If the small spatulate plateau is, indeed, a piece of the annual range of a core area located somewhere farther downstream, then why is it so much more extensive than that of the comb-stampers? Answers do not come readily to hand, but the question will be reopened in chapter 9 when all large spatulate motifs have been reviewed.

EIGHT

Double Tip Stylus and Variations

A visually distinct component of the non-rocker collection comprises sherds with lines of double-parallel small punctate impressions (fig. 8-1ab), executed in both stab-and-lift and stab-and-drag modes. The size of each punctate in the double row is comparable with the smaller (approximately 2–3mm) diameter of the small spatulate, but the shapes of the stylus tips are generally more pointed or irregular. These patterns are never mixed with single-row lines, and there can be no doubt that they form a category distinct from the small spatulate decorations reviewed in the previous chapter.

Proper identification of the stylus or, more probably, styluses used to make these impressions has eluded me, and remains a vexing problem. The first to be eliminated was the obliquely cut stick with a V-notch. This makes its own very distinct parallel row, to be described later. The following pairs of objects also failed to replicate the pattern: several sharpened sticks of various diameters, tip shapes, and spacing; several bone-shaft fragments of varied configurations, several porcupine quills, both tip and root ends cut to various angles. Eventually, one good replication was produced by pressing the upper incisors, still embedded in the maxilla, of a dassie (*Hyrax* sp.) into the clay surface. This duplicated only about a half-dozen patterns in the collection, however, so I set out to amass a large collection of micromammal skulls, which are a relatively common sight when walking in the Karoo veld. The upper and lower incisors of a modest list of field mice, rats, shrews, and mongooses were used in the experiment, and every effort was made to acquire both mature and juvenile skulls. In spite of all this, almost none of the skulls could be made to yield the required imprints. The only exceptions were two or three specimens of field mice that came close to replicating some very small tracks. I cannot claim to have exhausted all the possibilities, but remain wedded to the notion that most of

this category was indeed made with a variety of different micromammal incisors, only a few of which I have been able to match.

The point-plot of bowls decorated in this manner is given in figure 8-1c, which suggests a nearly ubiquitous distribution, broadly proportional to the overall density variations of the total non-rocker sample. The majority of those plotted here are in the stab-and-drag mode, with a minor, random scatter of stab-and-lift.

A subtle but visually distinct variation on this pattern can be achieved by canting the twin-stylus over to one side as it is moved across the clay surface. This produces a line of larger, deeper punctates and a parallel row of small shallow ones (fig. 8-2ab). I was able to produce the same effect with weatherbeaten micromammal skulls in which one of the two incisors was broken or split. I could not, however, exactly replicate any of the dozen or so rows represented in the collection. The distribution of this quite scarce variant is given in figure 8-2c, which suggests another bland and ubiquitous distribution. When both variants are mapped together (fig. 8-3), there does appear to be some scarcity in the southeast corner and again in the northwest, but the overall impression is that this technique represents background noise and not emblemic style. Conversion of this map to percentage frequencies per non-rocker cell (fig. 8-4) produces more patterning than the point-plot would suggest, however. A higher-frequency ridge occurs once again in the Elandskloof drainage, forming a pattern reminiscent of that seen for the small spatulate distribution (fig. 7-8), but which fails to covary exactly with it.

The same dilemma encountered in the interpretation of the small spatulate confronts us again. The high-frequency cells along the Elandskloof have lower sample totals, and the area itself falls between the sharply defined comb-stamp to the west and the

Figure 8-1a *(right)*. Example of twin-stylus decoration, possibly with a pair of micromammal(?) incisors still attached to the maxilla or mandible.

Figure 8-1b *(far right)*. Positive impression of figure 8-1a.

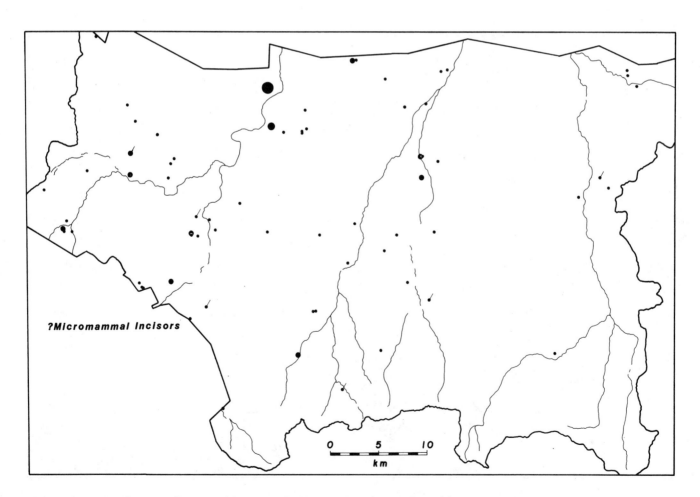

?Micromammal Incisors

Figure 8-1c. Distribution of sites yielding vessels decorated in the manner of figures 8-1ab.

Figure 8-2a *(far left)*. Example of twin-stylus decoration (possibly micromammal(?) incisors), in which the pair is canted to one side.

Figure 8-2b *(left)*. Positive impression of figure 8-2a.

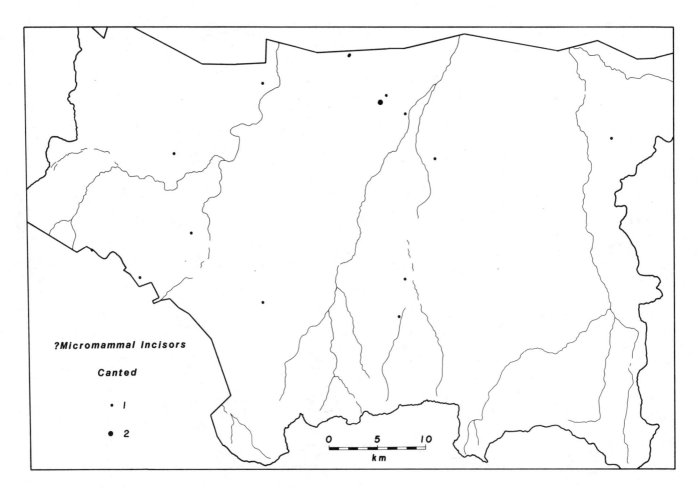

?Micromammal Incisors

Canted

• 1

● 2

Figure 8-2c. Distribution of sites yielding vessels decorated in the manner of figures 8-2ab.

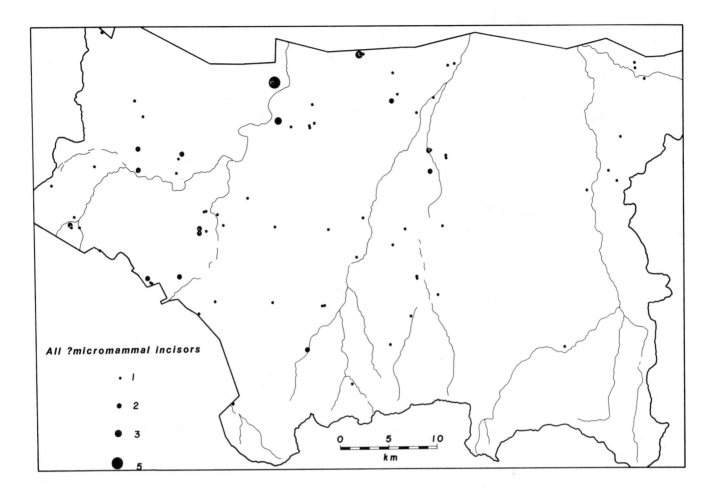

All ?micromammal incisors

· 1

• 2

● 3

⬤ 5

0   5   10
km

Figure 8-3. Distribution of all sites yielding vessels decorated with micromammal(?) incisors, both with vertical entry and canted entry.

large plain spatulate zone to the east. There remains a lingering doubt, therefore, that the Elandskloof "ridge" is nothing more than a spurious statistical distortion of what is really background noise.

At this juncture it is useful to turn to a related pattern labeled V-notch spatulate. As the name implies, this can be readily duplicated by cutting a V-notch in the edge of a thick, obliquely cut stick, then using it in a stab-and-drag mode (fig. 8-5ab). Of considerable interest here is the V-notch stick found in 1876 by Dunn (1931:92 and plate XIX) in a recently abandoned rockshelter in the Stormberg. It is seven centimeters long with a one centimeter diameter. One end is cut diagonal to the long-axis and the sharp end has a V-notch cut in it. Dunn asserts that this was definitely used to make the double-row impressions found on sherds in the Stormberg area, and his photographs of sherds from the area do suggest a remarkably good fit. However, this should not be confused with an eyewitness account, and is a functional inference much like any other still widely made by archaeologists. Dunn *may* have observed potmaking in Bushmanland in 1872, but he evidently never saw pot decorating in progress (ibid: 85). His observations in the Stormberg in 1876 were all archaeological, the local Bushmen having been virtually exterminated by the time of his visit.

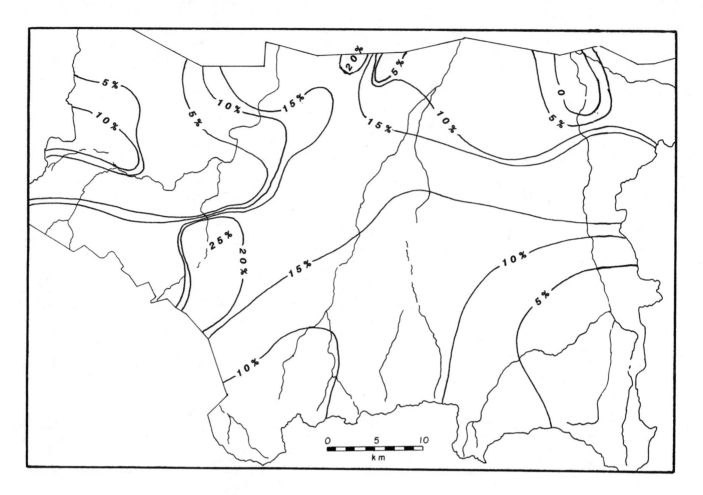

The track left by this stylus, used invariably in the stab-and-drag mode, looks superficially like the micromammal(?) incisor track, but the positive impression shows the V-notch spatulate form to good effect (fig. 8-5ab). The distinctive feature here is that the bottom of the notch is clearly visible in the impression, whereas the micromammal(?) incisor imprint shows the gap between the two tips continuing to the end of the imprint. This raises the very real possibility that my "micromammal" category is nothing more than a wide variety of sticks and bone fragments (split or notched or both) that have not been thrust deep enough into the clay to have captured the imprint of the notch base. I have not pursued this line of replication far enough to be absolutely certain that such an interpretation can be ruled out.

Such doubts are further reinforced when the point-plot of V-notch spatulate impressions is examined (fig. 8-5c). It is certainly widespread, but there is also a markedly strong showing in the Elandskloof drainage. The frequencies per non-rocker cell map out as typical random noise, however. The same applies to the much scarcer grooved spatulate (fig. 8-6ab), which can be easily replicated by carving a narrow groove in the oblique face of the cut stick, or even by merely splitting the end rather than notching it. In this case, five of the nine recorded specimens

Figure 8-4. Isopleth map of frequencies per non-rocker cell of all micromammal(?) incisor decorations.

110

Figure 8-5a *(right)*. Example of V-notch spatulate decoration.

Figure 8-5b *(far right)*. Positive impression of figure 8-5a.

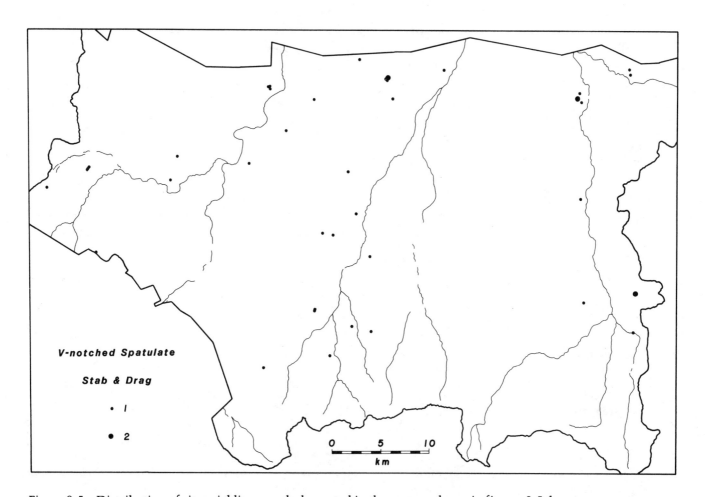

V-notched Spatulate

Stab & Drag

- • *1*
- • *2*

Figure 8-5c. Distribution of sites yielding vessels decorated in the manner shown in figures 8-5ab.

Figure 8-6a *(far left)*. Example of grooved spatulate decoration.

Figure 8-6b *(left)*. Positive impression of figure 8-6a.

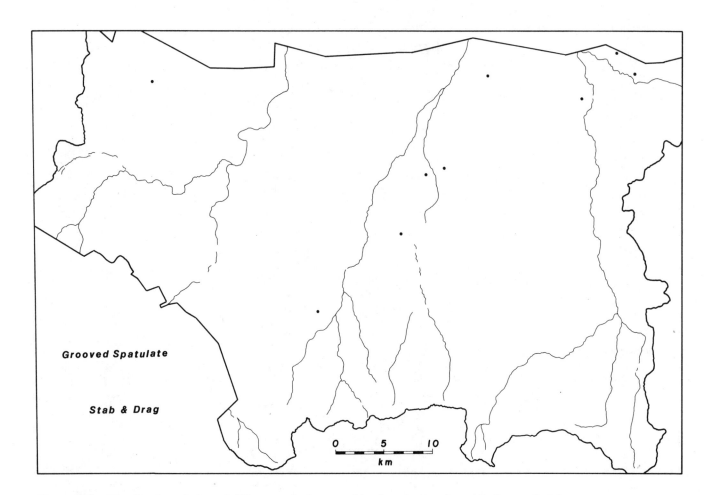

Grooved Spatulate

Stab & Drag

Figure 8-6c. Distribution of sites yielding vessels decorated in the manner shown in figures 8-6ab.

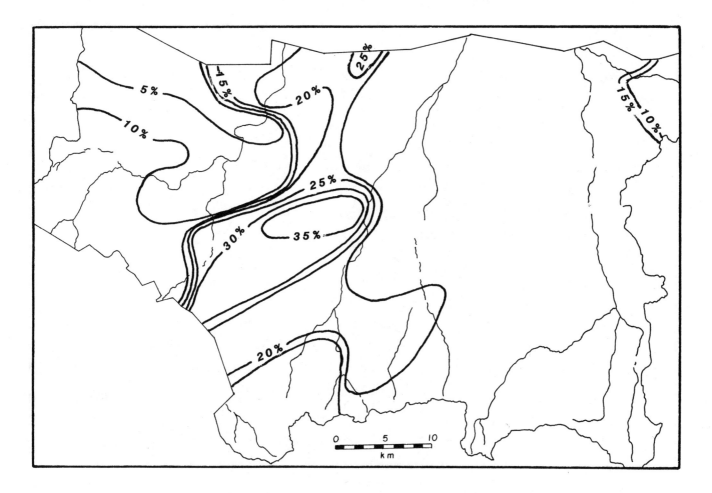

Figure 8-7. Isopleth map showing percentage frequencies per non-rocker cell of all twin stylus decorations combined.

come from the Elandskloof drainage (fig. 8-6c).

When all four variants (micromammal, canted, V-notch, grooved) are combined, and computed as percentages per non-rocker cell (fig. 8-7), the Elandskloof "ridge" emerges with a well-defined western drop-off shoulder, but a ragged drop-off to the east with a widespread 20 to 15 percent plateau covering almost half of the study area. The coherence of this pattern hints strongly that my subdivisions may have artificially broken down a single, highly variable class that does, after all, have some spatial coherence.

The twin-stylus frequency ridge invites comparison with that produced by the small spatulate subclasses (fig. 7-8). Although the latter is far better defined than the twin-stylus ridge, its crest is jagged with multiple spikes and saddles. When the two frequency plots are overlain (fig. 8-8) it is immediately apparent that the two ridges complement each other, that is the spikes of one fit into the saddles of the other. This configuration prompts a combination of the two to induce a smoother crest (fig. 8-9). This somewhat forced exercise produces some other intriguing features, particularly the two drop-off shoulders at 55 to 40 percent and again at 35 to 25 percent in the east and 35 to 15 percent on the west side. This two-step, double-shoulder profile offers a reasonably

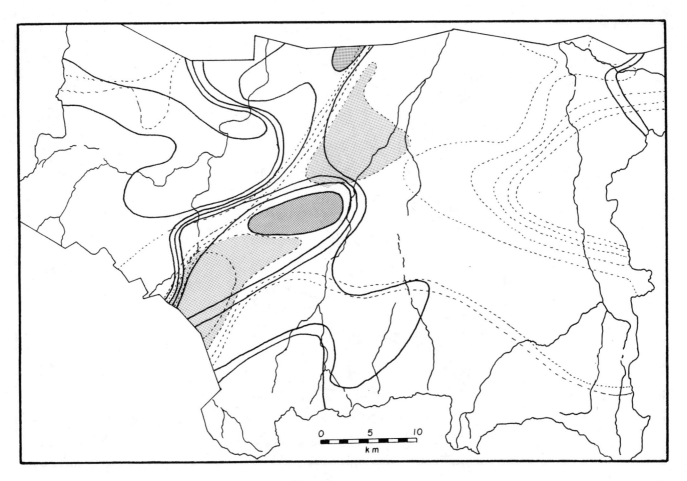

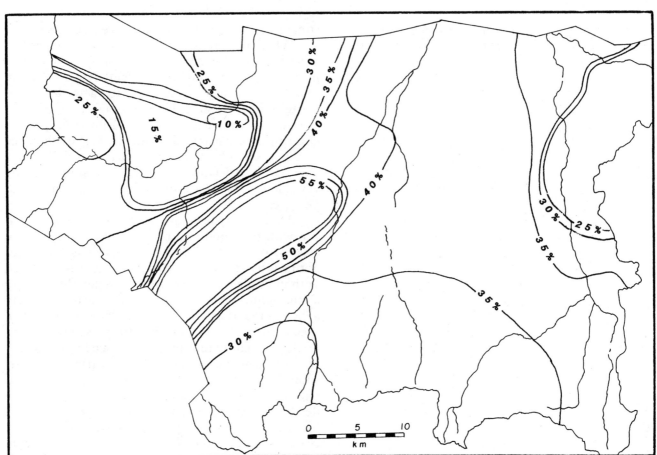

Figure 8-8. The isopleth map of all twin stylus decorations combined (thick line), overlaid by the isopleths for all small spatulate plus "cord" combined (dotted line), derived from figure 7-8.

Figure 8-9. Isopleth map showing the percentage frequencies per non-rocker cell for all twin-stylus plus all small spatulate decorations combined.

good fit with the expectations of the original territorial model (fig. 1-7) and this is certainly the most promising pattern to emerge from the last two chapters of analysis.

However, it would be premature to accept outright that parts of another "core area" have been captured, given the recurrent problems presented by this strip of land between the Zoetvlei-Seekoei and the Elandskloof. In this scenario, the purported "core area" comprises only cell Y (sample size = 10) and cell T (sample size = 18). The next highest frequency (44%) is cell S with only twenty vessels. These are the three smallest samples in the entire array of non-rocker cells, and their high frequency values could just as well be statistical aberrations. Once again, this combination "muddle in the middle" may be a spurious crest of background noise where the presence of both comb-stamp and large plain spatulate are much reduced.

What is needed now is an independent test of small spatulate and twin stylus distribution that is completely free of the influence of the other two dominant classes on either side of the ridge. In the following exercise, the mean number of vessels (with any of these decorations) per site was computed (1.7 vessels per site). Assumptions of the test are: (1) *if* the zone between the Zoetvlei-Seekoei and Elandskloof is a separate territory defined by a higher concentration of these decorative motifs, then it should contain more sites with two or more vessels, indicating a higher than expected yield; (2) *if*, on the other hand, the decorations concerned are nothing but background noise, then there should be an entirely random distribution of high-yield sites across the valley. The results are plotted in figure 8-10, which shows that only twenty sites (12% of all sites with these decorations) produced more than two vessels. Exactly half (10 sites) fall within the Elandskloof drainage, indicating a weak but definite tendency to cluster in this zone. Note also that high-yield sites are absent on the west side of the map. Of particular interest is that the two cells Y and T (which formed the high-frequency plateau in figure 8-9) contain no high-yield sites at all, suggesting that their contribution is, in fact, bogus. High-yield sites occur in all the other Elandskloof cells except V in the headwaters.

Although this angle of attack manages to sidestep the distorting influences of the other dominant non-rocker motifs in the collection, it is nevertheless subject to bias from individual sites with high overall yields. A brief inspection of the distribution of total non-rocker yields per site (fig. 5-2) will show that most of the sites plotted in figure 8-10 are indeed from rich sites as well. However, there are two important exceptions. First, this statement does not apply to the upper reaches of the Elandskloof, where there are no very rich sites. Second, it does not apply to the west sector, where there are many very rich sites, but

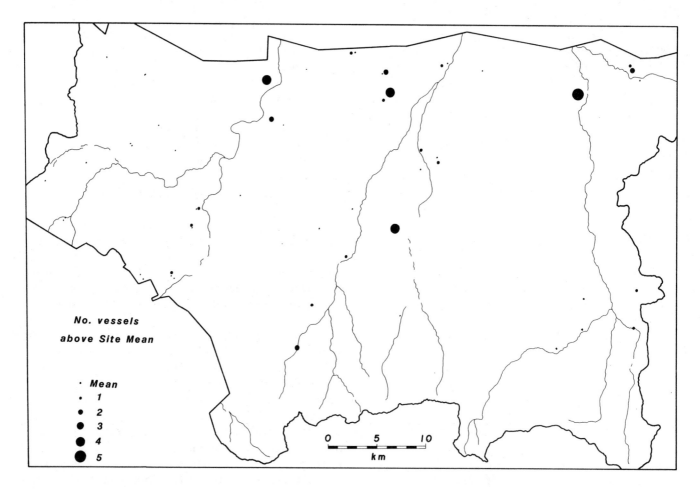

No. vessels
above Site Mean

· Mean
· 1
• 2
● 3
● 4
● 5

0   5   10
km

Figure 8-10. Distribution of sites with more than two vessels decorated with any twin-stylus variant or with any small spatulate variant.

none that yield above-average scores for the small spatulate and twin stylus combination. Thus it appears that the very rich sites do not invariably yield more of these motifs, nor do these motifs exceed expected yields only at very rich sites. In areas where rich sites are yielding above-average scores, there is a stronger correlation between the overall size of the non-rocker yield and the amount by which the average is exceeded. Thus the various sizes of the point-plots in figure 8-10 are a consequence of site richness, and have no bearing on the problem at hand. In the balance then, the case for a separate territory contiguous with those comb-stamp core areas already delineated, is rather weakly supported, and the case for a

"core area" over cells Y and T has no support at all. The fact that both small spatulate and twin-stylus patterns are found all over the comb-stamp region is the main spoiler. At this point it is pertinent to raise the possibility that comb-stamping disappeared first, and that the stylistic boundary shifted westwards through time. In Haaskraal shelter, a twin-stylus decoration was recovered from the top of the non-rocker levels and above the comb-stamp and small spatulate specimens (fig. 4-8). Of course, a case for chronological change cannot be built on this single example, but it certainly begs the question. This will be the central focus of future Seacow Valley research—we intend to excavate about a dozen such small shelters.

NINE

The Large Plain Spatulate Decorations

Casual inspection of sherds decorated with this motif would suggest that the stylus was nothing more than the potter's fingernail or thumbnail, pressed into the clay at various angles. However, there are grounds for suspecting that only a few sherds in this collection were treated in this way, and that a variety of similar-sized, but thicker, stylus tips were generally used. In either case, rows of relatively large (3–4mm) lunate impressions are the result, executed either in stab-and-lift or stab-and-drag (see chapter 7 for detailed definition of these terms). The bowl illustrated in figure 3-1 is typical of the seemingly haphazard layout of lunate rows, covering the entire side of the vessel.

Although ubiquitous in the upper valley, this set of motifs is clearly concentrated in the southeast corner, that is in the headwaters of the Elandskloof and Klein Seekoei drainages. When frequencies per non-rocker cell are calculated (fig. 9-1), the peak concentration appears under cells X and W—within a very clearly demarcated natural basin bounded by the Meiringsberg along the south edge of W, and the Rooiberg range on the west and north edge of X. Neither of these cells has especially large vessel totals, however, and the peak here could conceivably be sampling noise. What follows, however, should effectively dispel any such doubts. Furthermore, the case presented below is strengthened by the presence of mountainous barriers, devoid of human settlement on the south and east sides of the map. These were natural boundaries for each of the distributions to be analyzed—an advantage not encountered in any of the other segments of the valley.

Closer inspection of figure 9-1 reveals a gradual westward drop-off rate to a very uneven shoulder oscillating around the Zoetvlei-Seekoei line. At three points this shoulder laps against the second shoulder of the comb-stamp distribution (fig. 6-6), but it also laps partly against the first shoulder of the comb-stamp "core area," over cells F, G, and I. The fit be-

tween these two is, therefore, less than perfect, and this confusion is no doubt partly induced by the patchy small spatulate and twin-notch frequencies between the two. Thus, while the mountains to the south and east define those edges of a possible large spatulate "core area," its northern and western edges are too clinal and fuzzy to be at all convincing. However, another provisional data-set can be invoked to strengthen the case for a core-area edge close to the 35 percent isopleth:

There is an outcrop of silicified siltstone high in the Sneeuberg, which we have field-labeled "gray chert." While this adequately describes its appearance, it is probably not an accurate petrological definition. When first encountered, I took it to be a variety of porcelainite, and this may yet prove to be the case, when it is properly analyzed. The outcrop itself is entirely masked by slope scree, but small fist-size chunks can be quarried from the rubble. There is a fair amount of flaking debris, test-shot chunks, and core roughouts in the area, indicating that it was indeed quarried by passing hunters, in spite of its very remote locality on a steep mountainside, far from Bushman settlement. The stone itself has good flaking properties and quite good edge-holding characteristics, but is not especially desirable when compared to the standard hornfels. There are no grounds for supposing that it was specially sought out, and it is a rare occurrence on the sites where it has been observed (fig. 9-2). It may not be that every piece we have recorded was actually carried from the source, since it no doubt shows up sporadically in the gravels of the Elandskloof. Note, however, that we have not searched for it there, so this is not yet confirmed. Tentative though all these points may be, there can be little doubt that the westerly limit of its dispersal coincides remarkably well with the channel of the Elandskloof. This result helps to tip the balance in favor of a "core area" boundary that follows the

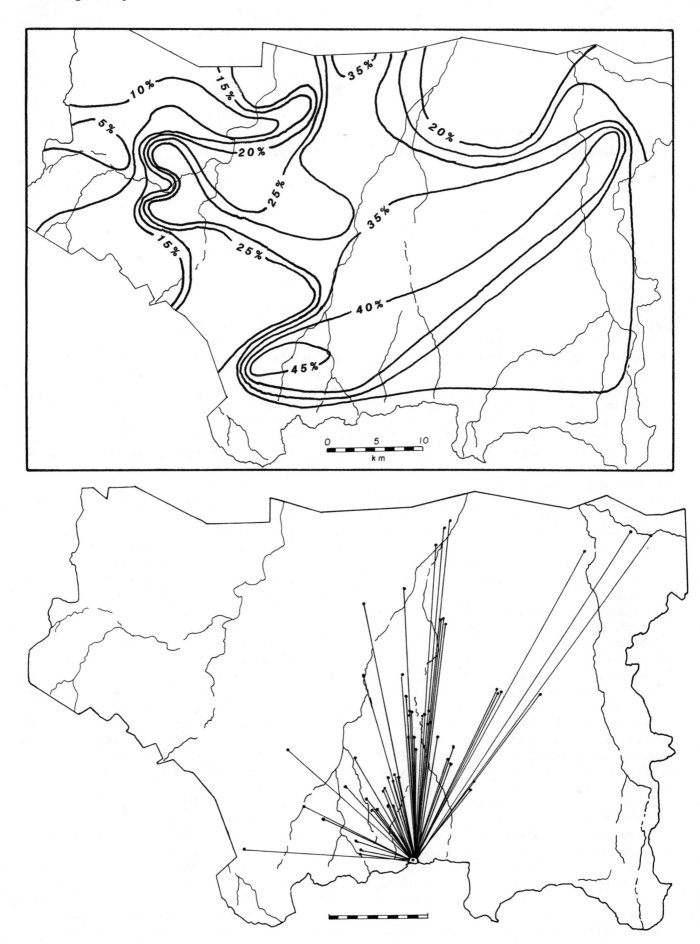

Figure 9-1. Isopleth map of percentage frequencies per non-rocker cell of all large plain spatulate decorations.

Figure 9-2. Map showing the distribution of the "gray chert" outcrop in the Sneeuberg range, with the positions of Smithfield surface sites on which "gray chert" artifacts have been observed.

stream channel, at least to the confluence of the east and west branches, with an "annual range" extending to the 25 percent isopleth or thereabouts. This will be the working hypothesis against which to examine the distribution of minor variants of the large plain spatulate motif. Those variants will now be reviewed before passing on to the frequency analyses.

First in line is the commonest variant, namely the *thin, oblique-entry, stab-and-lift.* Although the spatulate end is quite thin (fig. 9-3ab), I was completely unable to replicate this pattern with my own thumbnail, which is definitely thinner. All attempts to jiggle the nail in the clay failed to create a lunate impression that duplicated those I was getting from the sherds themselves. Of course, this may be a completely false analog in that the thumbnails of Bushman potters may have been considerably thicker than my own. This is not so unreasonable an assumption, given the breakage and callousing normal to a thumbnail subjected to daily foraging activities. If this was so, then the back of the nail was pressed at an oblique angle into the clay surface (air-dried, but not yet leather-hard) and pushed slightly away from the (potter's) body before lifting. If some other stylus was used, there are a couple of obvious choices. In 1876, Dunn (1931:93) asserted that a "flat-ended stick" was used, presumably an oblique-cut stick like that described in chapter 8, but without the V-notch cut in the tip. My own experiments also achieved excellent replication with the tip of the coronoid process of a mandible of a mongoose *(Herpestes ichneumon).* Although this would seem a rather abstruse candidate for a stylus, it should be remembered that remains of these creatures are encountered frequently when walking in the veld, as they are taken regularly by raptorial birds, and the heads are not ingested.

Be that as it may, the point-plot of vessels decorated in this motif (fig. 9-3c) is quite widespread, but they are notably absent along the far western rim (cells B, D, E, and K). There is also no very obvious clustering in the purported "core area." This also applies to a much scarcer subvariant in which the stylus was pushed into a wet soft clay surface, pushing up a small ridge ahead of the convex side of the imprint (fig. 9-4ab). Although this creates a rather distinctive appearance on the bowl surface, it was clearly not regarded as emblemic style, in that its distribution is widespread and completely random (fig. 9-4c). It probably reflects little more than laziness or haste among individual potters.

Rather more interesting is the *sharp, oblique-entry stab-and-lift* variant (fig. 9-5ab), which was probably executed with the thumbnail. Not only does this produce an imprint similar to those resulting from my own efforts, but its distribution (fig. 9-5c) is almost all west of the Elandskloof. This raises the distinct possibility that we are once again dealing with minor subterritories, rather like those that emerged

Figure 9-3a *(far left)*. Example of large plain spatulate stab-and-lift with oblique (diagonal) entry.

Figure 9-3b *(left)*. Positive impression of figure 9-3a.

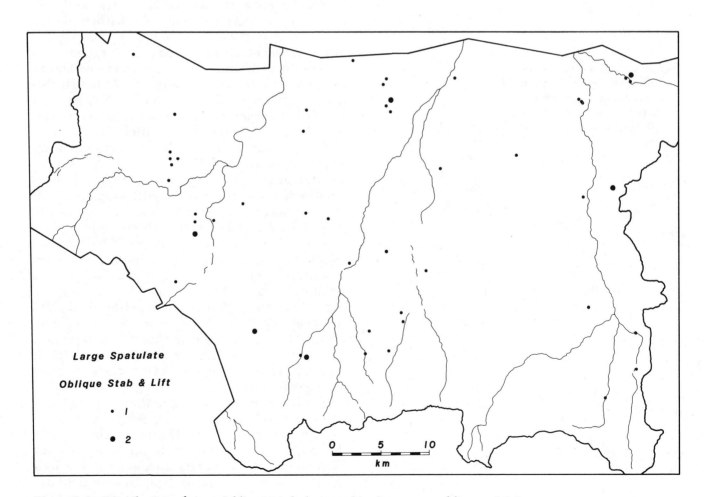

Figure 9-3c. Distribution of sites yielding vessels decorated in the manner of figures 9-3ab.

Figure 9-4a *(right).* Example of large plain spatulate, oblique stab-and-lift executed in wet or sticky clay.

Figure 9-4b *(far right).* Positive impression of figure 9-4a.

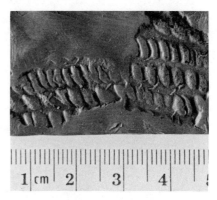

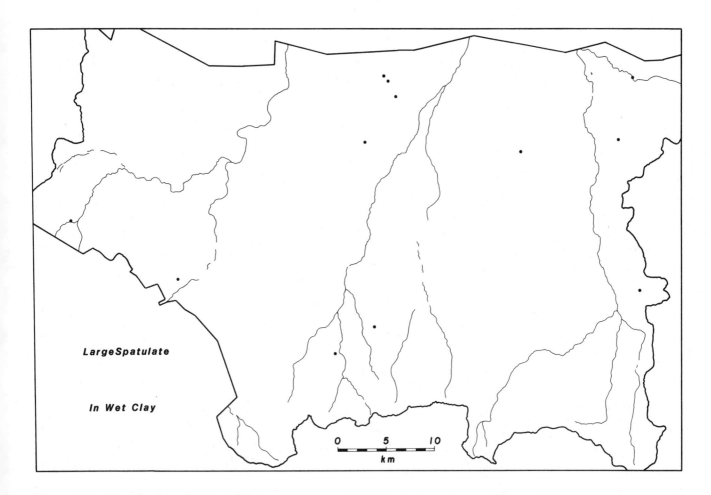

LargeSpatulate

In Wet Clay

Figure 9-4c. Distribution of sites yielding vessels decorated in the manner shown in figures 9-4ab.

121

Figure 9-5a *(far left)*. Example of sharpened large plain spatulate, oblique-entry stab-and-lift.

Figure 9-5b *(left)*. Positive impression of figure 9-5a.

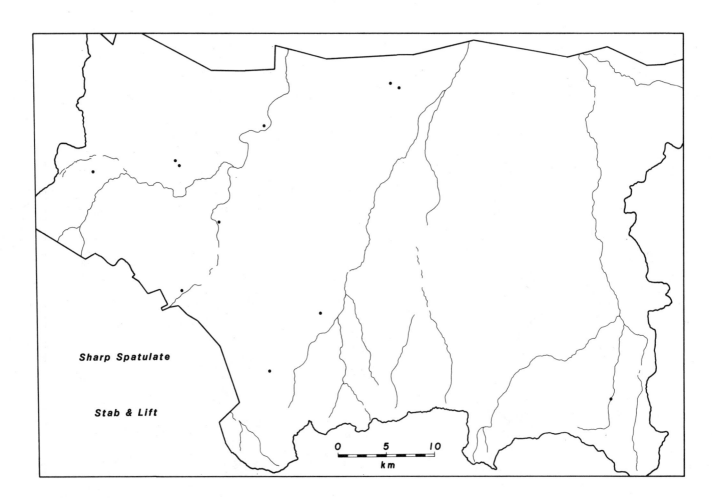

Sharp Spatulate

Stab & Lift

0   5   10

km

Figure 9-5c. Distribution of sites yielding vessels decorated in the manner shown in figures 9-5ab.

from the comb-stamp analysis (chapter 6). This question will be reopened later.

A subvariant of the last group can be formed from a small sample labeled *shallow, press-and-lift* which, as the name implies, is the result of letting the clay dry to leather-hard before starting work (fig. 9-6ab). Again, it is not certain that all this work was done with the thumbnail, and I had better replication successes with the same mongoose mandible mentioned above. The main reason for retaining this as a separate category is that its distribution, like the sharp variant, is mainly west of the Elandskloof (fig. 9-6c).

A more dubious variant labeled *thick, oblique-entry stab-and-lift* was created to accommodate a small sample decorated with a large spatulate too thick (fig. 9-7ab) to fit easily within the range of those mentioned thus far. It should be stressed, however, that there is no clear-cut separation between thick and thin variants, and the two grade into each other in a way that makes me doubt that a second analyst would separate them exactly as I did. I was able to closely replicate the thicker variant with the coronoid process of a dassie (*Hyrax* sp.) mandible, which has a slight ridged swelling at the tip. Like the thinner variant, however, its distribution (fig. 9-7c) is widespread and random.

The final variant in the stab-and-lift series is the *thin, vertical-entry stab-and-lift*, which produces a short, deep gash in the clay (fig. 9-8ab), rather than the lunate imprints left by all the other variants reviewed thus far. My first guess was that this had been done by jabbing the forefinger nail straight down into the clay (Rye 1981:93), then rocking the finger back and forth before removal. However, my own efforts to do this failed to approach the neatness of these gashes, and the positive impressions of my attempts were invariably more misshapen than those from the sherds. My trusty mongoose mandible came to the rescue once more, as this produced near-perfect replicas of the imprint. Turning now to its distribution (fig. 9-8c), there is a noticeable concentration in the purported "core area," but the variant is still very widespread. Nevertheless, this is the only variant to display any such patterning.

The remainder of this series is all executed in stab-and-drag, and much the same variants emerge, with all the attendant doubts and uncertainties about the identity of stylus tips. Retention of these categories is justified, however, because several of them show quite distinct distributions. First up is the *thin, oblique stab-and-drag* (fig. 9-9ab) with another very marked westerly distribution (fig. 9-9c). The same applies to an arbitrarily separated subvariant called *deep oblique stab-and-drag* (fig. 9-10ab), which clearly has no significance other than between-potter behavior, as its distribution (fig. 9-10c) overlaps with

that of the previous category. A very small sample decorated with a thicker tip (fig. 9-11ab) could be replicated with the same dassie jaw used in the stab-and-lift series, but this is so scarce that its distribution (fig. 9-11c) is impossible to evaluate.

One last variant is tentatively included in this series although the identity of the stylus remains in doubt. My first instinct was to lump it with the thin, oblique stab-and-drag, but following expert advice, I was later persuaded that it was *ostrich eggshell bead necklace-impressed*. The characteristic features are the very sharp edge of the channel sides and the very sharp, very evenly spaced lunate ridges (fig. 9-12ab), which suggest that a bead string was wrapped around the bowl and twisted so that the bead-row canted over and bit into the clay. Not having a necklace at my disposal, I was unable to attempt a replication of this, but was easily persuaded. Later on in the spatial analysis, this interpretation looked even more convincing as the small frequency spike of this variant over cell DD was repeated in the "cord-impressed" frequency map (chapter 7). When "cord and bead" were combined, a quite large, but completely isolated, spike could be created. However, further manipulations of the combined frequencies revealed a "notch" in the large spatulate stab-and-drag frequency shoulder, discussed later in this chapter. This notch occurred exactly over cell DD, and when the "OES" distribution (fig. 9-12c) was lumped in with the rest, the notch disappeared and the shoulder straightened out. This result persuades me that my first intuition was correct and that this "variant" reflects nothing more than obsessive neatness on the part of a few individual potters. The shallow stab-and-drag is also more likely to be the result of between-potter behavior, since it has a westerly distribution (fig. 9-6c) in keeping with the rest of the stab-and-drag.

This completes the descriptive review of the variants of the large spatulates and their raw distributions. It is already apparent that the thin and thick stab-and-lift motif is concentrated in the purported "core area" while the sharp and shallow variants, plus all the stab-and-drag work is concentrated in the purported "annual range" outlined earlier in this chapter. Clearly, the working hypothesis is already in trouble!

As a first rudimentary test of the "single core-area" hypothesis, the numerically dominant large spatulate variant in each non-rocker cell was isolated and plotted. This is the same elementary (but effective) procedure conducted in previous chapters—it simply ignores percentage values and selects the highest raw vessel count in each cell. The result is plotted in figure 9-13. Cell grouping is strong and clear in the east, and increasingly jumbled in the west, as large spatulate sample sizes per cell decline. The *vertical stab-and-lift* clusters well in the Elandskloof headwaters (cells UVWXY), and the *oblique stab-and-lift*

Figure 9-6a *(far left)*. Example of large plain spatulate with a shallow oblique press-and-lift technique.

Figure 9-6b *(left)*. Positive impression of figure 9-6a.

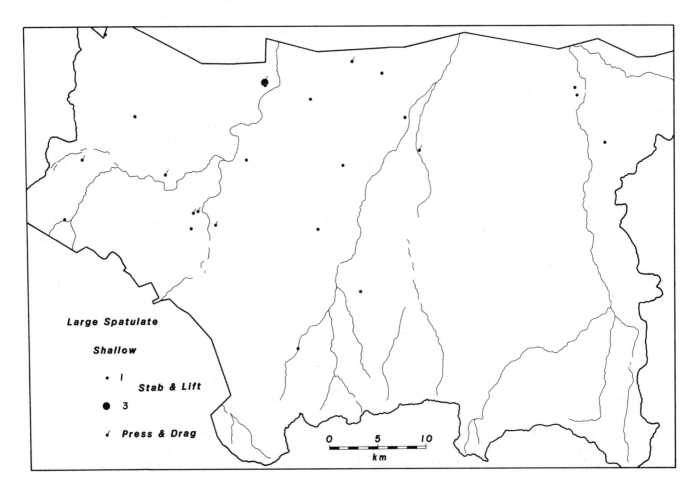

Large Spatulate

Shallow

• I   *Stab & Lift*

● 3

⌐ *Press & Drag*

Figure 9-6c. Distribution of sites yielding vessels decorated in the manner shown in figures 9-6ab. Sites yielding a press-and-drag variant are also shown.

Figure 9-7a *(right)*. Example of thick-edged large plain spatulate, oblique-entry stab-and-lift.

Figure 9-7b *(far right)*. Positive impression of figure 9-7a.

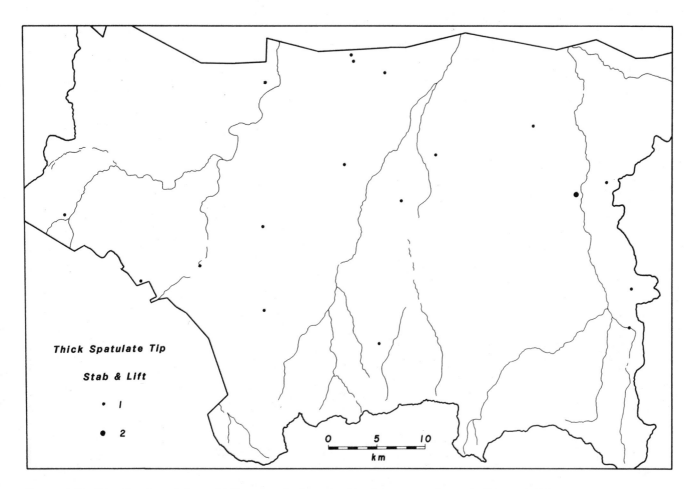

Thick Spatulate Tip

Stab & Lift

· 1

● 2

Figure 9-7c. Distribution of sites yielding vessels decorated in the manner shown in figures 9-7ab.

125

Figure 9-8a *(far left)*. Example of large plain spatulate, executed in vertical-entry stab-and-lift.

Figure 9-8b *(left)*. Positive impression of figure 9-8a.

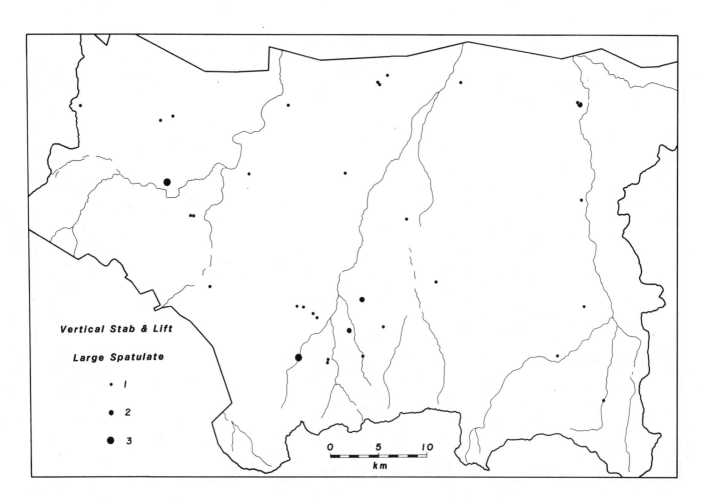

Figure 9-8c. Distribution of sites yielding vessels decorated in the manner shown in figures 9-8ab.

Figure 9-9a *(right).* Example of large plain spatulate stab-and-drag.

Figure 9-9b *(far right).* Positive impression of figure 9-9a.

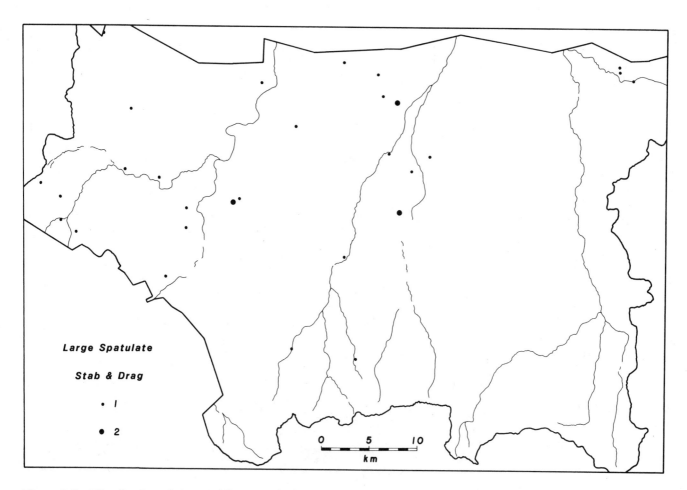

Large Spatulate

Stab & Drag

• 1

● 2

Figure 9-9c. Distribution of sites yielding vessels decorated in the manner shown in figures 9-9ab.

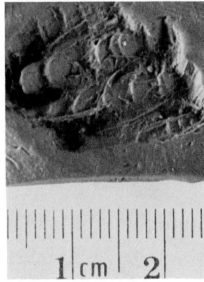

Figure 9-10a *(far left)*. Example of large plain spatulate, deep stab-and-drag.

Figure 9-10b *(left)*. Positive impression of figure 9-10a.

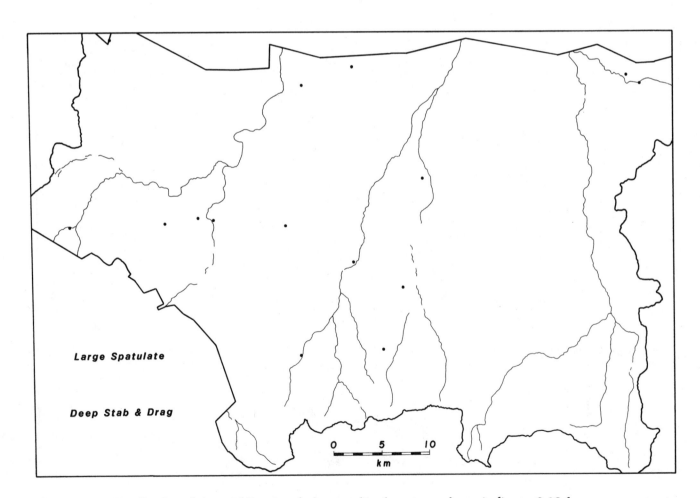

Large Spatulate

Deep Stab & Drag

Figure 9-10c. Distribution of sites yielding vessels decorated in the manner shown in figures 9-10ab.

Figure 9-11a *(right)*. Example of large thick-rimmed spatulate, stab-and-drag.

Figure 9-11b *(far right)*. Positive impression of figure 9-11a.

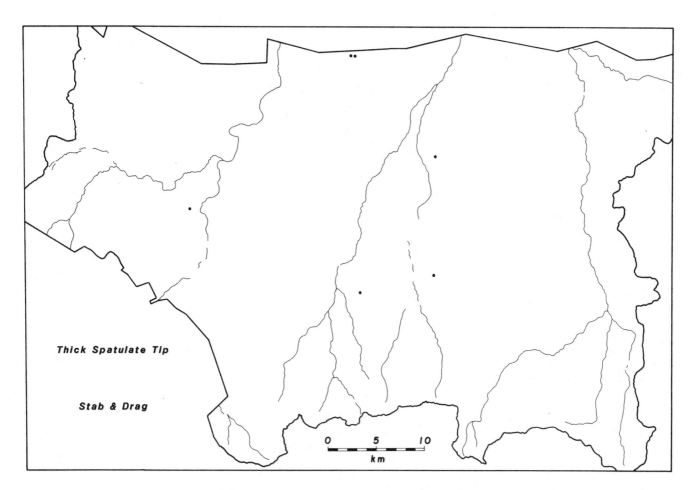

Thick Spatulate Tip

Stab & Drag

Figure 9-11c. Distribution of sites yielding vessels decorated in the manner shown in figures 9-11ab.

129

Figure 9-12a *(far left).* Example of so-called "ostrich eggshell bead necklace-impressed" decoration. It may in fact be large spatulate stab-and-drag executed with unusual neatness.

Figure 9-12b *(left).* Positive impression of figure 9-12a.

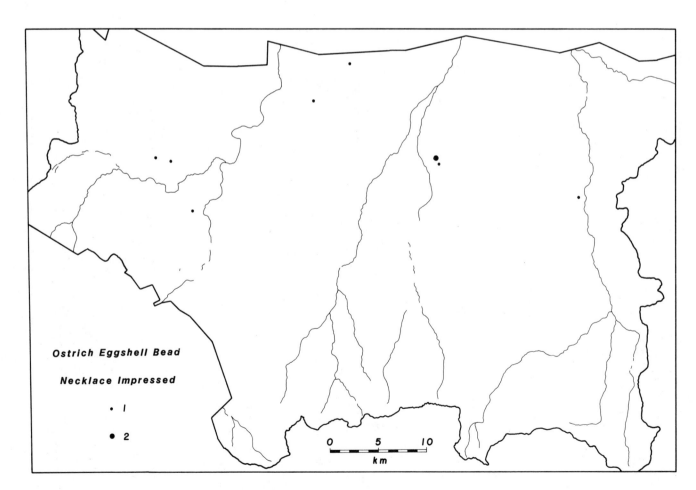

Ostrich Eggshell Bead

Necklace Impressed

· 1

● 2

Figure 9-12c. Distribution of sites yielding vessels decorated in the manner shown in figures 9-12ab.

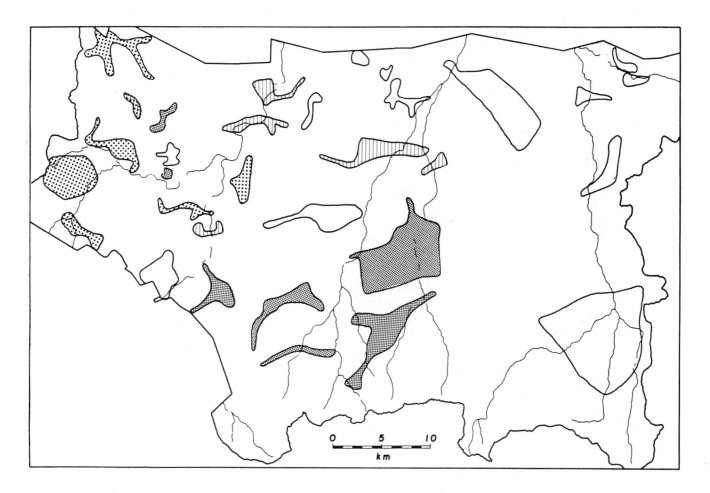

Figure 9-13. Dominant large plain spatulate subclass in each non-rocker cell: oblique stab-and-lift (white); vertical stab-and-lift (shaded); sharp/shallow (stippled); and stab-and-drag (vertical lines).

dominates the entire Klein Seekoei and the adjacent Tafelberg (cells NOPQ) on the north-central rim. The only unambiguous *stab-and-drag* grouping is at the far west rim (cells ABDEK), but sample sizes are so small here it is doubtful whether this has any meaning at all. This question will be resolved in the second test. Once more, there is a "muddle in the middle" between the Zoetvlei-Seekoei line and the Elandskloof. Even if the sharp and shallow and "OES" cells are lumped in with the stab-and-drag, this helps hardly at all to tidy up the picture.

Nonetheless, whichever way one views these results, they definitely refute the "single core area" hypothesis and hint at the existence of three subcores plus a chaotic intermediate zone. With this rival hypothesis in mind, we can now turn to the frequency maps of the purported subcores. Figure 9-14 shows the isopleths derived from computing percentages per non-rocker cell of the *vertical stab-and-lift* variant. The same cells (UVWXY) group together once again, with XY forming the highest concentration within the same natural basin described for the original "core area" of the purported single-core model (fig. 9-1). This time, however, cell CC in the Elandskloof drainage is included in the group. The stray cells in the jumbled zone dominated by this class show up only as minor spikes. Overall, this second test suggests that the UVWXY grouping has some merit, but the addition of CC is an untidy spoiler.

Turning next to the *oblique stab-and-lift* (fig. 9-15), there is really quite a poor fit with the results of the first test. Instead, the frequency concentration is over a triangular area WVZFF, with some outliers at O and T. Although there is a weak shoulder at the 20 to 15 percent isopleths, this is not sufficient to invoke the presence of a core area. This shoulder is far better defined when the oblique and vertical counts per cell are combined (fig. 9-16), and a second shoulder now appears at the 20 to 15 percent isopleths—a pattern which nicely fits the expectations of the territorial model.

The *stab-and-drag* frequency map (fig. 9-17) is at complete odds with the first test results, but reasons for this discrepancy are both predictable and unambiguous. The highest concentration of stab-and-drag is actually over cells O and U, both of which were masked, in the first test, by still higher counts for oblique stab-and-lift. Another concentration over cell I matches with the first test, however. The stab-and-drag grouping on the far west rim in figure 9-13 is now revealed as bogus—there is no concentration here, but merely a lack of any other variants to out-number the few stab-and-drag counts in each of these cells. This grouping can be discounted as a potential subcore, therefore. Likewise, there are too many iso-lated spikes on the remainder of the map in figure 9-17, suggesting more noise than signal.

In the next manipulation I added the "bead-impressed" component into the stab-and-drag counts, and a quite clearly defined concentration along cells OSTU and DD emerged (fig. 9-18), al-though there is still the anomalous outlier over cell I, yet to be explained. It is this improved patterning that first caused me to suspect that the "bead" impressions were nothing more than extra-neat stab-and-drag with a large spatulate, and that the original label was wrong. Perhaps the most striking feature of this fre-quency map is its resemblance to that of the small spatulate stab-and-drag (fig. 7-6) that shows a concen-tration in much the same region. This correlation raises the possibility that it was the *technique* (stab-and-drag) rather than the stylus (large or small spatu-late) that local potters recognized as emblemic style. When the two sets of frequencies are combined, the resulting pattern (fig. 9-19) shows a clear unambigu-ous upper shoulder suggesting a well-defined "core area" and there are fragments of what might be taken as a second shoulder. This goes some way to resolving the problems encountered in chapter seven when try-ing to make sense of the small spatulate decorations, grouped together (fig. 7-8), because the stylus was the same.

Figure 9-14. Isopleth map of per-centage frequencies per non-rocker cell of large plain spatulate, vertical stab-and-lift.

Figure 9-15. Isopleth map of per-centage frequencies per non-rocker cell of all large plain spatulate, oblique stab-and-lift (includes thick edge and wet clay subclasses).

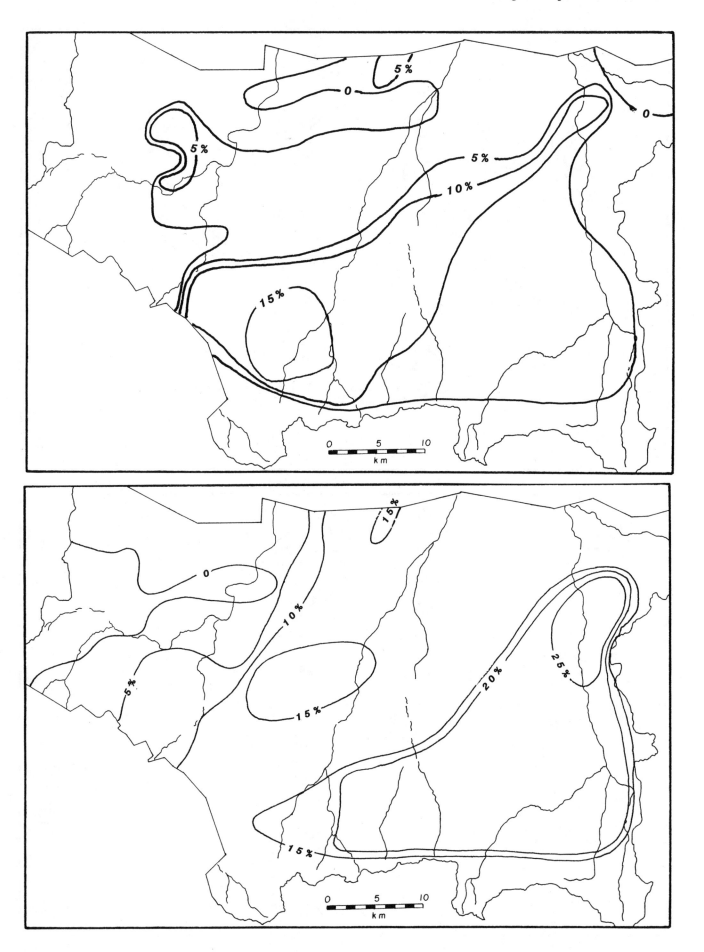

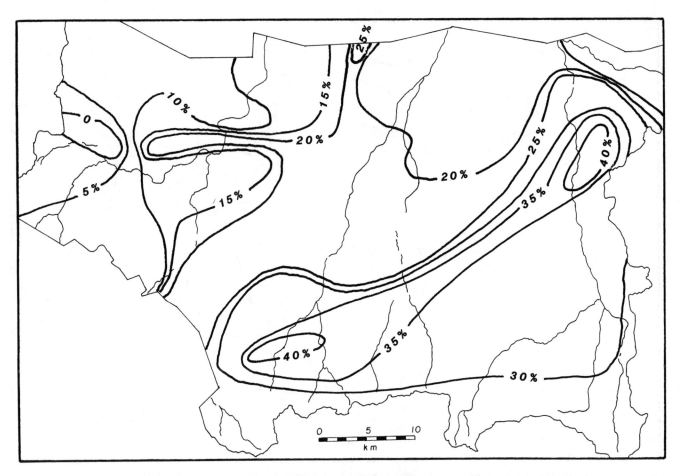

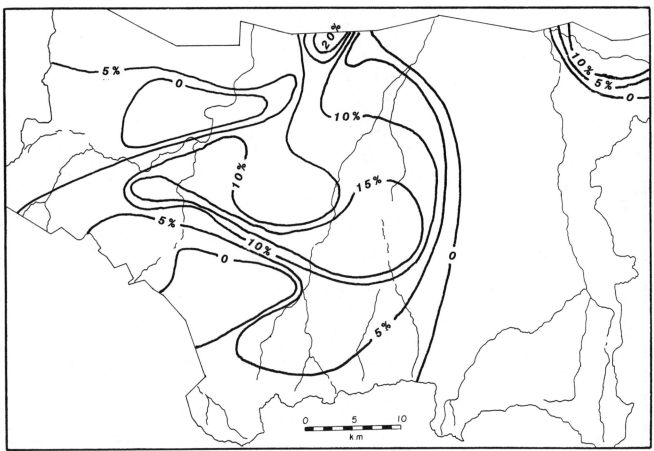

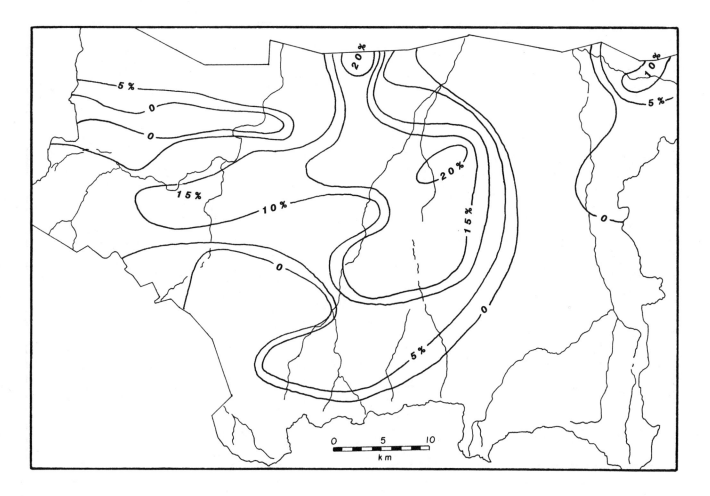

Figure 9-18. Isopleth map of percentage frequencies per non-rocker cell of all subclasses of large plain spatulate stab-and-drag, combined with the "ostrich eggshell bead necklace-impressed" variant.

Figure 9-16. *(above left)* Isopleth map of percentage frequencies per non-rocker cell of all subclasses of large plain spatulate stab-and-lift.

Figure 9-17. *(left)* Isopleth map of percentage frequencies per non-rocker cell of all subclasses of large plain spatulate stab-and-drag.

This result invites a similar treatment for the stab-and-lift technique, but when the large and small spatulate (oblique stab-and-lift) counts per cell are combined, the resulting isopleth map reveals nothing but multispike noise, with the usual overall decrease in frequency towards the west. The same result emerges when the large spatulate vertical stab-and-lift is added to the cell totals. Evidently the small and large spatulate decorations are spatially distinct in the stab-and-lift mode (large = signal, small = noise), as suggested by the overlays in figure 9-20.

It is now reasonably clear that two contiguous core areas can be derived from the large spatulate analysis. One is tucked into the upper valleys of the Elandskloof (cells XWV) and Klein Seekoei (cells ZFFCC). Potters in both valleys used large spatulate oblique stab-and-lift as an emblemic style, but those in the Elandskloof group distinguished themselves by more frequent use of vertical stab-and-lift. Again, the most parsimonious interpretation would be that these are two subcores, with each area occupied by a related band or two extended families within the same band. In this case, the entire core area has been captured on the map. The second core area is composed of cells OSU and is characterized by stab-and-drag decorations using both the large and small

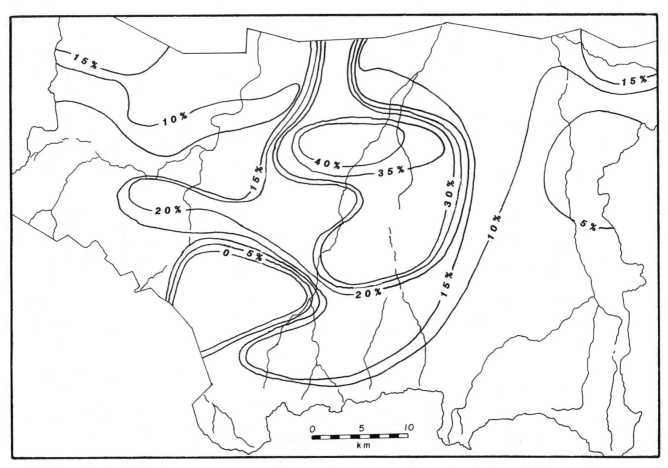

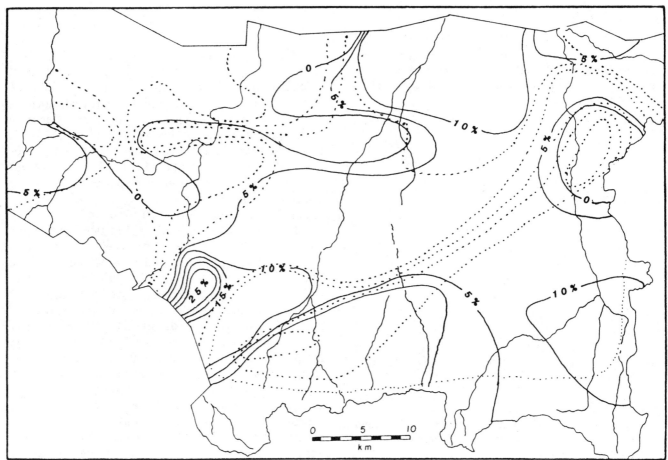

Figure 9-19. Isopleth map of percentage frequencies per non-rocker cell of all subclasses of small spatulate stab-and-drag, combined with all subclasses of large spatulate stab-and-drag.

Figure 9-20. Isopleth map percentage frequencies per non-rocker cell of all subclasses of small spatulate stab-and-lift (thick line), compared with all subclasses of large spatulate stab-and-lift (dotted line).

spatulate. There are no subcores visible, and it is truncated at the north end by the rim of the study area.

Although further extensive testing (along the lines of chapter 6) was carried out on the large spatulate component, no results emerged that suggested any improvements on the above conclusions. After some agonizing, I have elected to omit the details of all this testing, plus another set of laborious exercises. What follows is a brief summary of the essentially negative results derived from all this work. An exhaustive search was made of newly created cells of all spatulate (notched and unnotched), but too much noise was introduced by the notched specimens and the results were ambiguous. Next, these cells were modified to explore the ramifications of all stab-and-drag (notched and unnotched) with even more disastrous results. Finally, these modified cells were retained, but filled with counts of all stab-and-lift (notched and unnotched), with improved signal which at least distinguished between the oblique and vertical subcores, but with a good deal of spurious patterning of minor attributes such as stylus size, thickness, and notches. Most of these were exaggerated because of small cell sample sizes. Thus, the spatulate component has been approached from every conceivable angle, to ascertain that the approach used in this chapter has produced the simplest and most obvious pattern of all.

TEN

Porcupine Quill Decorations

Anyone walking regularly in the veld of the upper valley will encounter porcupine *(Hystrix africae-australis)* quills on a daily basis. They occur in patches, where nighttime fights have occurred, and quill numbers vary directly with the seriousness of the attack. Once shed, they seem to be of no interest to scavengers, and may also be more resistant to weathering than most bone remains. These factors no doubt contribute to their relative abundance. They are also highly visible in that the light and dark stripes create a stark contrast with the grey-buff tone of the surrounding veld. All this leads one to suspect that it may have occurred to Bushman potters to use them in various ways as styluses, especially as porcupines were regularly taken as food (chapters 2 and 3) leading to a regular supply of fresh quills.

Any given quill offers the would-be bowl decorator both a needle-sharp end and a blunter root end with a very characteristic bend and swelling that makes a quite distinctive punctate mark in clay. Also, quill roots vary in size and shape along the back of the porcupine. Towards the rump, there are more open tubular roots, displaying ragged edges. I have also collected quill roots that display a shallow longitudinal groove on one side, which peters out about 5mm from the root tip. Obviously, a wide variety of pen-quill shapes can be formed by cutting across the shaft of the quill. In spite of all this potential, it appears that quill decorations are rather limited in the upper valley—a result which in itself is quite significant. What follows is the description and point-plot of several decorative variants which, although looking quite dissimilar, have the quill stylus in common.

First up is the simple gash motif (fig. 10-1ab), which is easily replicated by holding a sharp tip perpendicular to the clay surface, then scoring the clay for about a centimeter. A row or band of vertically oriented gashes is applied below the rim of the bowl, and sometimes multiple bands cover most of the side.

With a little practice, it is a relatively simple matter to distinguish this mark from the large spatulate, vertical entry stab-and-lift (fig. 9-8ab), which has fewer ragged edges because the clay is pressed inward rather than gouged up. The scar is also generally shorter in length than the quill gash. Furthermore, the latter often have a slight turn at one end, replicable when the motion is speeded up, causing a slight flick of the wrist as the quill tip is withdrawn and moved to the next position in the row. Comparison of the positive imprints of these decorations leaves absolutely no doubt that they are differently executed.

The point-plot distribution of quill gash indicates a very clear concentration along the north rim of the study area (fig. 10-1c), and promises to yield a very sharp frequency drop-off shoulder comparable in clarity (but not distribution) to those of the comb-stamp point-plots. These will be explored further when the other quill variants are presented.

A scarcer variation on this is an oblique-entry gash, which again can be replicated with a sharp tip used in a slicing motion that fillets a narrow, thin flap of clay which nevertheless remains attached to the bowl surface (fig. 10-2ab). Although scant, its point-plot (fig. 10-2c) hints at a focus over cell AA—a recurrent theme in the following variants.

This is particularly obvious for the quill-grooved motif. Here, a root tip is drawn through the air-dried clay surface to form a round-bottomed channel with fine longitudinal ridges on the channel's inner surface, indicating that the tip has been drawn along it more than once. Sherds covered with these grooves (fig. 10-3ab) invariably show haphazard organization with grooves of different widths and depths criss-crossing the bowl surface. There are also a few with very light scoring in a leather-hard surface. If there is any overall plan to the motif, I have failed to come up with a large enough bowl fragment to see it. Of course such grooves could be readily executed with the end

Figure 10-1a *(right)*. Example of vertical gash decoration, probably done with the tip of a porcupine quill.

Figure 10-1b *(far right)*. Positive impression of figure 10-1a.

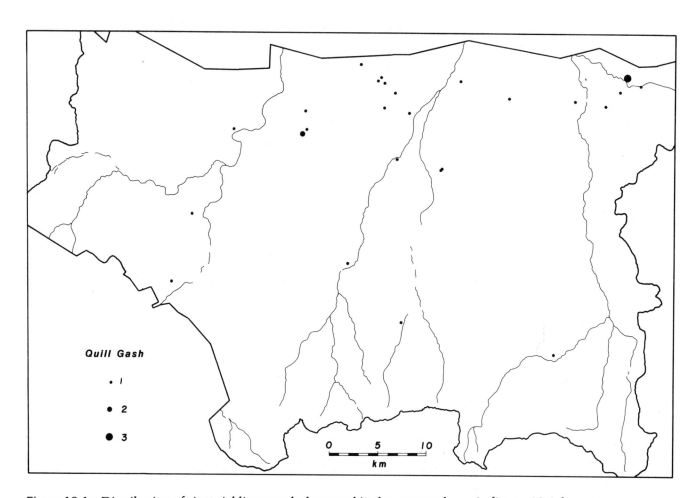

Quill Gash

• 1

● 2

● 3

0   5   10
km

Figure 10-1c. Distribution of sites yielding vessels decorated in the manner shown in figures 10-1ab.

Figure 10-2a *(far left)*. Example of oblique gash decoration, probably done with the tip of a porcupine quill.

Figure 10-2b *(left)*. Positive impression of figure 10-2a.

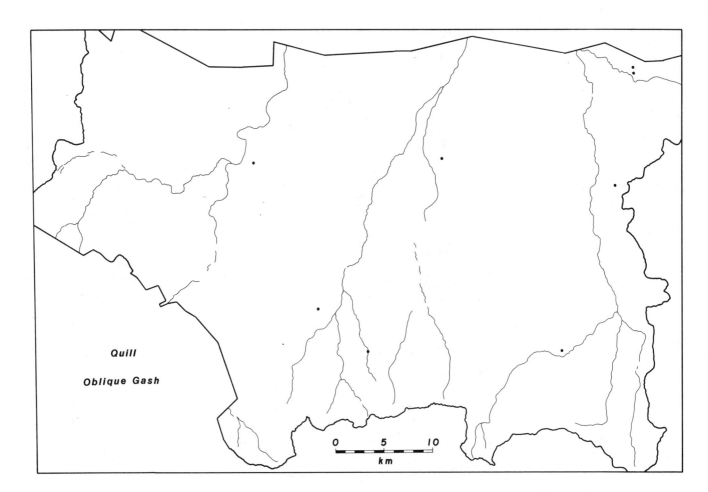

Quill

Oblique Gash

Figure 10-2c. Distribution of sites yielding vessels decorated in the manner shown in figures 10-2ab.

140

Figure 10-3a *(right)*. Example of random channel decoration, probably done with the blunt (root) end of a porcupine quill.

Figure 10-3b *(far right)*. Positive impression of figure 10-3a.

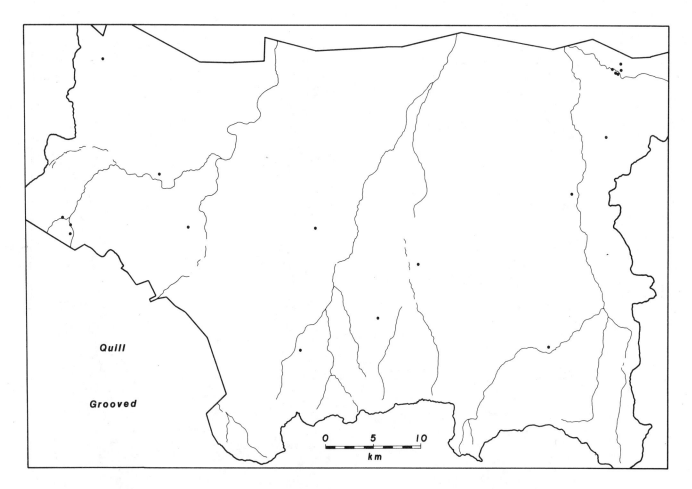

Quill

Grooved

Figure 10-3c. Distribution of sites yielding vessels decorated in the manner shown in figures 10-3ab.

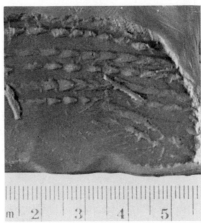

Figure 10-4a *(far left)*. Example of linear drag-and-lift, probably done with the blunt (root) end of a porcupine quill.

Figure 10-4b *(left)*. Positive impression of figure 10-4a.

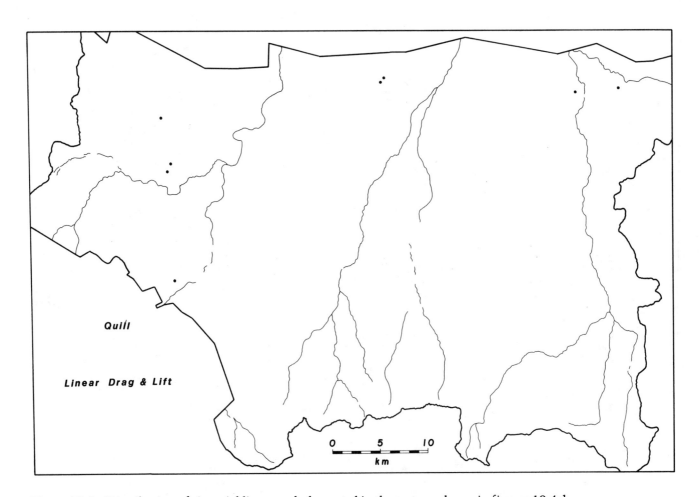

Quill

Linear Drag & Lift

Figure 10-4c. Distribution of sites yielding vessels decorated in the manner shown in figures 10-4ab.

Figure 10-5a *(right).* Example of small vertical punctate, probably done with the tip of a porcupine quill.

Figure 10-5b *(far right).* Positive impression of figure 10-5a.

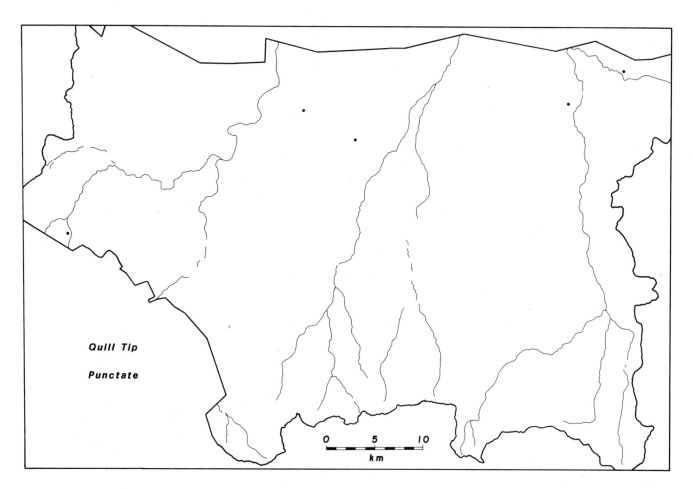

Quill Tip

Punctate

0   5   10
km

Figure 10-5c. Distribution of sites yielding vessels decorated in the manner shown in figures 10-5ab.

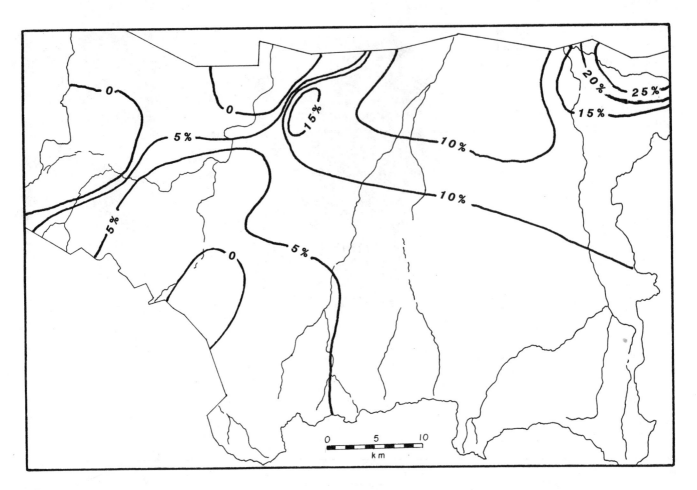

Figure 10-6. Isopleth map of the percentage frequencies per non-rocker cell of all quill decorations.

of a stick, also, but the strong overlap in distribution (fig. 10-3c) with other unequivocal quill decorations leads to a rather strong case that this, too, was made with the same stylus.

Another highly distinctive decoration can be replicated with a sort of linear drag-press-lift motion of the quill root tip. The result of this is a quite neat line (fig. 10-4ab) that was repeated around the bowl sides to form orderly rows. It is scarce, but has the same marked northerly concentration (fig. 10-4c). I struggled for some time to satisfy myself that this was not merely one extreme in the range of variation within ordinary pointed spatulate stab-and-drag (fig. 7-9ab), but the line separation (and the characteristic quill distribution) persuaded me that this was, indeed, a separate type.

The final variant is a straightforward vertical punctate in which a quill tip is held perpendicular to the clay surface and thrust in vertically to form a small prickmark (fig. 10-5ab). Specimens of this are extremely rare, but again are found in the same northerly belt (fig. 10-5c).

The counts per non-rocker cell for each variant

are so low, that percentage isopleth maps for each are hardly justified. When they are all combined, however, a quite orderly pattern emerges (fig. 10-6). There is a marked drop-off shoulder in the far northeast corner of the map, which encompasses cells AA, BB, and CC only. A minor fifteen percent spike occurs over cell N. In the light of this pattern it may be argued that the study area has nicked the corner of the "core area" of another territory, but such a proposition is not well supported by the presence of any visible second shoulder, which might designate the rim of its "annual range." Possibly the cell N "spike" is actually the rim of such a shoulder, also just nicked by the north rim of the map. Another option is to designate the northeast shoulder as part of the rim of the "annual range" of a core area still farther north and east, and outside the surveyed area altogether (figs. 2-1b, 2-1c). No amount of additional analysis of the existing maps can resolve this question, which requires that the entire study area be extended by more field collecting, and perhaps by further widening of the original survey.

ELEVEN

Motifs with Peripheral Distributions

A small residue of non-rocker motifs is considered together here not because they are related by stylus or technique, but rather because they are small in number and share a northerly spread on the distribution maps. This in turn suggests that the study area has captured only the outer fringes of their distributions —all of which must be centered somewhere in the middle reaches of the Seacow Valley.

The first to be considered is the center-notched large spatulate stab-and-lift motif, executed undoubtedly with a variation on Dunn's (1931) notched bevel-cut stick discussed in chapter 8. The main difference here is the shape of the notch, which was formed by sawing two parallel cuts in the sharp tip of the bevel edge, then breaking out the wood from between the cuts. This created a parallel-sided notch with a flattish bottom, in clear contrast to the V-notch form already described. When it is pressed into the clay surface, it makes a typical parallel row of punctate marks very like those placed in the twin-notch categories, but with the important difference that the flat base of the notch is clearly visible in the positive impression of the motif (fig. 11-1ab).

It is all but absent from the Klein Seekoei on the east side of the upper valley (fig. 11-1c), and when this rather meager sample is plotted as percentages per non-rocker cell (fig. 11-2), its isopleths form two highly suggestive lobes at the northern rim, close to the channels of the Groot Seekoei and the Elandskloof. This pattern may indicate that the study area has just nicked the outer fringes of a distribution centered somewhere farther north in midvalley. Other possibilities will no doubt occur to readers who have managed to wade this far through the narrative. The most obvious alternative is that it is just another variation of the twin-notched motifs treated in chapter 8. In all the preliminary manipulating and combining of data, this was indeed my invariable assumption. It was taken for granted that U-notch and V-notch were subvariants of

one type, and this combination was incorporated in the analysis based on all non-rocker cells (chapter 5). When their percentage values are combined, however, they produce a multispike isopleth map typical of random noise. This is the main reason that I decided to maintain the two as separate types and that the U-notch stylus was omitted from chapter 8, in spite of its very similar appearance to the other twin-notch patterns. It should also be mentioned here that they were separated for the analyses of all stab-and-lift and for all stab-and-drag, both of which failed to develop meaningful patterns. They were again separated for yet another abortive attempt to create patterns from huge cells composed only of all notched spatulate. Whether my decision was the right one or not can be resolved only by extending the northern rim of the study area.

Another "peripheral" design is the very scarce multinotch large spatulate. Although this imprint is quite distinct (fig. 11-3ab), the true identity of the stylus that made it has thus far eluded me. It may be that the beveled stick end was simply frayed, or battered, or nicked with a series of small notches or grooves, but I was able to replicate only one of these marks. I suspect the stylus was some object or objects taken, unaltered, from nature, possibly a ragged-edge tortoise scute, or even a large grass seed head, but these are just guesses. In any case, their scanty point-plot (fig. 11-3c) reveals another northerly spread, hinting that it may be a subvariant of the center-notched form discussed above.

Next in the series is a slightly more numerous sample of vessels decorated with a motif labeled ovoid stab-and-lift. Rows of shallow ovate dimples occur around the bowl, with quite wide spacing between rows (fig. 11-4ab). The long axis of the ovate is usually perpendicular to the row, but on a few recovered sherds it is oriented slightly diagonal to it. Imprints on some specimens are somewhat narrower

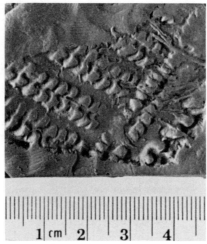

Figure 11-1a *(far left)*. Example of large U-notch spatulate stab-and-lift.

Figure 11-1b *(left)*. Positive impression of figure 11-1a.

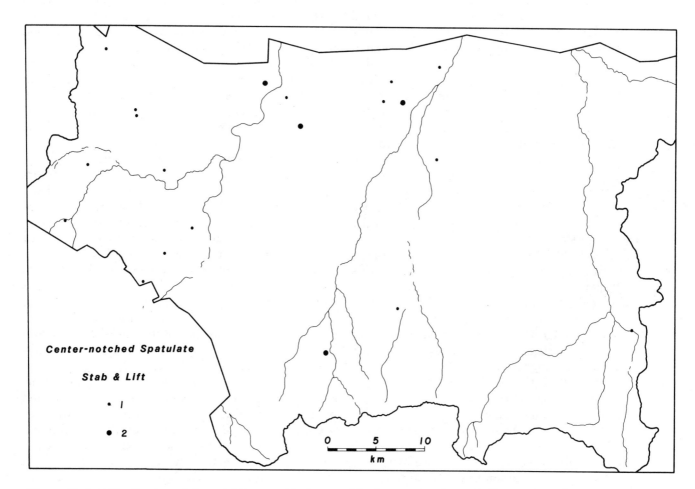

Figure 11-1c. Distribution of sites yielding vessels decorated in the manner shown in figures 11-1ab.

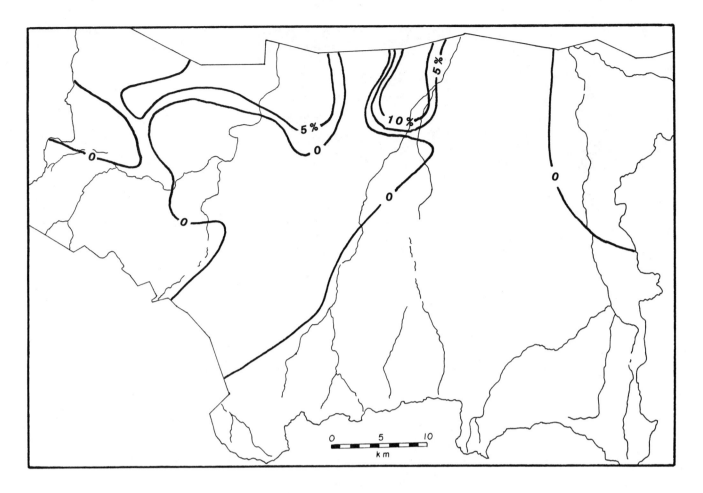

Figure 11-2. Isopleth map of percentage frequencies per non-rocker cell of large U-notch spatulate stab-and-lift.

than others. After much trial and error, I discovered that these could be easily replicated with the condyle of the very same mongoose mandible, the coronoid process of which I had used to replicate the large spatulate impressions (chapter 9). The process was broken off so that the condyle became prominent (fig. 5-1) and this was pressed vertically into the air-dried clay surface to form the imprint. Slight canting was enough to produce the narrower variant of this mark.

Its distribution (fig. 11-4c) lacks the unambiguous northerly spread of the others, and the isopleth map produces nothing more than low-level background noise (fig. 11-5). If a mongoose jaw was indeed the stylus used, then its distribution ought logically to overlap with the large plain spatulate stab-and-lift, but this is far from obvious (fig. 9-16). When the values for the two were combined, however, it must be admitted that the inner shoulder is enhanced and even the outer shoulder is rendered somewhat less jagged. Nonetheless, I hesitate to seriously proffer the combination at this stage, because the assumptions based on my replications strike me as rather too tenuous. The ovoid motif is retained separately in this chapter, therefore. Its point-plot suggests a riverine concentration; thus, it could conceivably be a northern fringe of some common motif in

Figure 11-3a *(far left).* Example of large multinotch spatulate stab-and-lift.

Figure 11-3b *(left).* Positive impression of figure 11-3a.

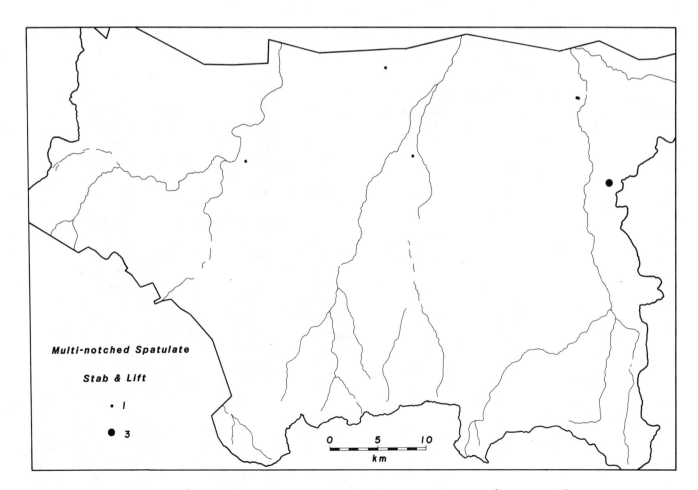

Figure 11-3c. Distribution of sites yielding vessels decorated in the manner shown in figures 11-3ab.

Figure 11-4a *(right)*. Example of ovoid-tipped stylus stab-and-lift.

Figure 11-4b *(far right)*. Positive impression of figure 11-4a.

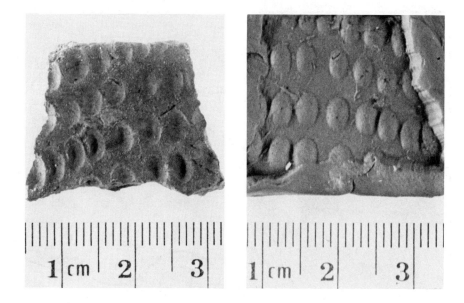

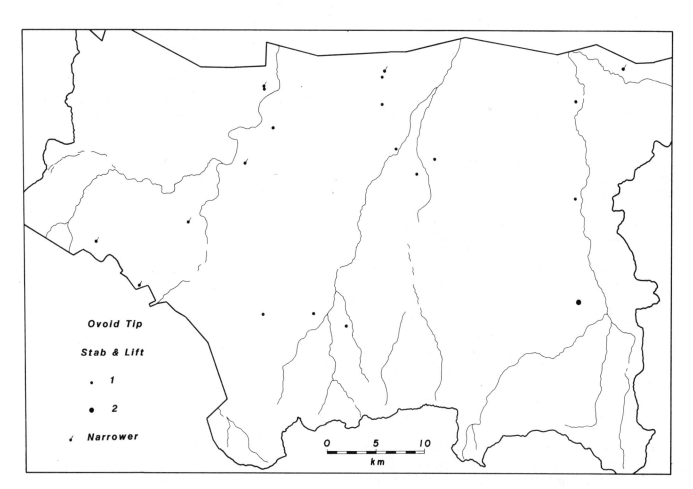

Figure 11-4c. Distribution of sites yielding vessels decorated in the manner shown in figures 11-4ab.

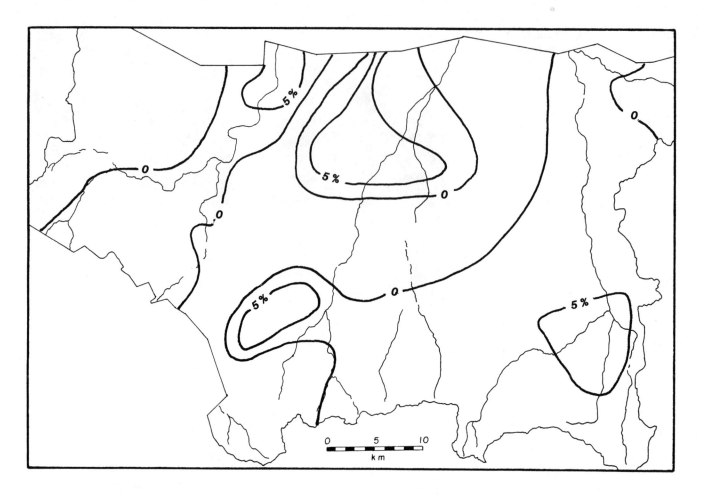

Figure 11-5. Isopleth map of percentage frequencies per non-rocker cell of ovoid tip stab-and-lift.

the central valley. Once again, further extension of the study area is the only way to test the merits of such a notion.

A subovoid stab-and-lift motif was executed in much the same way, but with a near-rounded stylus tip. Again, spacing is wide and rows are well separated (fig. 11-6ab). A few sherds have smaller imprints than those illustrated here. I was able to produce a fair copy of this imprint with the proximal humerus of *Procavia capensis*, but several micromammal species produce rounded limb bone ends that would have done just as well. It is impossible to distinguish the imprint of one from another. Also, there is no reason to exclude the rounded end of a whittled stick as a potential stylus. In any event, the point-plot (fig. 11-6c) shows this form to be rare, and my claim here for a northerly distribution is not very compelling. Given its scarcity and unique form, this remains the most suitable placement for it at present.

Finally, we come to a catchall category of blunt-tipped stylus work that was executed with a variety of broken stick ends or bone fragment ends, neither category yielding any consistent attributes such as width or tip shape. The stab-and-lift work (fig. 11-7ab) is relatively scarce (fig. 11-7c), but stab-and-drag (fig. 11-8ab) is rather more common (fig. 11-8c). Al-

Figure 11-6a *(right)*. Example of subvoid-tipped stylus stab-and-lift.

Figure 11-6b *(far right)*. Positive impression of figure 11-6a.

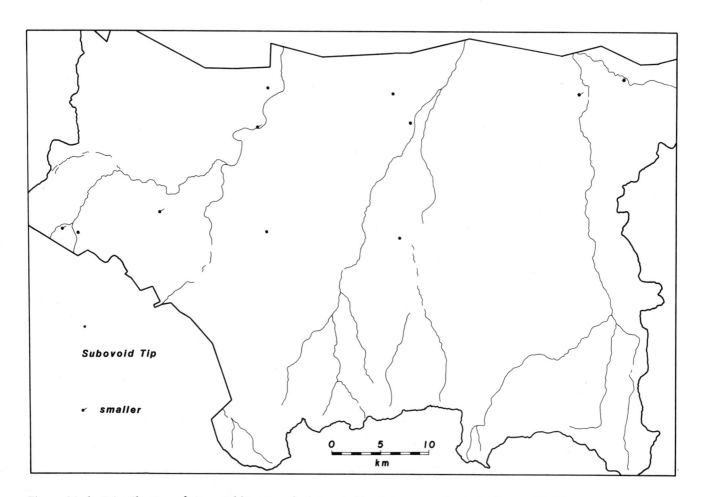

Subovoid Tip

↙ **smaller**

Figure 11-6c. Distribution of sites yielding vessels decorated in the manner shown in figures 11-6ab.

151

Figure 11-7a *(far left)*. Example of a blunted stylus (probably a stick or bone fragment) executed in stab-and-lift.

Figure 11-7b *(left)*. Positive impression of figure 11-7a.

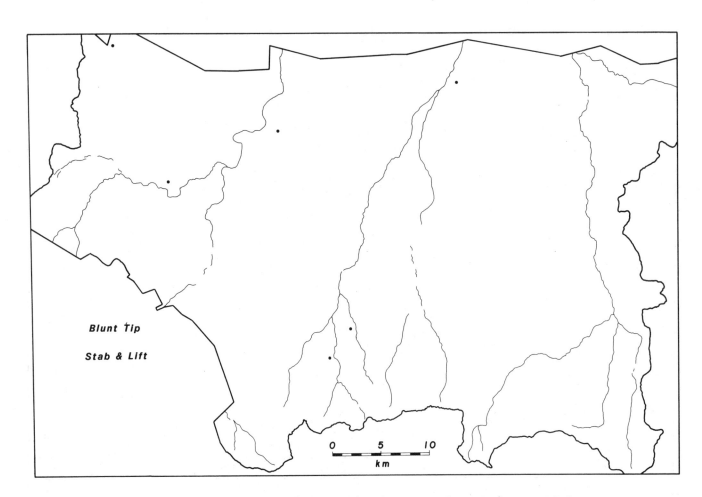

Blunt Tip

Stab & Lift

Figure 11-7c. Distribution of sites yielding vessels decorated in the manner shown in figures 11-7ab.

Figure 11-8a *(right)*. Example of a blunted stylus (probably a stick or bone fragment) executed in stab-and-drag.

Figure 11-8b *(far right)*. Positive impression of figure 11-8a.

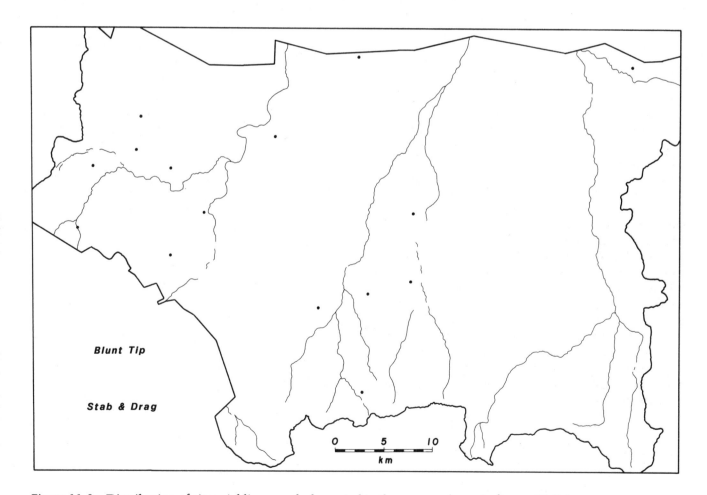

Figure 11-8c. Distribution of sites yielding vessels decorated in the manner shown in figures 11-8ab.

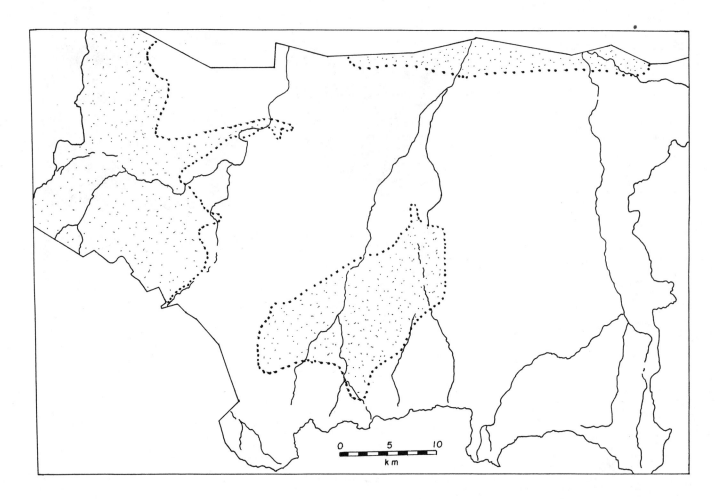

though there is no coherent reason that they should be treated as subvariants of a class, given the wide morphological variation of the stylus, their combined distribution may nevertheless be of passing interest. There are obviously too few of them to produce isopleths that will reveal anything other than low-level random noise. However, figure 11-9 simply plots distribution of the cell groups within which they occur, and only three such groups emerge. One shows a remarkable correlation with the distribution of comb-stamp wares, another covaries with the distribution of large spatulate vertical stab-and-lift, and a third overlaps with the quill group on the northern rim of the study area. It may not be too farfetched to suppose that potters in all three of these groups would, on occasion, use any old stick that came readily to hand as a stylus. This by definition is most certainly not emblemic style, but it raises the interesting possibility that nonemblemic motifs may yield low levels of concentration within different core areas, thus forming clusters that cannot be stylistically distinguished from one another.

Figure 11-9. Cell clusters containing small number of vessels decorated with blunted stylus tips (probably sticks or bone fragments).

TWELVE

The Rocker-Stamp Motifs

In both rockshelter excavations (chapter 4) rocker-stamp sherds were restricted to the top few centimeters of the deposits. No non-rocker motifs were directly associated with them. On these slender results, the rocker-stamp sample has been treated as a separate time-stratigraphic unit, independent of the non-rocker wares. At present it appears that rocker-stamping would have been the only technique seen in use by the first European trekboers when they entered the valley in the late 1700s. Thereafter, it persisted only for a few decades until the demise of the entire potmaking tradition. All told, rocker-stamping seems to have been in vogue for only a couple of centuries.

As the term implies, a notched shell edge (either mussel or ostrich egg) is rocked back and forth on the air-dried clay surface to create a zigzag scar around the bowl sides. The shell is "walked" across the surface to form a band of decoration much wider than any non-rocker row, and the work proceeds much faster, therefore. Perhaps as a consequence, bowl sides were almost completely covered by zigzag patterns, right down to the thick join between the baseplate and the sidewalls. It was never extended onto the baseplate itself, however. Band edges frequently overlap to create a confused and messy, textured surface that requires extra care in analysis. Most work proceeded around the bowl in more-or-less parallel bands, but rare rim sherds show that the shell was also sometimes walked vertically up the bowl sides.

The systematics of this motif are something of a nightmare as there are so many variables that come into play. Several stylistic attributes vary in size and are thus continuous rather than discrete. The analyst is faced with the difficult choice of laborious (and dubious) micromeasurements or arbitrary divisions into size categories that can easily lead to the creation of false types. I chose the latter course in the hope that

false classes would contain so few specimens that they could be weeded out. These hopes were only partly fulfilled.

It seemed to me that five variables most directly influenced the appearance of the decoration. My subjective ordering of their visual impact is as follows: (1) thickness of shell edge, (2) width of stride, (3) notch spacing, (4) notch beveling, (5) angle of entry.

Shell thickness is, of course, a continuous variable that I arbitrarily (and subjectively) divided into wide, blunt, and sharp. *Wide* scars are easily replicated with the edge of an ostrich egg fragment, but this does not preclude the use of a mussel shell that can be very easily ground flat on a rough stone. Care must be taken to distinguish between scars actually created with a wide shell edge, and those created with a thinner edge but with diagonal entry, thus spreading the clay. This must be checked with a positive imprint. *Blunt* scars, which form the bulk of the collection, are best replicated with a worn or slightly ground mussel shell edge. *Sharp*, as the term implies, can be replicated only with a fresh mussel shell edge.

Stride width means the distance that the shell was walked between each rocking motion. This could be quantified by measuring distances between the tips of adjacent strides, but I opted for a coarse subdivision into closed and open. Closed is the result of rocking the shell edge repeatedly over quite a small area, inducing a mesh-like pattern of punctates which, to the unpracticed eye, looks rather like basket-impressed patterning. *Open* is produced by deliberately turning the shell between each rocking motion. This speeds up the rate at which the surface is covered, and produces a very different effect.

Notch spacing was divided into *spaced* and *packed*, and *notch beveling* was divided into *crosscut* and *beveled*. These attributes are identical to those used for the comb-stamp decorations (chapter 6). Likewise, *angle of entry* was divided into *vertical* and

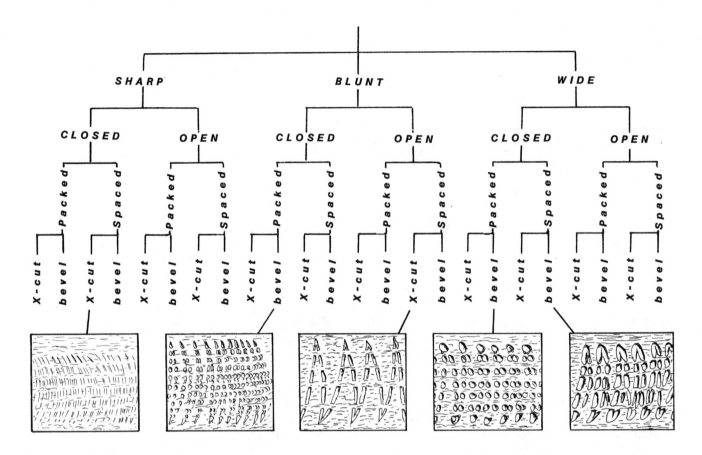

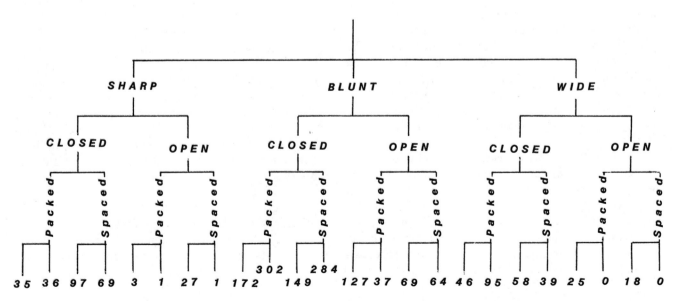

Figure 12-1. A sorting flowchart of the rocker-stamp decorations arranged in a hierarchy of attributes based on shell edge thickness, followed by stride width, notch spacing, and notch beveling. Common motifs are illustrated in the bottom row of frames.

Figure 12-2. The same hierarchy of rocker-stamp attributes shown in figure 12-1, with the number of vessels/panels decorated in each of the twenty-four "subclasses" (attribute combinations) derived from the sorting flowchart.

diagonal, as with the comb-stamp analysis.

If a sherd is classified according to one of these criteria for each of the five variables, it might fit into any one of forty-eight different permutations. Because this struck me as enormously cumbersome, I decided to ignore the angle of entry, on the very dubious grounds that this attribute had produced nothing of value in the comb-stamp analysis. This cut my sorting options down to twenty-four classes (fig. 12-1). When completed, only two classes proved to be devoid of vessels, and three others had so few as to be negligible (fig. 12-2). It must be stressed that the "classes" thus created are in fact nothing of the kind, but merely arbitrary groupings within a continuous fuzzy set of variables.

Another hazard of rocker-stamp classification is that the attribute combination tends to change as the potter works her way around the bowl. Especially sensitive is angle of entry and stride width. Most individual sherds contain only one attribute-set, but sherds from the same bowl show subtle changes so that there is a danger that two sherds from the same vessel may end up in different "classes." This was verified by a first blind test of the typology that proceeded as follows. All the decorated sherds from Haaskraal shelter were mailed to me in Dallas, where I classified them without knowledge of their exact position in the deposit. They were mailed back to Cape Town where the rocker-stamp sherds were built into a two-thirds complete bowl by Tim Hart. When refitted, this single bowl contains two sherds which I had classified as separate vessels. Admittedly both were somewhat worn sherds with shallow impressions, but the test proves that my rocker-stamp sorting technique is far from perfect, and there is a distinct possibility that the minimum vessel count is somewhat inflated by errors of this kind. For this reason the total rocker-stamp point-plot (fig. 12-3) is labeled as "panel or vessel" counts to signal some degree of uncertainty. It should be emphasized that no such difficulties were encountered with the non-rocker decorations.

The next task is to establish a suitable analytical framework of cells. The same criteria described in chapter 5 were applied in this exercise, but I lowered the optimal sample count to approximately twenty vessels or panels per cell, in an effort to reduce the number of overinflated cells. The result is a larger number of smaller cells (fig. 12-4), giving a much more even coverage of the entire area than was possible with the smaller non-rocker sample. Before discussing the distribution of various attributes within this framework, however, the overall distribution of rocker-stamping needs to be considered.

A rapid perusal of the figure 12-3 reveals that high-yield sites are again densely packed in the zone west of the Zoetvlei-Seekoei line and also along the north fringe of the study area. However, not every high-yield site that produced abundant non-rocker

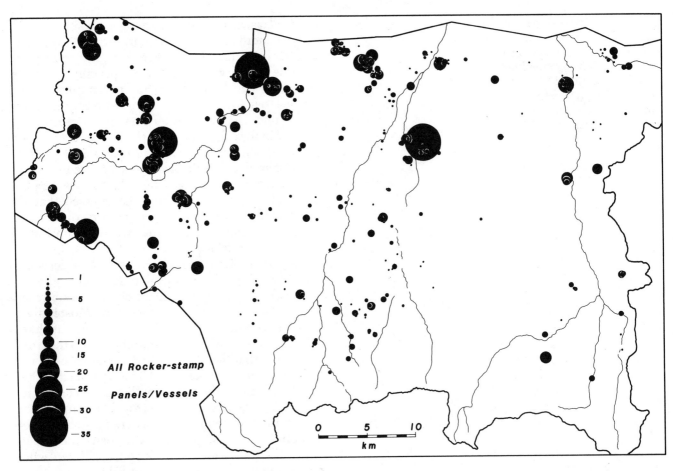

All Rocker-stamp

Panels/Vessels

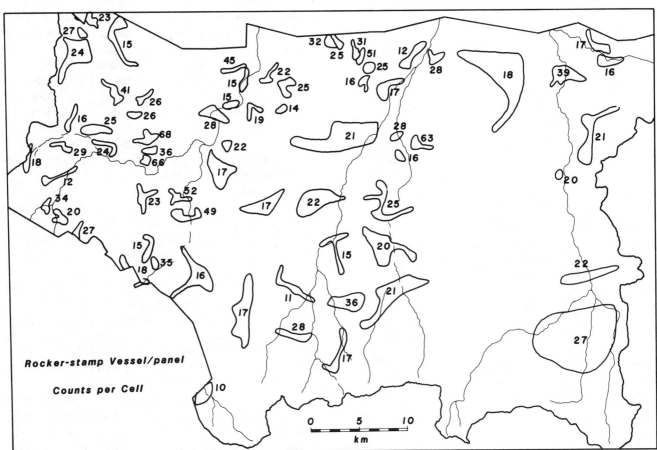

Rocker-stamp Vessel/panel

Counts per Cell

158

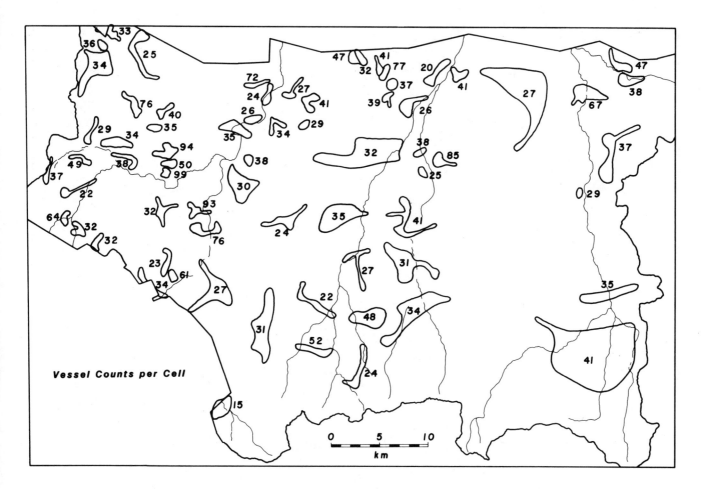

Figure 12-5. The distribution of total vessel cells, showing the numbers of all vessels (rocker, rock-and-lift, and non-rocker) in each cell.

Figure 12-3 *(above left)*. The distribution of all vessels decorated with rocker-stamp motifs in the upper Seacow Valley.

Figure 12-4 *(left)*. The distribution of rocker cells created by combining contiguous sites. Numbers reflect the minimum number of rocker-stamp vessels in each cell.

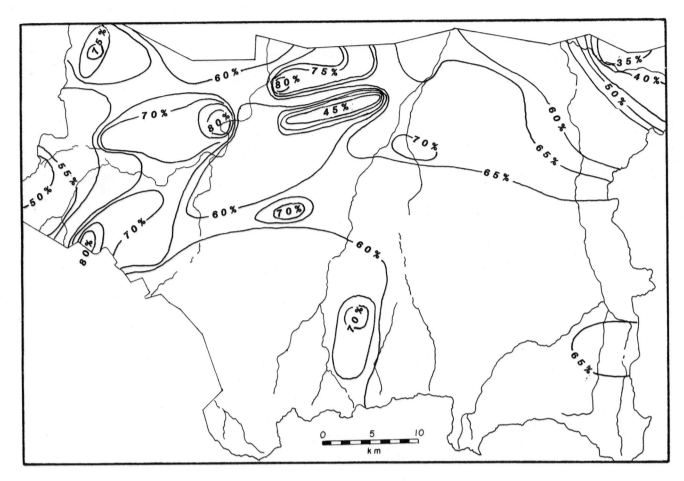

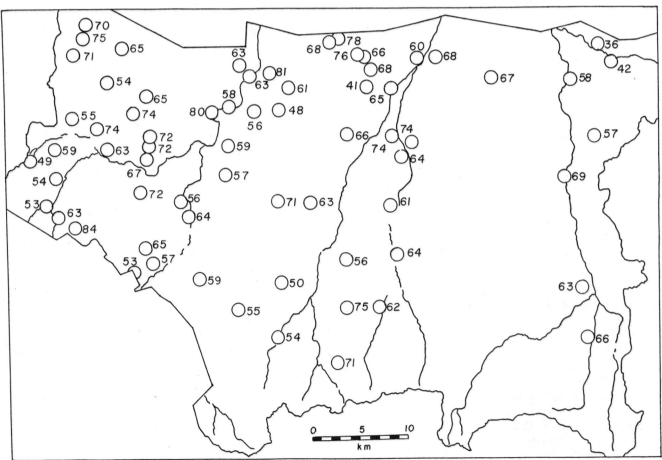

Figure 12-6. Isopleth map of percentage frequencies per total vessel cell of all rocker vessels.

Figure 12-7. Total vessel cells, showing the actual percentage values of rocker vessels per cell. Note that clusters of cells have remarkably similar values.

vessels is equally rich in rocker motifs, and vice versa. This is confirmed when figure 12-4 cells are filled with *total* vessel counts, that is, both non-rocker, rocker, and rock-and-lift counts (fig. 12-5) and rocker is plotted as percentage isopleths of the grand total for each cell (fig. 12-6). There are several marked spikes and troughs in the distribution that confirm that the drop-rate for rocker and non-rocker was by no means uniform in all parts of the valley, and suggest nothing more than random noise. However, one intriguing feature of this exercise, but difficult to explain, is the closely matching percentage values obtained for many contiguous cells (fig. 12-7). This suggests a grouping (apparently fortuitous?) like that shown in figure 12-8, but these of course have nothing to do with style. It should also be noted that identical grouping is possible for the non-rocker also (the rock-and-lift being a numerically insignificant category), but the values of the cell clusters are complementary to those for rocker. A minimal interpretation of these patterns is that the relative drop-rates (breakage-rates) of the two major classes were quite uniform over relatively large tracts of countryside. It will emerge later, however, that none of these cell-clusters exhibits any stylistic cohesion whatever. This is a puzzle worth exploring further, after the other rocker analyses have been reviewed.

Twelve of my arbitrary "classes" shown in figure 12-2 (those with the twelve highest sample sizes) were plotted as percentage isopleths, using the cell framework shown in figure 12-4. Every last one of them produced a patternless jumble typical of random background noise, complete with multiple spikes and dimples. Although some were more chaotic than others, not one map came even close to the sort of patterning achieved for so many of the non-rocker motifs. Satisfied that the "classes" are indeed meaningless figments of my own systematics, I then proceeded to plot isopleths for combinations using progressively fewer and fewer attributes. It was not until I reached single attributes, that any sort of broad patterning with reasonably well-defined isopleth shoulders began to emerge. What follows is a selection of maps of very basic attributes, there being little point in reproducing page after page of mapped noise.

The first isopleth map approaching the expectations of the model is that for *wide* shell edge only. Presumably most of this was made with ostrich eggshell, and a typical example is shown in figure 12-9ab. Unfortunately there are two concentrations (fig. 12-9c), rather than the one plateau called for by the model. The larger of the two covers the Elandskloof east branch and the Klein Seekoei, with a good shoulder running between the two Elandskloof branches and another separating the northeast corner from the Klein Seekoei. The second concentration seems to loop around and follow the Zoetvlei and Bo-Seekoei channels, as if concentrated along the riverbanks. A very

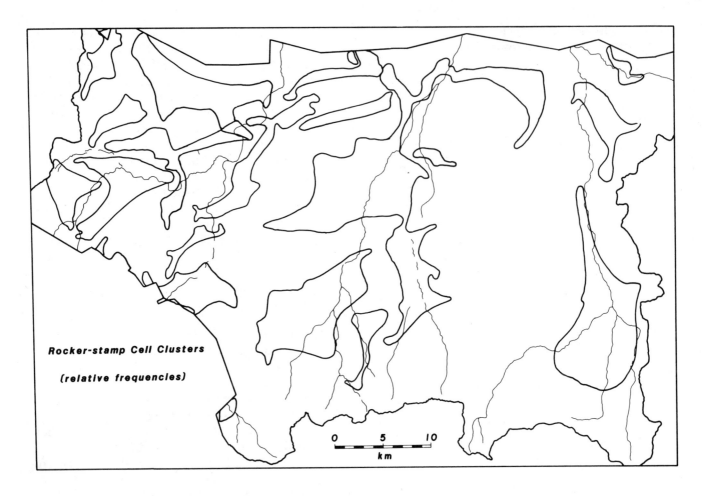

Rocker-stamp Cell Clusters

(relative frequencies)

Figure 12-8. Cell clusters suggested by the percentage frequencies shown in figure 12-7.

marked trough appears between the Elandskloof and Zoetvlei-Seekoei, and this swings to the northwest corner of the map. Every attempt was made to combine the *wide* attribute with others in a way that would allow a distinction to be made between these two concentrations, but without the slightest success.

Another single attribute that produced a small amount of clustering was the *sharp* edge. This is visually rather distinctive (fig. 12-10ab), but the resulting pattern also has far too many independent spikes in addition to the larger plateau between the Elandskloof and the Zoetvlei-Seekoei line (fig. 12-10c). The map for *blunt* (fig. 12-11ab) has been omitted as it represents noise without any redeeming features.

The other single attribute worth considering is *open stride,* which is also rather distinctive (fig. 12-12ab). The isopleth map shows a well-defined plateau covering most of the Elandskloof drainage with one shoulder running to the northwest corner of the map (fig. 12-12c). This is marred, however, by two massive spikes on the plateau and, worse still, a second minor cluster between the Zoetvlei and Bo-Seekoei. Of course the *closed stride* (fig. 12-13ab) produces a map that is the mirror image of this.

Figure 12-9a *(right)*. Example of rocker-stamp with sharp shell edge.

Figure 12-9b *(far right)*. Positive impression of figure 12-9a.

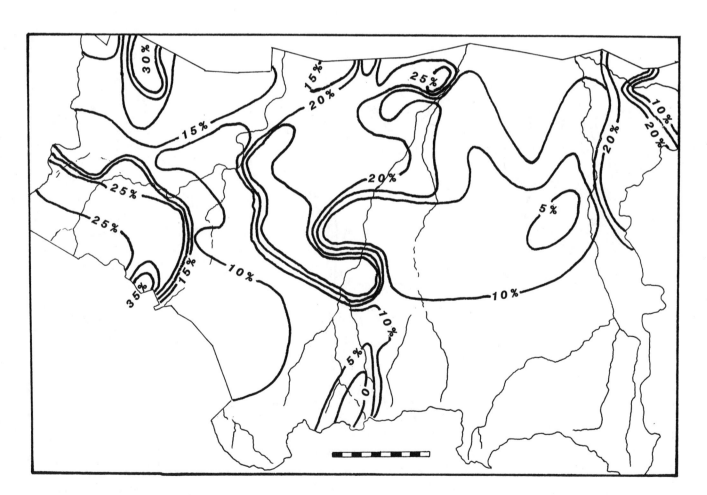

Figure 12-9c. Isopleth map of percentage frequencies per rocker cell of the sharp-edged rocker-stamp attribute shown in figures 12-9ab.

163

Figure 12-10a *(far left).* Example of rocker-stamp with very wide shell edge.

Figure 12-10b *(left).* Positive impression of figure 12-10a.

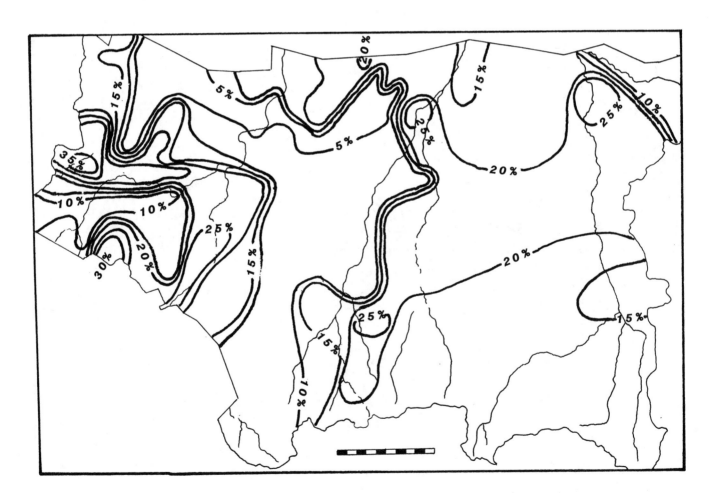

Figure 12-10c. Isopleth map of percentage frequencies per rocker cell of the wide-edge rocker-stamp attribute shown in figures 12-10ab.

Figure 12-11a. Example of rocker-stamp with blunt shell edge.

Figure 12-11b. Positive impression of figure 12-11a.

By way of symmetry, I have also included an isopleth map of the crosscut and bevel-notch ratios per cell (fig. 12-14). Crosscut notches form a plateau running diagonally from the Elandskloof headwaters to the northwest corner, but there is an independent spike on the north-central rim.

Finally, the isopleth map of the packed or spaced notch ratio (fig. 12-15) shows a slight preference for packed notches running east-west along the north rim, with another ridge on the southwest rim. These last two maps are included simply to illustrate why none of the attribute combinations seems to pattern out—ridges and plateaus of high frequency for each attribute crosscut those of several others, making for a crazy-quilt of values for combined attributes. Thus, individual attributes show better patterning than any given attribute combination, although none of them fits perfectly with the expectations of the model, thus none can be presented as candidates for true emblemic style.

One final attempt to wring some patterning out of this apparent chaos will be presented. This was a variant of the standard procedures outlined in chapter 1, in which attributes of one type (rocker) rather than lists of several types (non-rocker) were used to derive accumulative percentage differences between adjacent cells. In this test the percentage values (of rocker total per cell) are not all from the same calculations, but from several different ones. This means that the column of percentage values in each cell is likely to add up to considerably more than 100, and the results are not methodologically comparable to those for non-rocker cells (chapter 5).

The percentage values entered in each cell were for: wide, blunt, sharp (out of 100%); open stride (out of 100%); crosscut notch (out of 100%); and packed notch (out of 100%). Inevitably, the computed percentage differences are much higher than usual, but when values above the 70% difference level are plotted (fig. 12-16), the outcome is not total chaos—something of a surprise, considering all that has gone before. Most notable is the continuous separation line running north-south across the entire western sector of the map. It starts at the north rim west of the Groot Seekoei, crosses the river just west of the Bo-Seekoei and Zoetvlei confluence, and runs on down east of the Zoetvlei channel. Although not identical to the very marked non-rocker boundary line in this area, it is sufficiently close that I doubt that it is a coincidence. The second remarkable point is that the upper Elandskloof is again grouped with the Klein Seekoei drainage, and the northeast corner is separated, albeit weakly, from the Klein Seekoei itself. These results also mimic the much more emphatic patterns revealed in the non-rocker analyses. Likewise, the chaotic area between the Elandskloof and the Zoetvlei-Seekoei emerges as the "muddle in the middle."

These impressions are reinforced when percentage differences between all cells are computed, and the between-cell linkages are plotted at four levels below the 70% difference level (fig. 12-17). Note also that the familiar separation along the line of the Bo-Seekoei also emerges, and that the same north-central part of the map has the poorest clustering of all. These features, together with the separations already noted

165

Figure 12-12a *(far left)*. Example of rocker-stamp executed with open stride motion.

Figure 12-12b *(left)*. Positive impression of figure 12-12a.

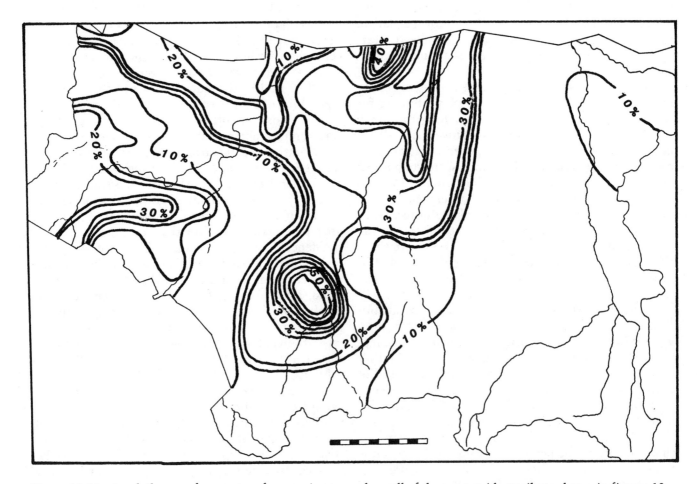

Figure 12-12c. Isopleth map of percentage frequencies per rocker cell of the open stride attribute shown in figures 12-12ab.

Figure 12-13a. Example of rocker-stamp executed in closed stride motion.

Figure 12-13b. Positive impression of figure 12-13a.

in figure 12-16, are very reminiscent of the recurrent patterns seen in the non-rocker analyses. Perhaps the most obvious departure is that the rocker linkages are more numerous and coherent on the east side of the valley, rather than the west (fig. 5-10).

What, then, are the characteristic attribute combinations that go with each of the traditional "core areas" if they were indeed the same ones seen in the non-rocker configuration? It is simply impossible to isolate any such combination. What is causing adjacent cells to cluster is a special mix of attribute frequencies, not a persistent association of attributes repeated from one vessel to another in that area. The causes of the clustering are, therefore, very different from those that created the non-rocker clusters—

which makes their similar clustering all the more remarkable. I for one find it quite difficult to construct a coherent argument to explain why this should be so, but I also find it hard to believe that the covariance is a spurious coincidence.

Two implications flow from these results. The first is that stylistic boundaries do not seem to have been much altered at the time when rocker-stamping became the standard decorative motif in all (?) parts of the upper valley. The second observation is that rocker attributes were combined in some way to signal group distinctions, but, for various reasons, their distribution has been smeared in such a way that the appropriate combinations are not discernible in my simplistic analysis.

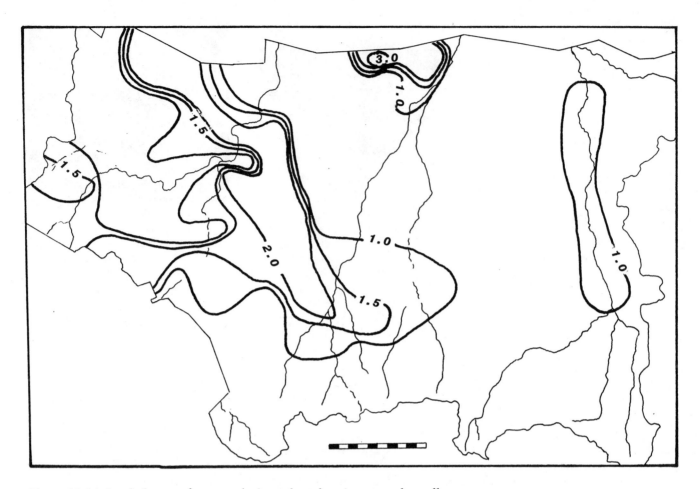

Figure 12-14. Isopleth map of rectangular/round tooth ratios per rocker cell. A value of 1.0 reflects a 1:1 ratio. Higher values indicate that rectangular tooth decorations outnumber round tooth decorations.

Figure 12-15 *(above right)*. Isopleth map of packed/spaced notch ratios per rocker cell. A value of 1.0 reflects a 1:1 ratio. Higher values indicate that packed notches (square and round tooth) outnumber spaced notches (elongated tooth) decorations.

Figure 12-16 *(right)*. Accumulative percentage differences between contiguous rocker cells, expressed as lines of varying thickness. Values less that 70 percent are omitted. The percentage values entered for each cell were: sharp, wide, blunt edges (100%); open stride (percent of total); rectangular tooth (percent of total); and packed notches (percent of total). Thus the maximum possible difference between two cells is 400 percent.

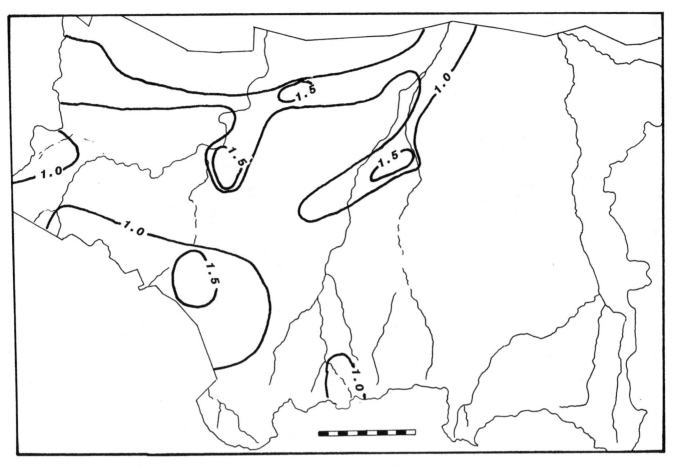

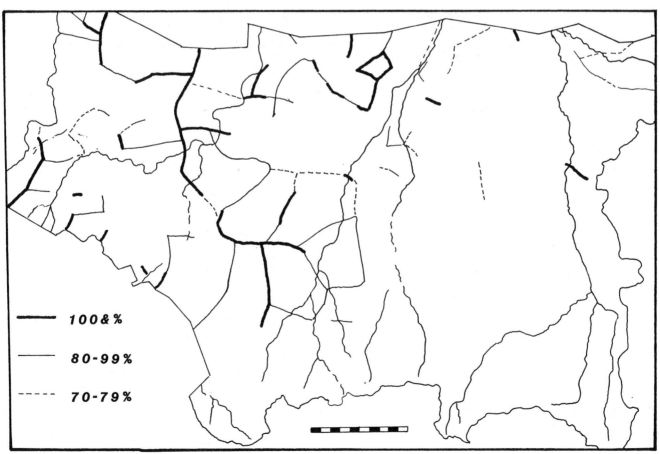

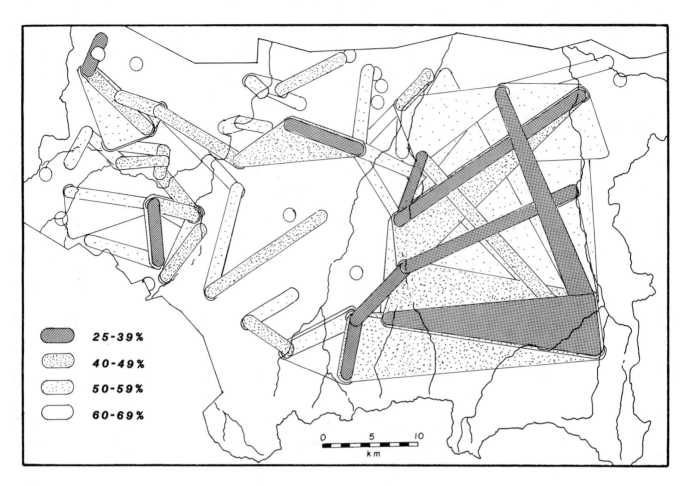

Figure 12-17. Accumulative percentage differences between all rocker cells, expressed as a cluster hierarchy of similar cells. Values of more than 70 percent are omitted. The percentage values entered for each cell were: sharp, wide, blunt edges (100%); open stride (percent of total); rectangular tooth (percent of total); and packed notches (percent of total). Thus the maximum possible difference between two cells is 400 percent.

THIRTEEN

Interpretations

In the introduction it was pointed out that this was only the second incremental step in a very long-term research project. The results are, therefore, intermediate rather than terminal, and they cannot be construed as conclusions in the full sense of the word. Instead, this closing chapter will point the way to future research opportunities by reviewing ideas and options that might help to explain what the motif boundaries actually meant to the upper Seacow River Bushmen themselves. It should by now be reasonably apparent that stylistic boundaries among mobile hunter-foragers *can* be detected in the archaeological record, given enough suitable data in a large enough study area. However, some understanding of the way boundaries are likely to reveal themselves in those data (clinal shoulders on isopleth maps) is essential. Using these criteria, boundary lines have been scored onto a 2,000 square kilometer map, and areas contained within those lines have been characterized by specific bowl decorations. A few areas can be further subdivided, with specific motif attributes concentrated in the subareas. Furthermore, zones of boundary overlap have been tentatively identified, and parts of some boundary lines have been flagged as more porous than others. It has also emerged that one of the boundaries (the Zoetvlei-Seekoei line) is more porous on its east side, and that vessel traffic from west to east was more restricted.

Implicit throughout the long cycle of analyses has been one bedrock assumption: that stylistic boundaries are equivalent to socioterritorial boundaries. This, it will be recalled, is inextricably bound up with the model proposed in chapter 1.

It is now time to explore the ramifications of that assumption, and to probe it for weaknesses. Rival interpretations of stylistic boundaries will be similarly explored in an attempt to undermine the territorial version. The path taken by this exploration leads through most of the thorny problems of interpretation raised, but not addressed, by the analyses. Are

some boundaries spurious? What causes boundary porosity? Did the Bushmen really see the motifs as group signatures? Did motifs have symbolic meaning? Why did bowl decorating begin? Why did it change? Why was rocker-stamping adopted universally towards the end? There are no quick answers to any of these questions, but they serve well to help isolate those lines of future research most likely to provide adequate tests of the model and its baseline assumptions.

Are some boundaries spurious? A rival model designed to support this position can be summarized as follows: *only the comb-stamp boundary is real*, because it is visible even on the point-plot map, and is replicated by the porcelainite dispersal map. All others have random, ubiquitous distributions, as suggested by the point-plot maps. If this is so, then the comb-stamp counts have been added onto the background noise of all other motifs. This addition in the west has set up a ripple effect on the frequency distributions of all the other principle (nonperipheral) motifs, passing eastwards. The ripple effect has caused spurious distortions of their random frequencies—which in turn created their various (bogus) drop-off shoulders in the isopleth maps. Several facts can be marshalled in support of this case.

First, most of the motifs are known to occur *outside the upper Seacow Valley*. None is unique to its purported "core-area." Unfortunately, good documentation is still extremely scarce and we have only the published photographs of Dunn (1931) to demonstrate this. His collecting areas were shown in figure 3-2. Present in his Camdebo collection are: large plain spatulate oblique stab-and-lift; large notched spatulate stab-and-lift or drag; small spatulate stab-and-lift or drag; pointed spatulate stab-and-lift. His Stormberg collection contains the same range, plus some near-complete rocker-stamped bowls, a large spatulate vertical stab-and-lift, quill gash, quill oblique gash, and comb-stamp. Several other comb-stamp photos are regrettably without proveniences, and there is a dubious V-notch stab-and-lift from Griquatown. No other published sherd illustrations, including my own from the Orange River Scheme area, are detailed or reliable enough for certain diagnosis, but the accession books of several South African museums are overloaded with entries for decorated Smithfield sherds collected from many hundreds of different localities. One obvious future research target is the plotting of these motifs throughout the central plateau to discover their maximum distributions.

Meanwhile, these meager available facts are loaded with implications for the territorial model. *If* potters intended their decorations to signal group membership (that is, emblemic style) then why were the same motifs being used in so many different places far beyond the reach of the Seacow Valley Bushmen? Also, were they regarded as emblemic style in the Camdebo, the Stormberg, and probably in hundreds of other regions besides? If they were, then was there some kind of reciprocal or information network that welded all the "comb-stamp bands" into a larger whole, and the "quill" bands into another whole, and so on? In our present state of knowledge, any such sociopolitical construct strains credibility to the limit. However, until we know the true extent of different motif distributions across the Karoo and beyond, these questions will continue to haunt the model.

Thus the rival (spurious boundaries) model gains considerable support from Dunn's photographs, and conjures up the possibility that density distributions of specific motifs (even the unchallenged comb-stamp) rise and fall in random swirling patterns throughout central South Africa. Under the terms of this scenario, my study area has captured one small segment of this large-scale frequency noise, and nothing more. The upper valley is still too small a picture, examined too closely, for us to see the wood for the trees. Thus, a second obvious research target should be the exhaustive statistical testing of all my assumptions. I hope, this will already be in process by the time these words are in print (see preface).

As a counterbalance to these doubts, there is the rather clear-cut correlation between parts of most stylistic boundaries and certain channels of the upper Seacow drainage. The use of stream-channels as mutual territorial boundaries by the !Kung San can be implied from published maps (fig. 1-1b), but this analog cannot be too heavily depended upon as there is no discussion anywhere in the ethnographic literature on whether visual landmarks are in fact consciously referred to by San to designate boundary lines. In the Karoo, where visibility is spectacularly greater than in the Kalahari (chapter 2), it would be far easier to visually monitor a boundary line, even if it was too much effort to actually patrol it. Thus, boundary lines might conceivably make more sense in this environment, rather than vaguely defined "dead ground" or unoccupied wastelands between adjoining territories.

What, then, of the stylistic boundary segments that do *not* covary with stream channels? One obvious possibility is that those other prominent linear features of this landscape, namely dolerite dikes, served as boundary markers as well. A rapid scan of the relevant sections reveals this to be only partly so, but there are enough good correlations that such an interpretation cannot be dismissed out of hand. The most obvious covariance between boundaries and dikes are shown in figure 13-1. Although these might be construed as spurious coincidence, their existence is quite damaging to the rival model when viewed in conjunction with the stream channel evidence. It is rather too much to believe that spurious boundaries (created either by frequency distortions or by larger-scale random noise) just happened to fall along two different kinds of linear feature on the landscape.

Also damaging to the rival model are the sizes of areas contained by the stylistic boundaries. Although no single area is completely circumscribed by boundary lines, the southeastern corner (characterized by large plain spatulate stab-and-lift) may be wholly captured by the study area. We must accept, however, that the unoccupied mountain chains on its south and east flanks are also true borders to the distribution. No matter what method is used to delineate this area, or those of its subcores, its measured area will invariably fall within the known range of territorial sizes for the !Kung and G/wi in the Kalahari, as can be quickly verified by glancing at figure 13-2. Again, if its configuration was manufactured from statistical distortions of a random distribution, can it be pure chance that this purported figment emerged at the appropriate size? This proposition is certainly testable. A third and obvious research target is to extend the size of the study area northwards, in an attempt to capture another complete spatial unit, this time entirely surrounded by stylistic boundaries. Further extension of the purported boundaries will go a long way to testing the merits of the rival scenario outlined above.

In balance, then, it seems more prudent to provisionally accept (subject to further testing) that the observed stylistic boundaries resulted from Bushman behavior and not from my own statistical manipulations of random noise. But are they also sociopolitical boundaries? More whole core areas in the sample will certainly add support to this assumption, but there are other possibilities. Another logical research target is the calculation of carrying capacity for delineated core areas. The goal here would be to discover the maximum Bushman population that a proposed core-area might support. Is a subcore, for example, capable of supporting a whole band or only an extended fam-

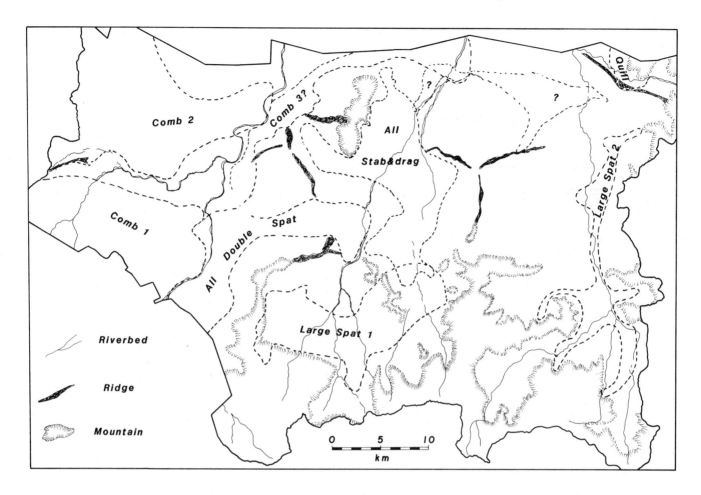

Figure 13-1. Summary map of proposed ceramic stylistic concentrations in the upper Seacow Valley, showing physical features between concentrations that may have served as visual references for territorial boundaries.

ily? Although hard numbers would help to substantiate or refute a territorial interpretation, it remains to be seen whether accurate estimates can be arrived at, considering that the habitat is no longer in its pristine state (chapter 2). Note also that optimal foraging models have no place in this endeavor, as the Bushmen are assumed to have operated well below maximum carrying capacity. Although difficulties abound, this is the *only* line of inference through which we can directly address the question of group size (cf. Martin 1983).

A first serious attempt to refute the socioterritorial model of stylistic boundaries may be embedded in another rival hypothesis that would also account for the presence of the same motifs far beyond the confines of the upper valley. In this model the basic assumption is that *motifs are part of a ritual or belief system* operating above the level of mere socioterritorial organization. In this scenario a particular motif had specific symbolic meaning associated with a trance experience, and was not meant to signal group membership. Thus, motifs cannot be emblemic style, but are instead created by potters belonging to many different bands scattered across the Karoo. A tenuous line of reasoning can be built in support of this notion, which may yet prove testable.

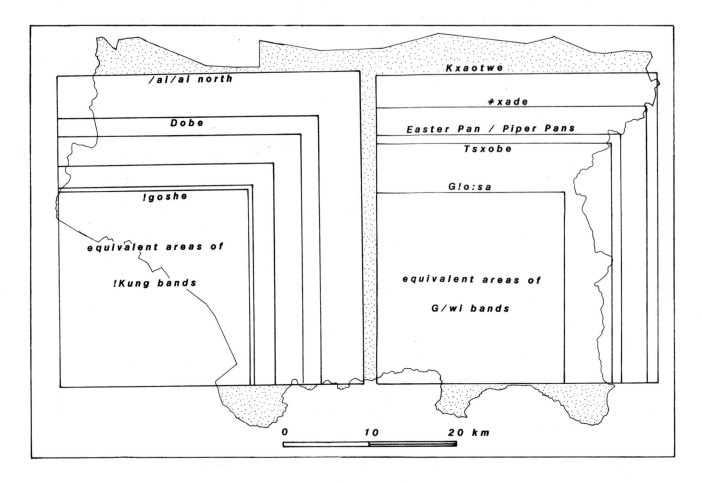

Figure 13-2. The upper Seacow Valley study area, with equivalent areas of recorded Kalahari San territories.

The considerable and growing body of research on the association between San trance-dance imagery and rock art (Lewis-Williams 1981) has recently focused on "form constants," that is, geometric hallucinations common to people of all cultures in the early stages of trance, neurologically induced by physical stress. Two of particular relevance to this model are zigzag lines and another group called nested catenary curves (Lewis-Williams 1986). Under the terms of this rival model, it would be entirely reasonable to interpret the rocker-stamp motif as a potter's rendition of the zigzag—also incidentally found among other "form constant" images commonly seen at dozens of rock art sites in the upper Seacow Valley. It would be equally plausible, under the same set of assumptions, to interpret the comb-stamp motif as the potter's rendition of nested catenary curves, a few of which also occur among the rock art images. It is, of course, now too late to test another more farfetched notion that juxtapositions between these decorations on the outside of the bowl, and boiling liquid on the inside had anything to do with the Bushman healer's commonly experienced sensation of "boiling" prior to his slump into full trance. Nevertheless, the viewpoint offered by this model raises some intriguing questions, most immediate of which is: why would certain trance images be distributed across the landscape in the patterns outlined in this volume?

Field testing of this model is quite a daunting prospect, but one obvious line of inquiry is a study of the upper valley rock art. If the model has any merit at all, then the imagery at rock art sites should covary with the pottery motifs. One early hint that this may have some potential comes from the observation that engravings are more common in the northwest, while paintings are more common in the southeast (fig. 13-3). Another research target, then, must be an analysis of the image-content of these sites. Even if covariance were to emerge from such a project, does it necessarily follow that the socioterritorial model is refuted? It could be that certain form-constants were adopted by different bands as group signatures—hence, their recurrence among bands so far apart that they are not likely to be exchanging information.

The same pair of rival models serve as complementary rather than competing frameworks within which to explain why pottery decoration came about in the first place. Potmaking was evidently in place in the Upper Karoo a few centuries before decorations first appeared. In terms of the socioterritorial model, group signaling would first appear under conditions of stress induced by scarce resources or population growth leading to overcrowding, or both (see chapter 1). The form-constant model would explain the same data by drawing on the analogs of Kalahari San trance-curing ceremonies, which increase in frequency, duration, and intensity whenever social tensions grow. It would follow that increased crowding would lead to conditions that might stimulate the production of trance-related symbols both on rocks and pots. This line of reasoning offers viable alternatives to the usual migration or diffusion sorts of explanation, and has the added virtue of being field testable. Test implications for this scenario are: sites with decorated ceramics will be more numerous than those with plainware; rock art will proliferate at the same time that pottery decoration appears; and/or the environmental and dietary record for the upper valley will show deteriorating conditions over the same period.

The search for such trends will require many more rockshelter excavations than the two mentioned in this volume. Several likely deposits from the upper valley have been earmarked for immediate attention, and work should be under way by the time this reaches print. These will also help to establish the chronology of non-rocker style changes and the association between those changes and any discernable shifts in environment. Another potential influence on stylistic change is the herder incursion during non-rocker times (chapter 4). More extensive excavation will certainly help to pin down the timing, duration, and areal extent of this incursion. This in turn will help to determine the weight of herder impact on each stylistic subcore in the upper valley.

Some of the rockshelters to be examined are in the Elandskloof drainage where there is substantial overlap between the large spatulate zone and twin-notch or small spatulate zone. It remains to be seen whether we can recover ceramic sequences from here that will allow an interpretation of that overlap. If it reflects a boundary shift through time, then motif sequences from deposits within the overlap strip should differ from those in the heartlands of the zones on either side of it. On the other hand, an overlap strip created along a porous boundary should produce "mixed" motif samples from all levels.

This excavation campaign will also attempt to address the intriguing problem of why the comb-stamp boundary is more porous on one side than the other. If sequences are forthcoming in all the right places, we should be able to test for the possibility that the comb-stamp boundary shifted westwards through time, and was "overrun" by the neighboring motifs. A case for this scenario will only be forthcoming if it turns out that comb-stamp underlies the other motifs at all sites near its eastern boundary—as was the case at Haaskraal.

These are all quite mechanical tests designed to pin down more precise chronologies. Although each is helpful in its own way, none will serve to explain the most fascinating question which is why pottery decoration became more uniform rather than more diverse during the last few centuries of the tradition. Available evidence hints ambiguously at a population increase through time, but there are alternative explanations for the marked increase in rocker-stamp over non-rocker vessels (chapter 4). Theory predicts that crowding should induce more emphatic group signaling, not less. Furthermore, the trekboer invasion of the late 1700s would surely have increased social stress, not reduced it. Thus, conditions seem ripe for the emergence of even more clear-cut boundaries than those discerned in the non-rocker record. What happened was the exact opposite.

If the depositional hiatus between non-rocker and rocker levels in the Haaskraal sequence is repeated elsewhere, then the possibility of some sort of abandonment episode may be seriously entertained. This, in turn, raises the possibility of a population turnover, leading to stylistic change brought about simply by in-migration. Another possible scenario worth investigating is the collapse of Bushman spatial organization caused by the trekboer takeover of upper valley waterholes. Early trekboer architectural remains are elusive but not inaccessible, and a fine-grained study of the advancing trekboer frontier across this landscape is certainly feasible. What remains uncertain at present is the chronological relationship between the first appearance of rocker-stamp motifs and trekboers. Our scant excavations suggest that the motif was already in place by the time European items show up in the deposits, but this needs to be demonstrated repeatedly in different parts of the study area.

Figure 13-3. Distribution of rock art sites in the central and upper Seacow Valley (after Sampson 1985:96).

Rock Engravings ■

Rock Paintings ○

0   5   1 0
k m

Clearly, there are many avenues of inquiry that promise to lead us closer to a viable interpretation of the meaning of stylistic boundaries. If they are indeed also socioterritorial borders, then the way is clear to firming up that interpretation. Meanwhile, these few lines etched out of the upper Seacow ceramics provide an excellent framework within which to begin a fresh round of inquiries into the meaning of style in stone artifacts. We are also poised to open inquiries into seasonal mobility patterns within circumscribed areas. Thus, the monograph comes full circle, ending with those two dominant concerns of hunter-forager archaeology, both of which filled its opening paragraphs—artifact typology and seasonal or subsistence systems. New research opportunities beckon.

Appendix

The summary map in figure 6-25 of chapter 6 shows all the isopleth shoulders for individual comb-stamp attributes, plotted as percentages of total comb-stamp vessels per enlarged cell. The individual isopleth maps from which these shoulders were derived are given below.

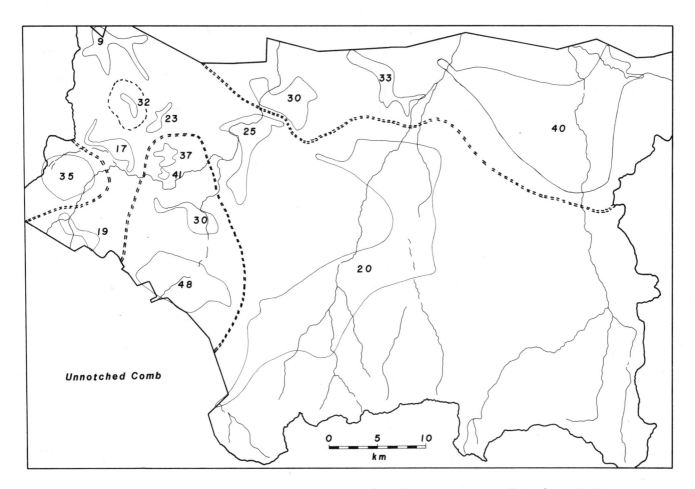

Figure A-1. Unnotched comb-stamp expressed as percentages of total comb-stamp per cell (see figure 6-22). Frequency drop-off shoulders are represented by double dashed lines.

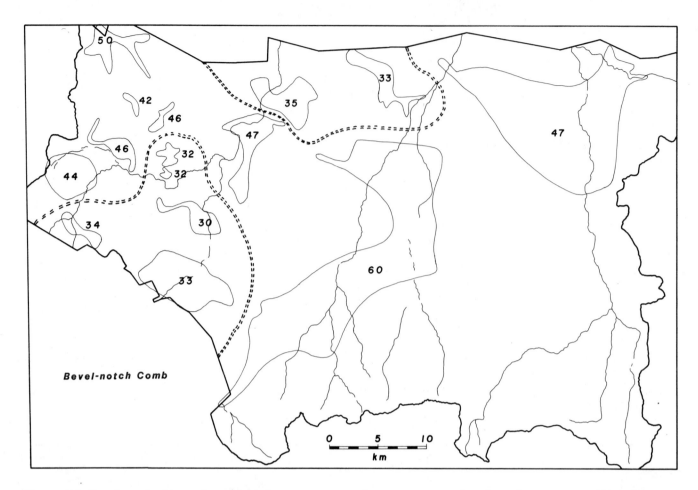

Figure A-2. Bevel-notched (round tooth) comb-stamp expressed as percentages of total comb-stamp per cell (see figure 6-22). Frequency drop-off shoulders are represented by double dashed lines.

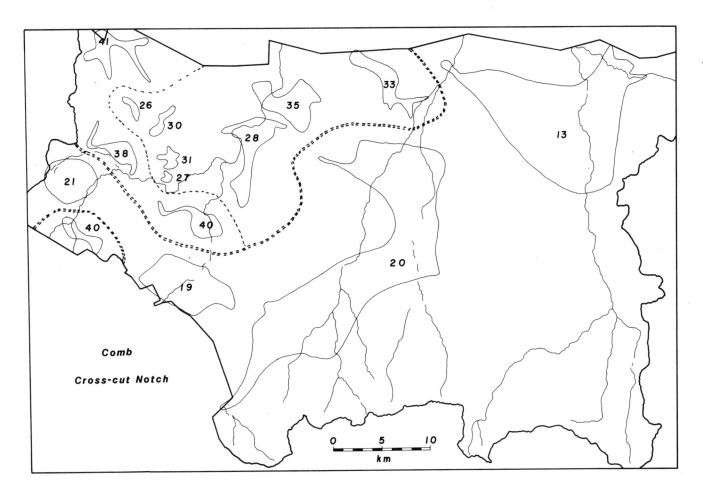

Figure A-3. Cross-cut notched (rectangular tooth) comb-stamp expressed as percentages of total comb-stamp per cell (see figure 6-22). Frequency drop-off shoulders are represented by double dashed lines.

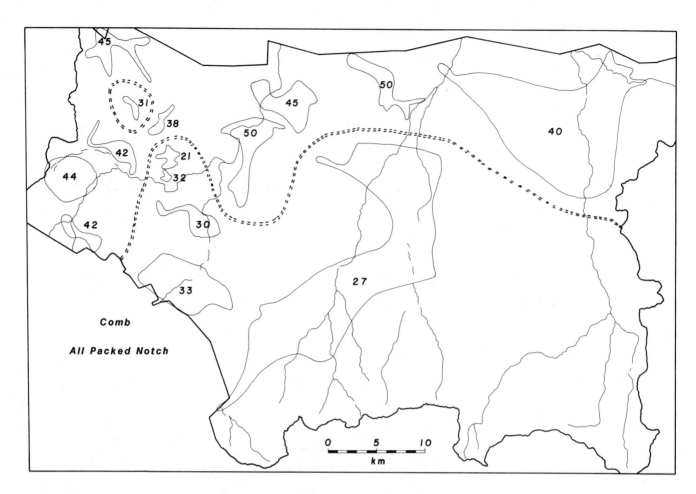

Figure A-4. Packed notch (square or round tooth) comb-stamp expressed as percentages of total comb-stamp per cell (see figure 6-22). Frequency drop-off shoulders are represented by double dashed lines.

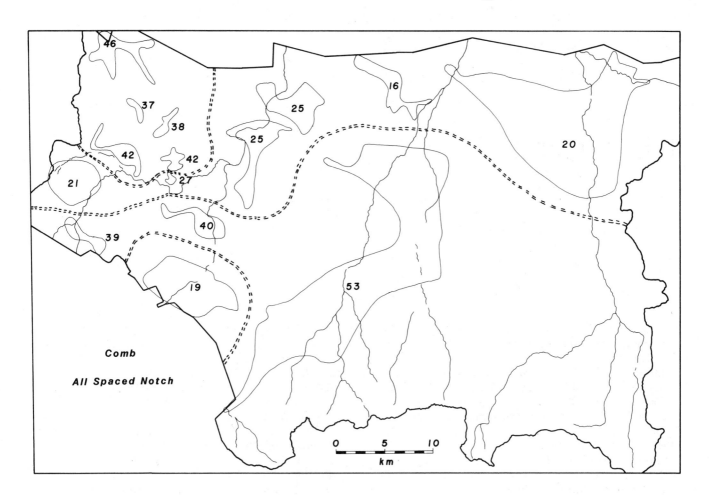

Figure A-5. Spaced notch (elongated tooth) comb-stamp expressed as percentages of total comb-stamp per cell (see figure 6-22). Frequency drop-off shoulders are represented by double dashed lines.

Bibliography

Acocks, A. J. P. 1975. Veld types of South Africa. 2d Ed. *Memoirs of the Botanical Survey of South Africa*, no. 40: 1–128.

Andresen, J. M., B. F. Byrd, M. D. Elson, R. H. McGuire, R. G. Mendoza, and E. Staski. 1981. The deer hunters: Star Carr reconsidered. *World Archaeology* 13: 31–46.

Ardrey, R. 1966. *The territorial imperative.* New York: Dell.

Ascher, R. 1961. Analogy in archaeological interpretation. *Southwestern Journal of Anthropology* 17: 317–325.

Ashley-Montagu, M. F., ed. 1973. *Man and aggression.* Oxford: Oxford University Press.

Bamforth, D. B. 1986. Technological efficiency and tool curation. *American Antiquity* 51: 38–50.

Barnard, A. 1979. Kalahari Bushman settlement patterns. In P. C. Burnham and R. F. Ellen, eds., *Social and ecological systems*, 131–144. London: Academic Press.

Barrow, J. 1806. *Travels into the interior of South Africa.* London: Cadell and Davis.

Baxter, P. T. W. 1975. Some consequences of sedentarization for social relationships. In T. Monod, ed., *Pastoralism in tropical Africa*, 206–228. London: Oxford University Press.

Beaumont, P. B., and J. C. Vogel. 1984. Spatial patterning of the ceramic Later Stone Age in the northern Cape Province, South Africa. In M. Hall, G. Avery, D. M. Avery, M. L. Wilson, and A. J. B. Humphreys, eds., *Frontiers: Southern African archaeology today*, 80–95. Cambridge Monographs in African Archaeology 10. Oxford: B.A.R. International Series 207.

Berndt, R. M., and C. H. Berndt. 1964. *The world of the first Australians.* London: Angus and Robertson.

Bettinger, R. L. 1980. Explanatory/predictive models of hunter-gatherer adaptation. In M. B. Schiffer, ed., *Advances in archaeological method and theory*, vol. 3, 189–225. New York: Academic Press.

Bigalke, R. C., and J. A. Bateman. 1962. On the status and distribution of ungulate mammals in the Cape Province, South Africa. *Annals of the Cape Provincial Museum* 2: 85–109.

Binford, L. R. 1978. *Nunamiut ethnoarchaeology.* New York: Academic Press.

———. 1979. Organization and formation processes: Looking at curated technologies. *Journal of Anthropological Research* 35: 255–273.

Binford, L. R., and N. M. Stone. 1985. "Righteous rocks" and Richard Gould: Some observations on misguided "debate." *American Antiquity* 50: 151–153.

Bishop, C. A. 1974. *The northern Ojibwa and the fur trade: An historical and ecological study.* Toronto: Holt, Rinehart and Winston of Canada.

Bleek, W. H. I., and L. C. Lloyd. 1911. *Specimens of Bushman folklore.* London: George Allen and Co.

Blundell, V. 1980. Hunter-gatherer territoriality: Ideology and behaviour in northwestern Australia. *Ethnohistory* 27: 103–117.

———. 1982. Symbolic systems and cultural continuity in northwest Australia: A consideration of Aboriginal cave art. *Culture* 2: 3–20.

Brooks, A. S. 1984. San land-use patterns, past and present: Implications for southern African prehistory. In M. Hall, G. Avery, D. M. Avery, M. L. Wilson, and A. J. B. Humphreys, eds., *Frontiers: Southern African archaeology today*, 40–52. Cambridge Monographs in African Archaeology 10. Oxford: B.A.R. International Series 207.

Brooks, A. S., D. E. Gelburd, and J. E. Yellen. 1984. Food production and culture change among !Kung San: Implications for prehistoric research. In J. D. Clark and S. Brandt, eds., *From hunters to farmers*, 328–348. Berkeley: University of California Press.

Brown, J. L., and G. H. Orians. 1970. Spacing patterns in mobile animals. *Annual Review of Ecology and Systematics* 1: 239–262.

Burchell, W. J. 1822. *Travels in the interior of southern Africa.* London: Batchworth Press.

Butzer, K. W. 1982. *Archaeology as human ecology.* Cambridge: Cambridge University Press.

Butzer, K. W., G. H. Fock, L. Scott, and R. Stuckenrath. 1979. Dating and context of rock engravings in southern Africa. *Science* 203: 1201–1214.

Campbell, J. 1815. *Travels in South Africa, undertaken at the request of the Missionary Society.* London: Black and Parry.

Caraco, T., and L. L. Wolf. 1975. Ecological determinants of group sizes of foraging lions. *The American Naturalist* 109: 343–353.

Cashdan, E. 1983. Territoriality among human foragers: Ecological models and an application to four Bushman groups. *Current Anthropology* 24: 47–66.

Clark, J. G. D. 1954. *Excavations at Star Carr: An early Mesolithic site at Seamer near Scarborough, Yorkshire.* Cambridge: Cambridge University Press.

———. 1975. *The earlier Stone Age settlement of Scandinavia.* Cambridge: Cambridge University Press.

———. 1980. *Mesolithic prelude.* Edinburgh: University Press.

Clarke, D. L. 1968. *Analytical archaeology.* London: Methuen.

Close, A. E. 1977. The identification of style in lithic artifacts from North East Africa. *Mémoires de l'Institut d'Egypte,* vol. 61.

———. 1978. The identification of style in lithic artifacts. *World Archaeology* 10: 223–237.

Cohen, M. N. 1977. *The food crisis in prehistory.* New Haven: Yale University Press.

Conkey, M. W. 1978. Style and information in cultural evolution: Toward a predictive model for the Paleolithic. In C. L. Redman, M. J. Berman, E. V. Curtin, W. T. Langhorne, Jr., N. M. Versaggi, and J. C. Wanser, eds., *Social archaeology: Beyond subsistence and dating,* 61–85. New York: Academic Press.

Davies, N. B. 1978. Ecological questions about territorial behaviour. In J. R. Krebs and N. B. Davies, eds., *Behavioural ecology: An evolutionary approach,* 317–350. Oxford: Blackwell.

Deacon, J. 1984. Later Stone Age people and their descendants in southern Africa. In R. G. Klein, ed., *Southern African prehistory and paleoenvironments,* 221–328. Rotterdam: Balkema.

De Atley, S. P., and F. J. Findlow, 1984. *Exploring the limits: Frontiers and boundaries in prehistory.* Oxford: B.A.R. International Series 223.

De Kock, W. J., ed. 1965. *Reize in de Binnen-landen van Zuid-Africa, gedaan in den Jaare 1803 door W.B.E. Paravicini di Capelli.* Cape Town: Van Riebeeck Society, vol. 46.

Driver, H. E., and W. C. Massey. 1957. Comparative studies of North American Indians. *Transactions of the American Philosophical Society* 47: 166–456.

Dunn, E. J. 1931. *The Bushman.* London: Charles Griffin & Co.

du Toit, P. J., J. G. Louw, and A. I. Malan. 1940. Nutritive value of the natural pasture of the Union of South Africa. *Farming in South Africa* 15: 229–232.

Dyson-Hudson, R., and E. A. Smith. 1978. Human territoriality: An ecological reassessment. *American Anthropologist* 80: 21–41.

Eibl-Eibesfeldt, I. 1974. Zur Frage der Territorialität und Aggressivität bei Jägern und Sammlern. *Anthropos* 69: 272–275.

Ellerman, J. R., T. C. S. Morrison-Scott, and A. W. Hayman. 1953. *Southern African mammals 1758–1951.* London: British Museum (Natural History) Trustees.

Ember, C. R. 1978. Myths about hunter-gatherers. *Ethnology* 17: 437–439.

Findlow, F. J., and J. E. Ericson. 1980. Catchment analysis: Essays on prehistoric resource space. *Anthropology UCLA* 10: 1–212.

Gendel, P. A. 1984. *Mesolithic social territories in northwestern Europe.* Oxford: B.A.R. International Series 218.

Godée-Molsbergen, E. C. 1916. *Reizen in Zuid-Afrika in de Hollandse tijd.* 3. s'Gravenhage: Martinus Nijhoff.

Gould, R. A. 1980. *Living archaeology.* Cambridge: Cambridge University Press.

Gould, R. A., and S. Saggers. 1985. Binford's idea of embeddedness in archaeology. *American Antiquity* 50: 117–136.

Gramly, R. M. 1977. Deerskins and hunting territories: Competition for a scarce resource of the northeastern woodlands. *American Antiquity* 42: 601–605.

Grayson, D. K. 1984. *Quantitative zoology: Topics in the analysis of archaeological faunas.* New York: Academic Press.

Green, S., and S. M. Perlman. 1985. *The archaeology of frontiers and boundaries.* Orlando: Academic Press.

Guenther, M. 1981. Bushman and hunter-gatherer territoriality. *Zeitschrift für Ethnologie* 109: 109–120.

Gutsche, T. 1968. *The microcosm.* Cape Town: Howard Timmins.

Hamilton, W. J., R. E. Buskirk, and W. H. Buskirk. 1976. Defense of space and resources by Chacma *(Papio ursinus)* baboon troops in an African desert and swamp. *Ecology* 57: 1264–1272.

Harner, M. 1980. *The way of the shaman.* New York: Harper & Row.

Hart, T. In preparation. Master's thesis, University of Cape Town.

Harvey, P. H., and G. M. Mace. 1983. Foraging models and territory size. *Nature* 305: 14–15.

Hassan, F. A. 1981. *Demographic archaeology.* New York: Academic Press.

Heinz, H. J. 1972. Territoriality among the Bushmen in general and the !ko in particular. *Anthropos* 67: 405–416.

———. 1979. The nexus complex among the !xo Bushmen of Botswana. *Anthropos* 74: 465–480.

Herbich, I. 1986. The mother-in-law in prehistory: Some archaeological implications of a study of a traditional west Kenyan pottery system. Paper given at Conference in Honour of J. Desmond Clark, Berkeley, California, April 1986.

Hiatt, L. R. 1962. Local organization among the Australian Aborigines. *Oceanea* 32: 267–286.

Higgs, E. S., and C. Vita-Finzi. 1972. Prehistoric economies: A territorial approach. In Higgs, E. S., ed., *Papers in economic prehistory,* 27–36. Cambridge: Cambridge University Press.

Hill, J. N. 1977. Individual variability in ceramics and the study of prehistoric social organization. In J. N. Hill and J. Gunn, eds., *The individual in prehistory: Studies of variability in style in prehistoric techniques,* 55–108. New York: Academic Press.

Hitchcock, R. K. 1982. Patterns of sedentism among the Basarwa of eastern Botswana. In E. Leacock and R. Lee, eds., *Politics and history in band societies,* 223–267. Cambridge: Cambridge University Press.

Hitchcock, R. K., and J. A. Ebert. 1984. Foraging and food production among Kalahari hunter/gatherers. In J. D.

Clark and S. Brandt, eds., *From hunters to farmers*, 328–348. Berkeley: University of California Press.

Hodder, I. 1977. The distribution of material culture items in the Baringo district, western Kenya. *Man* 12: 239–269.

———. 1982. *Symbols in action: Ethnoarchaeological studies of material culture.* Cambridge: Cambridge University Press.

Hodder, I., and C. Orton. 1976. *Spatial analysis in archaeology.* Cambridge: Cambridge University Press.

Hodson, A. W. 1912. *Trekking the Great Thirst: Sport and travel in the Kalahari desert.* London: T. Fisher Unwin.

Hogg, A. H. A. 1971. Some applications of surface fieldwork. In M. Jesson and D. Hill, eds., *The Iron Age and its hillforts*, 105–125. Southampton: Southampton University Press.

Horowitz, A., C. G. Sampson, L. Scott, and J. C. Vogel. 1978. Analysis of the Voigtpos site, O.F.S. South Africa. *South African Archaeological Bulletin* 33: 152–159.

Hughes, R. E., and R. L. Bettinger. 1984. Obsidian and prehistoric sociocultural systems in California. In S. P. De Atley and F. J. Findlow, eds., *Exploring the limits: Frontiers and boundaries in prehistory*, 153–172. Oxford: B.A.R. International Series 223.

Humphreys, A. J. B. 1979. The Holocene sequence of the northern Cape and its position in the prehistory of South Africa. Unpublished Ph.D. thesis, University of Cape Town.

Humphreys, A. J. B., and A. I. Thackeray. 1983. *Ghaap and Gariep: Later Stone Age studies in the northern Cape.* Cape Town: The South African Archaeological Society Monograph Series, no. 2.

Hutton, W. W., ed. 1887. *The autobiography of Andries Stockenstroom.* Cape Town: Juta.

Jacobi, R. M. 1979. Early Flandrian hunters in the South-West. *Devon Archaeological Society Proceedings* 37: 48–93.

Jochim, M. A. 1976. *Hunter-gatherer subsistence and settlement: A predictive model.* New York: Academic Press.

———. 1981. *Strategies for survival: Cultural behavior in an ecological context.* New York: Academic Press.

Kannemeyer, D. R. 1890. Stone implements of the Bushmen: With a description of Bushmen stone-implements and relics, their names, uses and mode of manufacture, and occurrence. *Cape Illustrated Magazine* 1: 120–130.

Keene, A. S. 1979. Economic optimization models and the study of hunter-gatherer subsistence settlement systems. In C. Renfrew and K. Cooke, eds., *Transformations: Mathematical approaches to culture changes*, 369–404. New York: Academic Press.

Kelley, R. L. 1983. Hunter-gatherer mobility strategies. *Journal of Anthropological Research* 39: 277–306.

King, G. E. 1976. Society and territory in human evolution. *Journal of Human Evolution* 5: 323–332.

Klein, R. G. 1979. Paleoenvironmental and cultural implications of Late Holocene archaeological faunas from the Orange Free State and north-central Cape Province, South Africa. *South African Archaeological Bulletin* 34: 34–49.

Laidler, P. W. 1929. Hottentot and Bushman pottery of South Africa. *South African Journal of Science* 26: 758–786.

Layton, R. 1986. Political and territorial structures among hunter-gatherers. *Man* 21: 18–33.

Leacock, E., and R. Lee, eds. 1982. *Politics and history in band societies.* Cambridge: Cambridge University Press.

Lee, R. B. 1965. *Subsistence ecology of !Kung Bushmen.* Unpublished Ph.D. dissertation, University of California at Berkeley.

———. 1972. !Kung spatial organization: An ecological and historical perspective. *Human Ecology* 1: 125–147.

Lewis, I. M. 1975. The dynamics of nomadism: Prospects for sedentarization and social change. In T. Monod, ed., *Pastoralism in tropical Africa*, 426–442. London: Oxford University Press.

Lewis-Williams, J. D. 1984. Ideological continuities in prehistoric southern Africa: The evidence of rock art. In C. Schrire, ed., *Past and present in hunter gatherer studies*, 225–252. Orlando: Academic Press.

———. 1986. Seeing and construing: A neurological constant in San rock art. *The longest record: The human career in Africa. Abstracts*, 54–55. Berkeley.

Lichtenstein, M. H. C. 1928–30. *Travels in southern Africa 1803–1806.* Cape Town: Van Riebeeck Society Publications, nos. 10–11.

Lorenz, K. 1963. *Das sogenannte Böse.* Wien: Handel.

Madden, M. 1983. Social network systems amongst hunter-gatherers considered within Norway. In G. Bailey, ed., *Hunter-gatherer economy in prehistory*, 191–200. Cambridge: Cambridge University Press.

Maggs, T. M. O'C. 1976. *Iron Age communities of the southern Highveld.* Pietermaritzburg: Occasional Publications of the Natal Museum, No. 2.

MacNeish, R. S., M. L. Fowler, A. C. Cook, F. A. Peterson, A. Nelken-Terner, and J. A. Neely. 1972. *The prehistory of the Tehuacan valley.* vol. 5, *Excavations and reconnaissance.* Austin: University of Texas Press.

Marshall, L. 1960. !Kung Bushman bands. *Africa* 30: 325–355.

Martin, J. 1983. On the estimation of sizes of local groups in a hunting-gathering environment. *American Anthropologist* 85: 612–629.

Monks, G. G. 1981. Seasonality studies. In M. B. Schiffer, ed., *Advances in archaeological method and theory*, vol. 4, 177–232. New York: Academic Press.

Orians, G. H., and N. E. Pearson. 1979. On the theory of central place foraging. In D. J. Horn, G. R. Stairs, and R. D. Mitchell, eds., *Analysis of ecological systems*, 155–177.

Parkington, J. E. 1972. Seasonal mobility in the Late Stone Age. *African Studies* 31: 224–243.

———. 1984. Changing views of the Later Stone Age of South Africa. In F. Wendorf and A. E. Close, eds., *Advances in World Prehistory*, vol. 3, 90–142.

Partridge, T. C., and T. Dalbey. 1986. Geoarchaeology of the Haaskraal Pan. In H. J. Deacon, ed., *Palaeoecology of Africa* 17: 69–78.

Peterson, N. 1975. Hunter-gatherer territoriality: The perspective from Australia. *American Anthropologist* 77: 53–68.

———. 1979. Territorial adaptations among desert hunter-gatherers: The !Kung and Australians compared. In P. C. Burnham and R. F. Ellen, eds., *Social and ecological systems*, 111–129. London: Academic Press.

Pheasant, D., C. G. Sampson, and A. Waibel. No date. Preliminary investigation of the source-tracking potential of hornfels from the central Orange River valley. Manuscript.

Price, T. D. 1981. Complexity in "non-complex" societies. In S. van der Leeuw, ed., *Archaeological approaches to the study of complexity*, 54–97. Amsterdam: Albert Egges van Giffen Instituut voor Prae-en Protohistorie.

Price, T. D., and J. A. Brown. 1985. *Prehistoric hunter-gatherers: The emergence of cultural complexity*. Orlando: Academic Press.

Reid, K. C. 1984a. Pots, Grass, Trips, and Time: Regrounding some old arguments. *Abstracts of the 83rd Annual Meeting of the American Anthropological Association, Denver, Co., November 1984*, p. 106.

———. 1984b. Fire and ice: New evidence for the production and preservation of Late Archaic fibre-tempered pottery in the middle-latitude lowlands. *American Antiquity* 49: 55–76.

Rivet, A. L. F. 1964. *Town and country in Roman Britain*. London: Hutchinson.

Rudner, J. 1968. Strandloper pottery from South and South West Africa. *Annals of the South African Museum* 49: 441–663.

———. 1979. The use of stone artefacts and pottery among Khoisan peoples in historic and protohistoric times. *South African Archaeological Bulletin* 34: 3–17.

Rye, O. S. 1981. *Pottery Technology: Principles and Reconstruction*. Washington: Taraxacum.

Sackett, J. R. 1982. Approaches to style in lithic archaeology. *Journal of Anthropological Archaeology* 1: 59–112.

———. 1985. Style and ethnicity in the Kalahari: A reply to Wiessner. *American Antiquity* 50: 154–159.

Sampson, C. G. 1967a. Excavations at Zaayfontein Shelter, Norvalspont, Northern Cape. *Researches of the National Museum, Bloemfontein* 2: 41–123.

———. 1967b. Excavations at Glen Elliott Shelter, Colesberg District, North Cape. *Researches of the National Museum, Bloemfontein* 2: 125–209.

———. 1970. *The Smithfield industrial complex: Further field results*. Bloemfontein: National Museum Memoirs, no. 5.

———. 1972. *The Stone Age industries of the Orange River Scheme and South Africa*. Bloemfontein: National Museum Memoirs, no. 6.

———. 1974. *The Stone Age archaeology of Southern Africa*. New York: Academic Press.

———. 1984a. A prehistoric pastoralist frontier in the upper Zeekoe valley, South Africa. In M. Hall, G. Avery, D. M. Avery, M. L. Wilson and A. J. B. Humphreys, eds., *Frontiers: Southern African archaeology today*, 96–110. Cambridge Monographs in African Archaeology 10. Oxford: B.A.R. International Series 207.

———. 1984b. Site clusters in the Smithfield settlement pattern. *South African Archaeological Bulletin* 39: 5–23.

———. 1985. *Atlas of Stone Age settlement in the central and upper Seacow valley*. Bloemfontein: National Museum Memoirs, no. 18.

———. 1986a. Model of a prehistoric herder-hunter contact zone: A first approximation. In M. Hall and A. Smith, eds., *Prehistoric herders in southern Africa*. Claremont, Cape: South African Archaeological Society Goodwin Series, no. 5.

———. 1986b. Veld damage in the Karoo caused by its pre-Trekboer inhabitants: Preliminary observations in the Seacow valley. *The Naturalist* 30: 37–42.

———. In press. Putting the wind up the Smithfield: Seasons of occupation inferred for sub-Recent Bushman surface sites. In John Bower and David Lubell, eds., *Environment and culture change in later African prehistory*. Oxford: B.A.R. Cambridge Monographs in African Archaeology.

Sampson, C. G., and B. Bousman. 1985. Variations in the size of archaeological surface sites attributed to the Seacow River Bushmen. *South African Journal of Science* 81: 321–323.

Schiffer, M. 1983. Towards the identification of site formation processes. *American Antiquity* 48: 675–706.

Schmidbauer, W. 1973. Territorialität und Aggression bei Jägern und Sammlern. *Anthropos* 68: 548–558.

Schoener, T. W. 1971. Theory of feeding strategies. *Annual Review of Ecology and Systematics* 3: 369–403.

Schofield, J. F. 1948. *Primitive pottery: An introduction to South African ceramics, prehistoric and protohistoric*. Cape Town: South African Archaeological Society, Handbook Series 3.

Schoon, H. F., ed. 1972. *The diary of Erasmus Smit*. Cape Town: Struik.

Schrire, C. 1980. An enquiry into the evolutionary status and apparent identity of San hunter-gatherers. *Human Ecology* 8: 9–32.

———. 1984. *Past and present in hunter gatherer studies*. Orlando: Academic Press.

Sealy, J. C., and N. J. van der Merwe. 1985. Isotope assessment of Holocene human diets in the southwest Cape, South Africa. *Nature* 315: 138–140.

Silberbauer, G. B. 1981. *Hunter and habitat in the central Kalahari Desert*. Cambridge: Cambridge University Press.

Smith, E. A. 1983. Anthropological applications of optimal foraging theory: A critical review. *Current Anthropology* 24: 625–651.

Soja, E. W. 1971. *The political organization of space*. Association of American Geographers, Commission on College Geography, Resource Paper, no. 8.

Steward, J. H. 1942. The direct historical approach to archaeology. *American Antiquity* 7: 337–343.

Stiles, D. 1979. Paleolithic culture change: Experiment in theory and method. *Current Anthropology* 20: 1–21.

Stow, G. 1905. *The native races of South Africa*. London: Swan, Sonnenschein & Co.

Tanner, A. 1973. The significance of hunting territories today. In B. Cox, ed., *Cultural ecology*, 101–114. Ottawa: Carleton Library, no. 69.

Thomas, D. H. 1986. Contemporary hunter-gatherer archaeology in America. In D. J. Meltzer, D. D. Fowler, and J. A. Sabloff, eds., *American archaeology: Past and future*, 237–276. Washington and London: Smithsonian Institution Press.

Tindale, N. B. 1974. *Aboriginal tribes of Australia.* Berkeley: University of California Press.

Turner, D. H. 1978. Ideology and elementary structures. *Anthropologica* 20: 223–247.

Tyson, P. D. 1978. Rainfall changes over South Africa during the period of meteorological record. In M. J. A. Werger, ed., *Biogeography and ecology of Southern Africa,* 55–70. The Hague: Junk.

van der Merwe, P. J. 1937. *Die noordwaartse beweging van die boere voor die Trek (1770–1842).* Pretoria.

van Riet Lowe, C. 1929. The Smithfield Industry in the Orange Free State. In A. J. H. Goodwin and C. van Riet Lowe, eds., *The Stone Age cultures of South Africa. Annals of the South African Museum* 27: 151–206.

van Rooyen, T., and T. du T. Burger. 1974. Plant ecological significance of the soils of the central Orange River Basin. *South African Geographic Journal* 56: 60–66.

Wadley, L. 1986. Private lives and public lives: A social interpretation for the Stone Age. *The longest record: The human career in Africa. Abstracts,* p. 97. Berkeley.

Wellington, J. H. 1955. *Southern Africa: A geographical study.* Vol. 1, *Physical geography.* Cambridge: Cambridge University Press.

Werger, M. J. A. 1978. The Karoo-Namib region. In M. J. A. Werger, ed., *Biogeography and ecology of Southern Africa,* 231–300. The Hague: Junk.

White, I. M. 1977. From camp to village: Some problems of adaptation. In R. M. Berndt, ed., *Aborigines and change: Australia in the 70's,* 100–105. Canberra: Australian Institute of Aborigine Studies.

Wiessner, P. W. 1977. *Hxaro: A regional system of reciprocity for reducing risk among the !Kung San.* Ann Arbor: University Microfilms.

Wiessner, P. 1983. Style and social information in Kalahari San projectile points. *American Antiquity* 48: 253–276.

———. 1984. Reconsidering the behavioral basis of style. *Journal of Anthropological Archaeology* 3: 190–234.

———. 1985. Style or isochrestic variation? A reply to Sackett. *American Antiquity* 50: 160–166.

Wilcox, A. R. 1963. *The Rock Art of South Africa.* Johannesburg: Nelson.

Wilmsen, E. N. 1973. Interaction, spacing behavior, and the organization of hunting bands. *Journal of Anthropological Research* 29: 1–31.

Wilmsen, E. 1983. The ecology of illusion: Anthropological foraging in the Kalahari. *Reviews in Anthropology* 10: 9–20.

Wilson, M. L. 1986. Notes on the nomenclature of the Khoisan. *Annals of the South African Museum* 8: 251–266.

Winterhalder, B. and E. A. Smith, eds. 1981. *Hunter-gatherer foraging strategies: Ethnographic and archeological analyses.* Chicago: University of Chicago Press.

Wobst, H. M. 1974. Boundary conditions for Paleolithic social systems: A simulation approach. *American Antiquity* 39: 147–178.

———. 1976. Locational relationships in Paleolithic society. In R. H. Ward and K. M. Weiss, eds., *The demographic evolution of human populations,* 49–58. London: Academic Press.

———. 1978. The archaeo-ethnology of hunter-gatherers or the tyranny of the ethnographic record. *American Antiquity* 43: 303–309.

Woodburn, J. 1972. Ecology, nomadic movement and the composition of the local group among hunters and gatherers: An East African example and its implications. In P. J. Ucko, R. Tringham, G. W. Dimbleby, eds., *Man, settlement and urbanism,* 193–206. London: Duckworth.

———. 1982. Egalitarian societies. *Man* 17: 431–451.

Yellen, J. E. 1976. Cultural patterning in faunal remains: Evidence from the !Kung Bushmen. In D. W. Ingersoll, ed., *Experimental archaeology,* 271–331. New York: Columbia University Press.

———. 1977. *Archaeological approaches to the present: Models for reconstructing the past.* New York: Academic Press.

Yellen, J. E., and H. Harpending. 1972. Hunter-gatherer populations and archaeological inference. *World Archaeology* 4: 244–253.

Yengoyan, A. A. 1976. Structure, event and ecology in Aboriginal Australia: A comparative viewpoint. In N. Peterson, ed., *Tribes and Boundaries in Australia.* Canberra: Australian Institute of Aboriginal Studies.